Haynes

Restoration Manual

Morris Minor and 1000

T0364969

Lindsay Porter

First published by G. T. Foulis & Co. as *Morris Minor & 1000 Purchase and Restoration Guide*, 1985

Reprinted by Haynes Publishing with new cover and minor amendments as *Morris Minor & 1000 Restoration Manual*, 2001

A catalogue record for this book is available from the British Library

ISBN 978 1 78521 857 6

Library of Congress catalog card number 85-81670

Haynes Group Limited
Haynes North America, Inc

www.haynes.com

Printed in the UK

Jurisdictions which have strict emission control laws may consider any modification to a vehicle to be an infringement of those laws. You are advised to check with the appropriate body or authority whether your proposed modification complies fully with the law. The publishers accept no liability in this regard.

While every effort is taken to ensure the accuracy of the information given in this book, no liability can be accepted by the author or publishers for any loss, damage or injury caused by errors in, or omissions from, the information given.

The manufacturer's authorised representative in the EU for product safety is:

HaynesPro BV
Stationsstraat 79 F, 3811MH Amersfoort, The Netherlands
gpsr@haynes.co.uk

Dedication

I would like to dedicate this book to Anders Ditlev Clausager and the British Motor Industry Heritage Trust.

Without their devotion to cataloguing, preserving and presenting the history of much of the industry, often taking it straight from the manufacturer's records saved from the scrapheap, much of our knowledge of motoring history would be lost for ever.

Contents

Foreword by John Frye

My first contact with the world of the Morris Minor began whilst a student, when my grandmother thought I needed a car to go with the London image. Accordingly, I purchased a '61 Traveller, codenamed 'Buzzard' (after my grandmother).

During 1973-1977, whilst lecturing in South Africa, I took the Buzzard with me, and added something in excess of 100,000 miles before she expired. During 1976, I managed to find a Series II Saloon shell, which I rebuilt from the viable remains of the Buzzard, christening the result 'Victoria' (last outpost of empire, and of the inevitable female gender). Whilst visiting a friend (illegally) in Soweto, Victoria and I got stuck in a ferocious African storm. Four shadowy figures emerged from nowhere, and heaved Vickers into a nearby shed, face to face with a '51 MM. They got us going in half an hour — such are the feelings of camaraderie inspired by these remarkable cars.

Since 1977, I have been teaching in Norwich. No, Vickers was not left behind (how could I?) — now with 351,000 on the clock from the Buzzard, bloodied but unbowed, she is just about due for a dose of Lindsay Porter's restoration expertise.

Lindsay has already produced (among others) an impressive volume on Sir Alec Issigonis's other mighty Mog, the Mini, and his latest companion to this, *Morris Minor Guide to Purchase and DIY Restoration*, is equally impressive.

I believe that Sir Alec is on record somewhere for claiming the Mini as his favourite brainchild. Well, there must be several hundred thousand 'parents' throughout the world whose first love is for his original 'jelly-mould' conception, the Minor. Surveying the historical information that Lindsay Porter has put together, one cannot fail to be inspired by the excellence of the photographic record as well as the written documentation. There is no doubt that Minors *look* nice, and the recent achievements of the Morris Minor Owners' Club in individual and team events at the big car shows demonstrate that the judges think so too.

If you are a proud Minor owner, or if you are thinking of joining that happy band, then Lindsay Porter's book really should grace your bookshelf. The level and accuracy of technical information is as comprehensive as your insurance policy should be. In particular, I like the detailed illustration of restoration processes, with clear photographs and clear instructions.

Perhaps the book's greatest asset is its simplicity: no unwarranted assumptions are made about what you do or don't know, so that in each case the instructions start from the basics. To experts and beginners alike, and to the vast majority who, like me, lie somewhere between the two, I would thoroughly recommend this admirable book.

**John Frye
Chairman, the Morris Minor Owners' Club**

Introduction & Acknowledgements

The Minor is an amazing motor car but at the same time it represents a typically British paradox. Based on a design that was well ahead of the contemporary competition and so soundly engineered that it gained a justifiable reputation for going on and on, it was, nevertheless, a failure in sales terms. That may seem a strange thing to say about a car that sold to well over one-and-a-half million satisfied customers world-wide, but when you consider that the Minor was built for over twenty years and that the VW Beetle, the Minor's nearest competitor in concept terms, sold twenty times as well as the Minor, the failure becomes clear.

From the enthusiast's point of view, however, the situation is rosy, for sufficient cars were built to make it worthwhile manufacturing spares for the Minor and, indeed, the spares situation is better than for many modern cars. Unlike the case for the Beetle fanatic, however, who could, at a pinch, import a brand new car from South America where Beetles are still being built, the prospective owner of a sound, reliable Minor has to go in for restoration — and if you want to do it properly, this is the only book that shows you how in the sort of detail the restorer needs to know.

No one example of a car could ever show the full range of problems that can be encountered in restoration work, so this book shows a number of Minors of all different types, and every commonly encountered aspect of restoration work — as well as a goodly number of uncommon ones — are covered here.

Almost every restoration photograph was taken by myself at The Morris Minor Centre, Bath, which is the best equipped, best informed and best organised restoration set-up I have yet encountered. Nevertheless, we all have our own ways of doing things, and where I feel that an alternative or preferable way of working exists, I have said so. Moreover, there must be other Morris Minor specialists who are capable of carrying out a first-class restoration of a Morris Minor. Still, the Minor Centre is where I went for advice, photographs and information and as this book shows, they gave a great deal.

My thanks are due, therefore, to all the welders, the panel beaters and sprayers, the trimmers, mechanics and the parts staff, and the management; all of these were unfailingly friendly and helpful in spite of what must have been a somewhat intrusive presence!

Thanks are especially due to Charlie Ware, founding father of the Morris Minor Centre, whose ideas and beliefs on the production and maintenance of durable goods and their influence on manufacture, design and employment are ideas and beliefs whose time is just starting to come.

Thanks are also due to all of the suppliers mentioned in this book, all of whom have given their assistance in the preparation of this and other restoration guides.

Members and officials of the Morris Minor Owners' Club have been most helpful and friendly whenever approached for advice; special thanks are due to John Frye and Ray Newell, and those unknown owners whose cars I 'snapped' in the rain at an MMOC Rally.

Finally, but not least, my thanks as always to the invaluable efforts put in by my wife, Shan, in helping to bring this book together.

**Lindsay Porter
Upper Sapey,
Worcester**

Using this book

The layout of this book has been designed to be both attractive and easy to follow during practical work on your car. However, to obtain maximum benefit from the book, it is important to note the following points:

1) Apart from the introductory pages, this book is split into two parts: chapters 1 to 6 dealing with history, buying and practical procedures; appendices 1 to 7 providing supplementary information. Each chapter/appendix may be sub-divided into sections and even sub-sections. Section headings are in italic type between horizontal lines and sub-section headings are similar, but without horizontal lines.

2) Step-by-step photograph and line drawing captions are an integral part of the text (except those in chapters 1 and 2) — therefore the photographs/drawings and their captions are arranged to "read" in exactly the same way as the normal text. In other words they run down each column and the columns run from left to right of the page.

Each photograph caption carries an alpha-numeric identity, relating it to a specific section. The letters before the caption number

are simply the initial letters of key words in the relevant section heading, whilst the caption number shows the position of the particular photograph in the section's picture sequence. Thus photograph/caption 'DR22' is the 22nd photograph in the section headed "Door Repairs".

3) Figures — illustrations which are not integral with the text — are numbered consecutively throughout the book. Figure captions do not form any part of the text. Therefore Figure 5 is simply the 5th figure in the book.

4) All references to the left or right of the vehicle are from the point of view of somebody standing behind the car looking forwards.

5) The bodywork repair chapter of this book deals with problems particular to the Morris Minor. In concentrating on these aspects the depth of treatment of body repair techniques in general is necessarily limited. For more detailed information covering all aspects of body repair it is recommended that reference be made to the Haynes 'The Car Bodywork Repair Manual' also by Lindsay Porter.

6) Because this book concentrates upon restoration, regular maintenance procedures

and normal mechanical repairs of all the car's components, are beyond its scope. It is therefore strongly recommended that the Haynes *Morris 1000 Owner's Workshop Manual* should be used as a companion volume.

7) We know it's a boring subject, especially when you really want to get on with a job — but your safety, through the use of correct workshop procedures, must ALWAYS be your foremost consideration. It is essential that you read, and UNDERSTAND, appendix 1 before undertaking any of the practical tasks detailed in this book.

8) Before starting any particular job it is important that you read the introduction to the relevant Chapter or Section, taking note of the 'tool box' and 'safety' notes. It is recommended that you read through the section from start to finish before getting into the job.

9) Whilst great care is taken to ensure that the information in this book is as accurate as possible, the author, editor or publisher cannot accept any liability for loss, damage or injury caused by errors in, or omissions from, the information given.

1 Heritage

Parentage

It has been quite amusing to see the mad rush by all the leading car manufacturers to produce the definitive 'super-mini': Metro, Polo, Corsa/Nova, and in the USA GM's 'Saturn' project, have all been searching for the ultimate 4-seater, capable of good performance, good roadholding and low cost with attractive styling. Some would argue that they have all been beaten to it − and by several decades, too! The 1948 Morris Minor, created by the Greek-born genius of small car design, Alec Issigonis, set a standard for space utilization coupled with superb standards of efficiency that were new in concept and years ahead of the car's competitors at the time. Nowadays, the Morris Minor is taken very much for granted to the extent that it is the epitome of old-fashioned values. In 1948, it was anything but old-fashioned (especially when compared with Morris cars that had gone before) but was a car that solved problems that William Morris's Nuffield empire had hardly realized were in existence!

William Morris started to make his name before the First World War when he set up in business to build the 'Bullnose' Morris Oxford. Never an innovator, he concentrated upon rapid assembly of largely bought-in parts and an aggressive pricing and sales approach towards selling a basically conventional car. The method worked, and by 1925, in fierce competition with the 'enemy' at Austin, 54,000 Bullnose Morrises were sold, making the car Number One in the UK's hit parade.

The cash generated by this success led Morris to expand his range and, in 1928, he launched a small car to compete with the tremendously successful 'baby' Austin, the Austin Seven. Once again, the car was fairly conventional in appearance and construction (even if the coil ignition and dry-plate clutch were actually up-to-date), except for the engine, which was actually an overhead camshaft unit. This startling innovation had little to do directly with the almost reactionary William Morris but was developed at Wolseley, the company which had gone bankrupt and then been bought out by Morris in the receivers court. Wolseley had always been an innovative company and their Wolseley Hornet 6-cylinder engine apparently made an ideal power source for the new Minor when cut down to 4-cylinders, which reduced its capacity to 847cc with a bore and stroke of 57 × 83mm. The engine's most unusual feature was the camshaft drive which was taken off the crankshaft, and which also formed the rotor for the dynamo. Unfortunately for Morris, the camshaft drive also proved to be the engine's Achilles heel, for its design promoted oil leakage. Oil seal technology of the time was far behind today's levels, and the felt seals then used were notorious for doing no more than slowing the steady trickle of oil out of the engine. (Indeed, some owners resigned themselves to the fact and drove around with a little tray mounted to catch the wasted oil which was poured back in to the engine after every journey of any length.) The car body could be had as a tourer, fabric or steel bodied saloon, or as a 5cwt van.

Other than as predecessor to 'our' Morris Minor, the pre-war Minor's main claim to fame was as the source material for the first MG Midget, the first in a long line of traditional British sports cars: nippy rather than startlingly fast; robust rather than exotic, but always

produced as *affordable* enjoyment. MG (the initials stood for Morris Garages, the company with which Morris had started in business in Dingwall Street, Oxford) started as something approaching a car builder by rebodying the boringly conventional Bullnose Morris as a sporting tourer, and when the overhead cam Minor came along, MG's managing director, Cecil Kimber, took what was to be a momentous and inspired decision for the future of the sports car. The Minor was rebodied with spartan bodywork and cycle wings, the chassis was altered, and the engine mildly tuned to give 20bhp. Introduced in 1928, the M-type Midget spawned a long line of successors, one of which, the Austin-Healey 'Frogeye', almost repeated history some thirty years later in its relationship with the Morris Minor 1000 – but that's another story!

The overhead camshaft Minor lasted until 1930, when a sidevalve version of the engine was fitted giving a more sluggish performance but the kind of reliability that buyers sought. By 1934, when production ended, the car had gained hydraulic brakes and a four-speed synchromesh gearbox.

If the first Minor bequeathed only its name to the post-war Morris Minor, later cars from the Morris stable began to demonstrate features which were to find their way into the Minor in due course.

One of those cars was the Morris Eight, which was introduced to attempt to stem the drop in sales which Morris were suffering. The man responsible for its introduction was another product of the Wolseley company, and one who was destined to have the most profound impact upon the shape of the British motor industry after the war: he was a production engineer by the name of Leonard Lord. Lord's task was to introduce a competitor to the new family car from Ford, the 8 HP, and to do it in double-quick time. This he did in his typically uncompromising way; he arranged to copy it! The 1935 Eight was a family saloon with a 918cc

sidevalve engine and cart-spring suspension front and rear. The four-cylinder engine was an extremely rugged, simple and reliable unit and provided the power source for the Morris small-car range for years to come. By 1938, it was deemed necessary to redesign the Eight, and the Morris Eight Series E was introduced. Based around the same 918cc engine, the new Eight had more modern, rounded bodywork, and (following the contemporary trend) shrunken running boards and headlamps blended into the wing shape. Interestingly, the chassis, unlike that of its predecessor, was supported by the bodywork, giving semi-unitary construction. In the same year, its stablemate the Series M Ten was introduced with similar styling but with full unitary construction – making it the first Morris to be built without a chassis and giving Morris their first experience of this American-inspired construction method.

It is interesting to note that Alex Issigonis, designer of the post-war Morris Minor, joined Morris in 1936 at a time when development of Morris's latest chassis innovations were getting well under way. Just before Issigonis joined Morris, a new system had been introduced whereby car design was divided into 'cells' each being headed by an engineer responsible for a logical subdivision of the new car. So it was that Issigonis was appointed to be responsible for new Morris cars' suspension work. A year before Issigonis had joined Morris, in 1935, the MG design team had been incorporated into the Morris set-up and so Issigonis was to make important contacts with two people whose ideas were eventually to have an important bearing upon the Morris Minor: one was H.N. Charles and the other was a young engineer by the name of Jack Daniels.

But for now, Issigonis was preoccupied with his first project, the suspension for the new Morris Ten Series M, the company's first unitary construction car. For this car, Issigonis designed and tested a coil spring and wishbone independent front suspension and

fitted a steering rack in place of the traditional steering box and its attendant link rods. Issigonis was said to have been bitterly disappointed when management decided that his suspension and steering designs were not sufficiently well developed for use in the new Ten and introduction was put off by Morris until 1939 when the new system was scheduled to appear fitted to a new MG saloon. In the event, of course, the MG YA did not appear until 1947 because of the intervention of a world war, but the design was to form the basis for MG sports car front suspension right up to the last MGB some forty years later. This new suspension arrangement was significant from the point of view of the Morris Minor story, too, because it had the unconventional feature of a wishbone supporting the bottom of the kingpin with the top supported by the shock absorber arm – a principle to be found in revised form on the Minor itself.

Design

The Nuffield managing director, Miles Thomas, prided himself on the fact that during the war the Nuffield group directed almost all its efforts toward munitions production and he felt anger – perhaps born of pique – that Austin, perfectly legitimately, carried on producing and designing cars. In fact, Morris also involved themselves in car design because Thomas was determined that they should have a new, small car to replace the venerable Eight as soon as possible after the war. So right from the early years of the war Thomas had discussions with Chief Engineer A.V. Oak and involved Issigonis from the outset. It became obvious that Issigonis had some pretty interesting ideas of what he wanted from small-car design and so, once Miles Thomas was committed to the idea of developing a new car, Issigonis was given *carte blanche* to

design the car the way he wanted it. He was given his own separate small design department and two draughtsmen, Jack Daniels, the ex-MG man, who was to work on mechanical components, and body man Reg Job.

Of the two men, Daniels was probably the more significant in the Minor story because of the work he had carried out on torsion bars for front suspension use.

Both Issigonis and Daniels had been influenced by H.N. Charles who had designed in 1933-34 the racing R-type MG with all-independent torsion car suspension. So strong was the influence that when Jack Daniels designed the gargantuan tank, known only as the Tortoise, which had 13 inch armour plate and a weight of around 85 tons, he employed torsion bars – 128 feet of them and up to 2⅜ inches in diameter.

In another way, too, the work of H.N. Charles was to influence Issigonis and Daniels when it came to designing the Minor's front suspension. The Series M Ten, the car which did *not* use Issigonis's design of front suspension, used instead a half-elliptic spring front beam axle, designed by H.N. Charles. Charles rid the car of many of the traditional problems experienced by cars with this type of front suspension by using softer springs to give a better ride, with an anti-roll bar to cut down on shimmying and other undesirable axle movements. Issigonis, investigating means of improvement, mounted a couple of sandbags on the Series M Ten front bumper, whereupon he found that handling actually improved. All of these developments – the torsion bars, the soft suspension, the nose-heaviness, were to have a profound impact upon the Minor.

At first, though, the name 'Minor' was nowhere to be seen, the prototype and development name being 'Mosquito'. Issigonis was determined from the first that the Mosquito would do the job of carrying people in comfort and safety in a superior way to that of any small car that had gone before.

His aim, in the very best sense, was to build a car that was simply effective – not for design or production engineers, nor for aesthetes or motoring writers but for those who were to use the car. So, it had to contain the maximum passenger space within the minimum length, it had to be inexpensive to produce yet it had to be safe and sufficiently rapid. But the car's looks, its engineering virtuosity and its sheer performance did not matter, or more correctly, if Issigonis' former objectives were achieved, he was absolutely certain that the latter objectives would automatically follow.

Mosquito had to have ample room for its passengers which meant that wheel arches, which protruded badly into available space on most cars, had to be reduced in size. The obvious corollary was that wheel sizes had to be reduced, and so they were reduced from the 17 inch size fitted to the Morris Eight Series E all the way to 14 inches. These days, that size sounds unremarkable (and in fact it is a measure of Issigonis that he, perhaps like Sinclair a generation on, would introduce the apparently outlandish only for it to be accepted as the norm) but the smallest wheels then in use were on the Fiat baby car, the 'Topolino', which used 15 inch wheels. There were no purpose built wheels available, so Issigonis leant on his already well-established contacts at Dunlop to produce very special wheels and tyres for his prototype. (He was to do the same twenty years later when he designed the Mini to run on the equally outrageous 10 inch wheels.)

The wheels were a perfect example of a component that, being 'right' for one part of the Issigonis plan, was absolutely right for several other parts, too, rather like a piece in a jigsaw puzzle having a different shape along every edge, each perfectly fitting its neighbours. Not only did they provide more room for the occupants, they also improved the car's road holding by lowering its centre of gravity. They improved the car's ride (and made it

easier to get away with soft suspension) by reducing the unsprung weight, which affects the tendency of the wheels to 'bounce' and which requires stiffer damper settings to balance out, and they made the tyres cheaper to buy which reduced the cost of the car. It is said that Issigonis insisted upon small wheels simply because, for the size of the car, they looked right, but to an engineer, looking right means something of a deeper significance than mere visual appearance . . .

Mosquito's soft front suspension was again a multi-faceted thing. Cars built without a chassis are far less prone to flexing than those with a chassis, so they need softer suspension settings to cope with road shocks. But Issigonis had also learned from Charles's suspension design of the Series M Ten and from the work of Maurice Olley, a British suspension expert working in the United States, that softer suspension coupled with extra nose-weight gave better cornering stability (although over a certain point, you get too much understeer – the car tries to go straight on at corners!) but he knew that independent front suspension was essential to avoid the axle shimmying that H.N. Charles had gone to so much trouble to avoid on the Ten. And then again, independent front suspension could be cheaper to produce, it allowed the engine to be pushed further forwards to make better use of passenger space – and having the engine further forwards gave the extre nose-weight one was also looking for. Issigonis, it would seem, was a man whose design solutions only worked in neat, virtuous circles!

During the war, Issigonis had got in on the torsion bar act by building a personnel carrier based on Morris Ten components but with all-independent torsion bar suspension. With the experiences of Jack Daniels, torsion bars were almost inevitable for the new car especially since designers were still nervous about chassisless cars, and Issigonis was happier about feeding

suspension loads back into the main structure of the car, whereas coil springs would have pushed the loads into the front of the vehicle. To take the torsion bar loads, the new car was fitted with a sturdy I-section cross-member which ran across the mid-point and which was also used to take the car jack, mounting points being built into the ends of the cross-member. It seems that Issigonis also contemplated using torsion bars for the rear suspension, in which case the same cross-member could have taken rear suspension loads, too. In other words, a mounting point was chosen, which allowed the greatest possible torsion bar length; the longer the bar, the greater the diameter could be, which prevented the risk of breakage. Instead, conventional leaf springs and a rigid axle were used at the rear, probably for reasons of cost, independent rear suspension being far from cheap to develop and produce, the only unconventional note being the placing of the rear shock absorbers on the axle itself which had the undesirable side-effect of adding unsprung weight to what, in any case, was to become notorious as a lively axle.

The front suspension assembly also comprised a bottom link which was bolted to the front 'chassis' leg and a top link which doubled as the shock absorber arm. And in another move to feed loads back into the main structure of the car (and leave more room for a flat-four engine?) the shock absorbers themselves were bolted to the bulkhead.

Other mechanical areas were the subject of considerable speculation by Issigonis and his assistants. An all new engine was developed for the car using a flat-four format on which barrels could be swapped to give simple capacity alterations; a principle not dissimilar to that of a certain German people's car built with similar aims in mind to those of the Minor. Not only were these engines built and run in 800cc and 1100cc capacities (although by all accounts they were under-powered and underdeveloped by Morris Engines at Coventry who

could be biased and wilful to a degree which is unthinkable today), it is actually true that the shape of the underbonnet area was designed to take the Issigonis engine and, as a result, when Morris management decided not to use the flat-four engine, access to the conventional engine was phenomenally good. To digress from strict matters of design for a moment, it is worth pointing out that Herbert Morris, by now relabelled Lord Nuffield, was still in nominal charge of his empire, even though his influence was negative, conservative to a high degree and ultimately destructive. If it had not been for the energies of Miles Thomas there seems little doubt that the Mosquito would never have lived as the Morris Minor and it is said that Nuffield virtually despised Issigonis, refusing even to remember his name properly and referring to him ill-temperedly as 'Issy, Issy-wassisname'. Under the circumstances, getting the Minor into production at all seems to have been a small miracle — expecting the new engine to be used when Nuffield, the personally mean but institutionally incredibly generous man, could see nothing wrong with the old side-valve unit, would have been to expect too much! And it must be admitted that getting an unconventional car accepted by the stick-in-the-mud British buying public would perhaps have been a tall order if it had been fitted with an untried engine, too.

The Mosquito bodyshell was developed as an incredibly complex structure by today's standards. From just about every angle, the car was a mass of curves (a 'poached egg', Nuffield was said to have called it) which meant also that it was inherently strong and capacious. It had a strong bulkhead, particularly well stressed beneath the bulkhead top where the dash and other supporting panels made a large box structure and, beneath the rear panel shelf, a rear bulkhead gave extra rear-end torsional rigidity. The floorpan was conceived as a relatively smooth structure but with a great number of individual parts beneath the box-section sills.

These had a lightened inner membrane and an outer structure which screwed into place and formed the last, vestigial remnants of the pre-war running boards. Box sections ran from the I-section cross-member to the front of the car to help support the torsion bar and engine weight, and more box-sections snaked along the rear wheel arch to support the rear spring rear mountings. A further boxed cross-member fitted beneath the rear seats to help support the rear spring front mountings which were fitted directly to the floor.

The Mosquito/Minor project was nearing completion when Issigonis suddenly decided that he would like to see the car made wider. He went to the workshop, it is said, announced that the car was to be cut in half and moved apart — nearer-apart until, with the two halves four inches apart, he decreed that the Minor now looked just right. Many of the body press tools were already completed so Reg Job had to widen the roof along its apex (where it ran horizontal anyway), widen each side of the floorpan by 2 inches, and add a flat strip to the bonnet, which is the reason why it has always had its distinctive raised flat right down the middle. The most amazing thing about the exercise is that, at this late stage, Chief Engineer A.V. Oak and Miles Thomas let Issigonis get away with it. There is no doubt, however, that the increase in track made the car handle so much better and gave the occupants the extra width to go with the immense amount of leg room that helped to make the Minor such a capacious little car.

Introduction

The 1948 Motor Show at Earls Court saw the introduction of the Minor after Reg Hanks (who had succeeded Miles Thomas as Morris's MD a year earlier) finally persuaded Lord Nuffield to relent and allow the new car to be

introduced. The show also saw the introduction of the Jowett Javelin, designed by Gerald Palmer who had worked at Cowley until 1942. The Javelin was uncannily similar to Issigonis's original thinking for the Mosquito/Minor, having all-torsion bar suspension, a flat-four engine set well forwards and similarly beetle-like styling. The highly innovatory Javelin cost around twice the price of a Minor, however!

Other stars of the show were the XK120 with its exciting (and seemingly everlasting) dohc 6-cylinder engine and, of more significance as a competitor in the market-place, the all-new Austin Devon with its overhead valve engine.

The Minor was initially produced only as a saloon or a convertible and no heater was available even as an optional extra. The great majority of Minors were exported, Australia topping the list in spite of the low power output of the pre-war Morris 8 engine. On the other hand, the Minor reputation for reliability was built, in these early days, on a system of production line checks and quality control that meant that the Minor had the best guarantee claims record of any British car. With its high levels of (summer) comfort, space and road holding, the Minor earned from *Autocar* the comment, 'The design has raised the breed of small cars to a much higher level!' They were presumably encouraged by the belated introduction of a heater (October 1950) and a kit to enable those who had already shivered through the depressing winters of 1948 and 1949 to give themselves the welcome present of a little warmth.

Man behind the Minor

The story of the Morris Minor is so tied up with the work of Alec Issigonis, that it is well worth digressing a little at this point and taking a look at the man himself and how his thinking on the Minor fitted into a pattern of thought that was to be a lifetime's preoccupation.

The days are gone when the inspiration, let alone the design effort, behind an individual car can be ascribed to one man. The Colin Chapmans, Herbert Austins, W.O. Bentleys and the Donald Healeys of today are now cut down to anonymity in the motor car world where the financial safety of the manufacturer must be the prime consideration. Alec Issigonis must rank among the greatest of all innovators being responsible for not one but two 'landmark' motor cars, and with ideas enough for more.

Alec Issigonis was born in Smyrna (Izmir) in 1906 as a British subject with a German mother and in line to inherit the family business. When Germany occupied his homeland during the First World War, young Alec lived under house arrest while the Germans commissioned his grandfather's factory. After the war, his family was forced to flee and abandon all they had as Greece and Turkey fought one of their periodic wars over possession of disputed territory. At 15, Issigonis arrived in England and attended Battersea Technical College where he gained a grounding in basic engineering in spite of a glaring and self-confessed weakness in maths.

In 1928, he began work in a London drawing office draughting a design for an automatic clutch. Humber showed an interest in the clutch but in the end rejected it and 'head hunted' Issigonis instead. In 1936, Issigonis made the significant move to Morris at Cowley, his pre-Second World War work there culminating in his design for the MG YA front suspension which was not actually put into use until after the cessation of hostilities but which was good enough to find favour in a line of cars including the MGA and then, in refined form, the MGB.

After spending the war years allowing his fertile mind to consider a wide range of military vehicle applications, Issigonis's first moments of wide acclaim came with his design for the new Morris Minor. Unfortunately, the Minor's engine and gearbox failed to match the performance potential of the rest of the car until the Austin Morris merger into the British Motor Corporation in November 1951 made the cross-fertilization of an Austin engine into the Morris Minor a possibility.

During 1951/52, however, Issigonis produced an experimental front-wheel-drive Minor with engine, clutch and gearbox transversely all in a line and a final drive beneath. Issigonis never drove the prototype, but it was completed and used as an everyday car by Jack Daniels, one of the Minor development team. Daniels was later to claim that this prototype Minor played a key role in the conception of the Mini, because not only was its handling outstandingly good but also, so the story goes, it was parked outside Leonard Lord's office window every day!

Shortly after the BMC merger, Issigonis moved temporarily away from BMC and joined Alvis where he designed a sports saloon with an almost frightening specification. It was to be capable of over 110mph and boasted a 3.5-litre V8 engine, a two-speed gearbox with overdrive on each gear and – significantly – hydrolastic-type suspension.

In November 1955, Lord lured Issigonis back into the BMC fold with the promise that he could start again where he had left off with the Minor, and have a free hand in designing an all-new small car which would rejuvenate BMC's ageing model line-up. Issigonis gathered around himself a small team including, once again, Jack Daniels. Issigonis already had a number of established concepts about what a small car should have as its major attributes such as front wheel drive (he had long-standing regard for the Citröen Traction Avant), small, space-saving wheels and wheel-arches, rack and pinion steering, front-heaviness, and a general high regard for function rather than fashion. With that much established, Issigonis began, unconventionally but typically, by considering the ergonomic

requirements of four passengers, finding the space needed by them and designing a bodyshell to fit.

In Ancient Greek, there are no words to differentiate between 'Art' and 'Craft'; they were considered to be one and the same thing. Issigonis, the modern Greek, was a man capable of drawings of great artistic merit which although far removed in appearance were every bit as effective as 'technical' drawings. The fact that Issigonis was capable of truly creative thought and yet was an engineer with the technical insight and determination to make things work in a highly successful manner, went some way towards proving the ancients right. Being right and looking right were, to Issigonis, one and the same thing; a rare view in our modern society where, aesthetically speaking, 'black box' has succeeded Bauhaus.

Minor developments

The addition of a heater (standard overseas; optional in the UK) in 1950 has already been mentioned, but even before the car's introduction, the first development was planned. Californian regulations stated that from early 1949 all headlamps fitted to cars were to have a minimum height of 24 inches above the road and, since there was no way that Minor headlamps could be retained in their original grille mounted position, they were fitted in special pods in the tops of the wings. From that year, all United States cars received headlamps in the raised position and UK cars were similarly equipped from the 1950 Motor Show. At the same time, Lucas 7 inch headlamps were fitted in place of the original 5 inch items, while sidelamps — formerly in the headlamp bowls — were fitted in the grille where headlamps had once been. Issigonis was said to have always hated the loss of his smooth lines but, quite by chance, the new headlamp

positions took away the slightly squint-eyed appearance and gave the Minor its timeless visual quality. The 1950 Show also saw the introduction of the four-door Minor (although it had been planned at least four years earlier), fitted with a few extra fixtures and fittings as befitted its more up-market status. In spite of still being powered by the same thoroughly outdated engine, the Minor was selling extremely well and in fact totalled half of the entire output of the Nuffield Organisation and, as well as being sold all over the world, production from kits (supplied from Cowley) was started in the Irish Republic, Australia, Denmark, India, Holland and New Zealand. However, more changes were on the way!

Series II — the A-series introduced

For many, many years, Morris' greatest competitor was the Austin Motor Company. Both businesses had started from nothing to become among the largest motor manufacturers in the world, each under the proprietorial control of one man. The fierce rivalry between Herbert Austin and William Morris was even continued in another incarnation after Herbert Austin's death. Amazingly, a similarly tough-minded, equally successful (and equally brilliant, judged on his own merits) engineer named Leonard Lord had taken over the running at Austin upon the founder's dotage, but only after having been fired from the Nuffield Group and heavily humiliated by Morris himself. From pre-war days, Leonard Lord had dedicated himself to establishing the primacy of Austin and, by modernizing his design departments and model ranges, expanding the company's areas of activity and making production facilities among the best in the world, he had achieved his goal. At the same time he had long seen that it was senseless for Austin and Morris to

engage in a war of attrition and that, given the efficiencies of the kinds of mass-production systems that he was busy having installed, there was no room for two separate companies building similar cars aimed at a similar market and so cutting each other's maximum potential into two. William Morris had a founder's pride and an old man's stubbornness and refused to countenance a merger. Leonard Lord retaliated by piling on the pressure, launching a direct competitor to the Minor in the form of the Austin A30, fitted with a new 803cc overhead valve engine and pushing William Morris to the point where he gave in and sanctioned a merger with Austin, forming the British Motor Corporation.

Austin were predominant in every way and stamped their influence overpoweringly upon the Nuffield group. So, the Minor went from a management whose chairman hated the car, in spite of its commercial success, to a management who were emphatically *not* Morris people and with whom the Nuffield staff found it excruciatingly difficult to co-operate.

One of the earliest effects of the merger was for BMC to scrap the horribly outdated sidevalve Minor engine and to substitute the overhead valve A-series unit. This small Austin engine had been developed as a post-war version of the Austin Seven power source using a layout largely derived from the 1948 Austin A40 Somerset engine, the 1943 Austin 16 engine and the 1939 Austin Truck engine. Introduced in 1950, the A-series engine was a crucial part of Leonard Lord's engine strategy and he must have been delighted with the opportunity to use Longbridge's production facilities to the full by installing the A-series engine in a car that was to sell to over 50,000 customers in 1953 and was to double its sales in the next four years. The new engine increased power at the flywheel from the 27.5bhp of the 918cc sidevalve Morris engine to 30bhp for the 803cc Austin overhead valve

engine, while torque was also very marginally increased. The extra power, such as it was, was used by BMC to give extra acceleration and an almost unchanged top speed. Nowadays it is fashionable to criticize the large gaps between the gears of the Austin gearbox fitted to the Series II Minor and the general lack of engine power, but in its day, acceleration was acceptable and the use of a common engine size for all Minors and A30s must have kept costs down (although, in fact, Longbridge had considered the use of different capacities right at the start of the A-series design exercise, including 948cc and 848cc as fitted to the Mini). But once again, that's another story!

Incidentally, production and use of the sidevalve engine did not cease overnight. Initially, only those Minors destined for export were fitted with the more modern engine, production of the sidevalve Minor Series MM hanging on until early 1953.

At the time of the merger, Morris were getting ready to fit an overhead valve conversion to the venerable, long-stroke Morris Eight engine and had bought tools to increase production to the levels of over a thousand per week. Although the conversion itself was tried and tested and in use in the Wolseley 8HP, there is no doubt that the engine itself, based as it was upon the ancient Ford Eight design, was of too old-fashioned a design, lacked development potential and was inefficient to produce. And so what if production levels *could* have been raised to 1000 per week? Within four years, twice that number of Minors were to be built.

Even though Jack Daniels is quoted as saying that the Austin engine 'wasn't a good engine', that statement can be seen to have reflected sour grapes rather than sound engineering judgement. Of course, the A-series engine was a very fine engine indeed (unless getting on for 10 million customers have been deceived!) and added typical Austin engine reliability to that of the Minor. Technically, it

was quite an interesting unit. Back in the late nineteen-thirties Leonard Lord had decided that Austin should attack the truck market with more vigour, but he found himself with the same problem as when, at Morris, he had been given the brief of introducing a new small car: there was no engine; or at least, nothing suitable! Whilst at Morris, he had decided blatantly to copy the Ford 8 engine and now, at Austin, he pulled off the same trick by copying the GM/Bedford 'Stove Bolt' overhead valve truck engine. The point of doing so was that he short-circuited much of the lengthy design process whilst morally and legally sailing close to the wind, of course. The only major concession to change made to the Austin engine was that the camshaft position was moved from the left-hand to the right-hand side of the engine (viewed from the front) which meant that problems of squeezing a quart into a pint pot were encountered. For the finest of reasons, Austin engineers wanted to keep all their electrics (plugs, plug leads, coil, distributor) on the left side of the engine with manifolds — which mean volatile fuel and heat — on the other. The practical outcome was that pushrods, inlet and exhaust ports *and* some of the head studs had all to pass through one side of the head. Room was made by siamese-ing some of the ports, which should have been a disaster but wasn't — in fact Austin engines were always relatively efficient. During the war, the truck engine design was cut down to four cylinders from the original six and used in the Austin 16, then in the Hampshire/Hereford and Austin-Healey 100. It was scaled down to 1200cc for use in the A40 Devon/Dorset and Somerset, reduced still further to 803cc for the A-series engine and then scaled back up to 1200/1500cc for the B-series.

The original truck engine has been out of production for some time although it is still the last car engine that some people ever go near as it was finally used in the Austin Princess, many of which are

still used as hearses even today. The B-series ceased UK production in 1980, although it is still in production in India, but the A-series engine has had the most amazing life-span and is still used with credit in the Austin Metro, smaller-engined versions of the Maestro and, of course, the ageless Mini.

What a coincidence that one piece of Leonard Lord's bare-faced plagiarism, the Morris 8 engine, should be turfed out by an engine that was derived from another piece of typical Leonard Lord enterprise!

Original Longbridge thinking on the A-series engine was for an ultra-simple, ultra-lightweight, aluminium sidevalve engine with oil pump mounted directly on one end of the camshaft and distributor on the other. In the end, only the camshaft-mounted oil pump idea survived, the rest of the engine being in the now-typical Austin mould. The crankshaft ran in three 'thinwall' bearings, the first British production engine to do so, and the cylinder head was designed by Harry Weslake, an independent consultant who had long worked for Austin and whose work was instrumental in making the A30 combustion chambers so efficient.

1953, the year in which all Minors finally 'went' Series II, was a good year for the car in other ways, too. Not only were the 'Commercial' Minors introduced in van, pick-up and chassis-cab form, ready for the customer to fit his own body, but the Minor range was completed by the introduction of the Traveller in October. The Minor Traveller followed the announcement a year earlier of the 'woodie' Morris Oxford and was based upon the floorpan of the Minor saloon. From the door shut-pillar area back, the framework provided structural support and was most certainly not merely a cosmetic accessory.

The Traveller was introduced with a number of modifications which were to find their way onto the rest of the range in the coming months: wheel hubs, front and rear, were separated from the brake drums, while the new-type road wheels were held on by nuts instead

of studs which made wheel changing a far simpler exercise. New swivel pins were fitted and the Austin 'banjo' type of rear axle replaced the Morris split-case item. All Series II cars received a small body modification which has largely gone unnoticed: Minor Series MM's scuttle panels had wrapped around the sides of the car, reaching down to the line of the wing tops, but Series II bonnets were designed to overlap the now inset scuttle sides, the bonnets themselves abutting the leading edges of the front doors. It is worth noting, therefore, that post-MM bonnets will not fit Series MM cars!

In October 1954, the Series II Minor was given a host of small-scale modifications plus one body change which apart from its split windscreen, gave the Minor the appearance with which most people identify today — the vertical slats were wiped form the face of the grille, the vertical grille mouldings were angled in at the bottom (and grille and front wing shapes modified to suit) and an array of five horizontal, painted grille slats fitted over the radiator aperture. The 803cc engine, perhaps good enough for 1952, was, however, looking distincly sluggish when compared with the 1956 opposition . . .

A thousand, a million, and more

In October 1956, the increasing number of critics — especially overseas — who felt that the Minor would benefit from the use of a larger engine were at last rewarded. The A-series engine was increased in size to one of the larger sizes envisaged when it was first designed: 948cc. However, although there seemed to be plenty of room between the tiny 58mm (2.28in) wide 'pots' of the 803cc engine, a decision was taken to strengthen and improve the engine generally. The block was a new casting with bores 1 & 2, and 3 & 4

siamesed in pairs — that is to say that there was now no longer a water jacket between those pairs of cylinders. While this feature was not essential in order to achieve 948cc from the original block, it followed Austin's approach to the B-series engine and it meant that the changes necessary for a further capacity increase had already been carried out. The crankshaft was also new, with larger diameter big-end bearings; stiffer con-rods were fitted; and lead-indium bearings were substituted for the 803cc's white metal — again following B-series practice. This meant that the oil filtration system had also to be changed. The 803cc engine with white metal bearings used a bye-pass filtration system whereby the flow of oil from the oil pump was passed through an internal main gallery and part-diverted through a very fine filter whilst most passed through the bearings. Thus the oil was very thoroughly filtered — but only a little at a time so there were usually small particles in circulation. With white metal bearings this hardly mattered since the particles would bed themselves into the relatively soft white metal causing no damage to the crank. The much longer lasting lead-indium was, naturally enough, much harder and so a new way of filtering the engine, using the coarser but quicker 'full-flow' filtration system, had to be introduced. Although the basic layout of the head was unchanged — and *couldn't* have been changed without completely redesigning the engine — valve sizes were increased, the combustion chamber shapes were increased in size whilst still using Harry Westlake's patented design (and in fact a label on the rocker box told you so!), and the SU carburettor size was increased from the 1⅛ inch used on all previous Minors to the 1¼ inch size used on all subsequent cars.

The new engine was a dream and represented a high-point in A-series engine design. Others were more powerful but none was quite as smooth, economical and well-balanced while the 948cc engine was still, in its day, sprightly

enough. It pushed out 37bhp at the flywheel and its increased torque enabled it to pull from a ridiculously low speed in top gear and to go on pulling to well over 70mph. At the same time, BMC fitted an improved gearbox with gear ratios to match the increased power (top speed in third gear was now not far short of the Series II Minor's overall maximum), better synchromesh and a remote gearchange giving a sensibly short, positive gearstick in place of the long, spindly pudding-stirrer previously used.

The new, more powerful Minor was called the Minor 1000 but it would seem, incredibly, that the 803cc Series II remained in very limited production for at least seven or eight more years as a specially adapted invalid's car. Presumably the prejudice which assumed that disabled folk wouldn't want to drive as rapidly as those sound in wind and limb was not appreciated in 1956, but at least the car was a distinct improvement over the even more offensively crude 2-stroke buggies made available by the government (although one might note that *they* are preferable to the zero provision of today!)

Structurally, the Minor received one more change, the last it was ever to see. The split windscreen, which though it seems charming now, was hopelessly old-fashioned in 1956, was replaced by a larger, curved, one-piece screen but, extra-ordinarily, the old opposed-action windscreen wipers were still fitted, leaving a great central chunk of windscreen unwiped! The rear window was also made much larger and the rear wings covered more of the rear wheels. Brakes, tyres and suspension were quite unaltered but the dash *was* changed. Glove locker lids were fitted to both sides of the perfectly symmetrical dash, but with one small problem — the steering wheel wouldn't allow you to open, by more than a couple of inches, the locker lid fitted behind it, and even then it involved hand contortions in order to grab hold of the ridiculously tiny handle whilst reaching through the steering wheel

spokes. Apprentice-quality design was starting to let the Minor down! In overseas markets, for instance, there was no external lock on the left-hand (driver's) door, so the driver had to slip the internal catch on the left-hand door and scramble out of the 'British' driver's door, locking it behind him. Similarly, although the indicator switch was moved to a steering column stalk and the horn button positioned on the end of it to allow 'hands-on' horn operation, road testers complained that the horn push spring was so strong that you had to take your hand off the wheel anyway in order to exert sufficient pressure on the thing! Still, BMC were trying, and rear passenger access was improved in 2-door cars when the front passenger seat backrest was made to fold flat onto the seat base which then tipped right forwards and out of the way. Semaphore indicators were still fitted as standard to UK cars, although flashing indicators incorporated in the sidelights were standard for export cars and were optional in the home market, too.

In 1960, the one-millionth Morris Minor was built. Although American companies had achieved this figure many times over with some models, as had Volkswagen and Renault in Europe, it was a British 'first' and BMC, and the British public, became quite excited about the event. The millionth Minor was built a couple of days before Christmas 1960, which enabled BMC to benefit from the post-festivity dearth of news in most newspapers and so receive extra publicity for their achievement. They capitalized on the fact by building 350 cars, numbered out of sequence as 1,000,000 to 1,000,350 and painting them a revolting shade of lilac with an equally hideous white interior. At least they were noticed! 'Minor Millions' were also given special 'Minor 1 000 000' badges but were otherwise bog-standard 2-door cars, 320 of them being home-marked right-hand drive and the remainder exported. The publicity seemed to have had no effect whatever on sales because the 1960 figure of 95,000 cars, itself 20,000 down on two years previously, slumped to 60,000 in 1961 and fell steadily from then onwards. The reasons are not hard to see.

The Renault Dauphine, introduced in the fifties had an appeal never before seen in a European car. In spite of the fact that it handled abysmally and corroded at an amazingly rapid rate, the car had something that the Minor's designers had never heard of – consumer appeal! In 1959, the Mini came onto the market and, quite by chance, it too acquired 'chic'. The same year saw the Triumph Herald's appearance; a car which set its own high standards in consumer-orientated appeal. A similar sort of package had been offered by BMC when the Farina-styled Austin A40 appeared and then a modern mechanical layout was allied to updated styling with the introduction of the Austin/Morris 1100, a car that was to be a big seller – almost as big a seller as the new small-ish Ford, the Cortina, launched in the same year, to accompany the direct Minor competitor, the Anglia 105E, with its distinctive forward-sloping rear window. Given the circumstances, it now seems amazing that the poor old Minor sold as well as it did, especially since it was consigned by management to the back-burner and left to simmer virtually unchanged.

Just one more major change was on the cards, although it was simply a matter of the Minor getting caught up in company rationalization rather than there being any plans to modernize the Minor.

In October 1962, the engine was increased in capacity to 1098cc along with the A-series engines used in the Austin A40, A35 van and the Sprites and Midgets so that they all used what was fundamentally the 1100 block. Once again, valve sizes were increased and the crankcase strengthened, along with a tougher crank and centre main bearing thrust washers. The crank itself was stronger, with thicker webs while the clutch was enlarged in diameter in order to cope with the increased power. The transmission was greatly improved and altered to meet the changing needs of motorists in the new motorway era. In spite of a 30 per cent increase in bhp, the new Minor 1000 was not significantly faster than its predecessor because higher gearing gave more relaxed, long-legged cruising instead. Modification to the gearbox internals meant that baulking whilst going into first gear was far less likely and, at last, this was a synchromesh system that worked properly! Front brake drums were increased from 7 inch to 8 inch diameter but suspension wheels and tyres remained the same. Unfortunately, there was a disappointing side effect of the increased power on tap (getting on for *twice* the power of 1948!) combined with two fewer rear leaf springs on saloons and convertibles, a change brought about in the late fifties in the interests of passenger comfort. The rear end would tramp badly if the car was accelerated hard in a low gear, (especially in the wet), whilst cornering or when climbing a steep hill. This occurred especially when the rear shock absorbers were past their best, when the results could be embarrassing if not downright dangerous!

At long last, the Minor was given some sensible mods. There was a fresh air heater, a self-supporting bonnet stay (although the boot lid, illogically, still needed a prayer for calm weather to get it propped open and the boot loaded) and the amber flashing indicator lamps were large and unmistakable – and expensive to replace if cracked! The glove lockers no longer had fiddly lids but were, as *Autocar* complained, of the self-emptying variety if the driver made a sharp getaway. A few months after the 1098cc engine was fitted, the wipers were at last made to operate conventionally and key-operated door locks were fitted to both front doors.

Over the remaining years of the 'Swinging Sixties', the one thing that *didn't* swing was the Minor! As its sales fell and it continued to

remain undeveloped, its profits fell accordingly. Consequently, following the Leyland-dominated merger with BMC, the Minor Convertible was one of the first of a long line of obsolete cars — in technical and marketing terms — that were to be axed by the new management when it was dropped in mid-1969. The two- and four-door saloons followed just over a year later and, in April 1971, after getting on for 23 years of production, the last Traveller — the last Minor of all — left the production lines.

The commercials

As already mentioned, the first Minor commercials were introduced in May 1953 to replace the ancient Morris Eight — based 'Series 2' Vans which had been kept in production. The three models of LCV (Light Commercial Vehicle) served a vital part of the domestic market as well as notching up a large number of sales to local authorities and the 'utilities'; the General Post Office and PO Telephones being major buyers.

Quite apart form the glaringly obvious differences in body styling, the Minor LCVs differed in at least one other major respect, too — they were based upon a separate rear chassis. Where the Minor saloon and Traveller's chassis stopped at the main crossmember, the LCV's chassis continued right through to the rear of the vehicle, sweeping up and over the line of the rear axle. The rear spring shackles fitted around the rearmost part of the chassis while the front shackles fitted pins on the chassis sides. Connecting both of the pins was a tubular section to add rigidity and provide support for the bed. The petrol tank was found slung between the rear of the chassis members. Theoretically, van and pick-up bodies are simple to remove (from the cab-back), but given the all-corroding ravages of time, that in practice is no longer the case!

Among the commercials, early

GPO vans are probably the most collectable, the most rare — and certainly the most distinctive! Their driver's side windscreen was built with top hinges to give improved visibility, when opened, in a good old-fashioned 'pea-souper' fog, and the headlamps were mounted separately on MM-style rubber front wings, giving them for all the world the appearance of a bull frog.

The original 803cc LCVs were of 5cwt capacity but in October 1962 payload was increased to 6cwt. Like the Traveller, the LCVs retained their 7-leaf rear springs until 1968 when an extra leaf was added, front suspension was strengthened, wheels and tyres increased in size to give a 5.60 × 14 inch dimension, and maximum payload increased to 8cwt. Very soon afterwards, the only ever 'Austin' Minor was offered for sale in the form of the Austin 8cwt van. It had an Austin badge on the bonnet, rocker box and steering wheel, a typically Austin crinked radiator grille and plain, anonymous hub caps.

Nowadays, keeping a Minor commercial on the road is little more difficult than keeping a 'private' vehicle in tip-top condition. In fact, when you consider the absence of interior trim and the presence of stout chassis members, it can be considerably easier in some respects. Minor Pick-ups are probably the most 'collectable' of the non-GPO commercials, but as yet the commercials range as a whole has not attracted the same sort of interest from enthusiasts as the 'domestic' range. They are, however, vehicles that combine the ruggedness of the Morris Minor with the attributes of a chunky, roomy light van or pick-up and so many of them are still in everyday, workaday use.

Riley, Wolseley and Australian variants

At first glance, there is nothing to

connect the Minor with the Riley 1.5 or the Wolseley 1500, but beneath the skin, the connections are there all right and for the restorer, the structural part of the story is almost exactly the same. And, similarly, there is the story of the Morris Major and Austin Lancer, built in BMC Australia's plant at Victoria Park, Sydney and again with a larger engine on a Minor chassis/floorpan.

Almost from the first days of the Minor, folk had tried increasing its performance to match its roadholding abilities but it was not until 1957, when in April and November the Wolseley and Riley were announced, that BMC produced cars to match the Minor 'chassis' potential.

The Wolseley Fifteen-Hundred, as it should properly be known, was taller than the Minor, and 3¾ inches longer, but used a virtually standard Minor floorpan, suspension and steering, although every single outer body panel was different. Because the Wolseley had a squarer shape than the egg-like curves of the Minor, 3 inches more width was available with a little more headroom, although the distance from front to back seats was reduced for rear seat passengers because of the more heavily upholstered seats used. Polished wood veneer cappings added to the air of opulence in the car, but the biggest change to the car's character came from the use of the B-series Austin engine in place of the Minor's A-series. With 1500cc and 50bhp on tap, performance was much better than the Minor's in spite of the extra-high final drive ratio in the Minor rear axle which gave delightfully relaxed high speed cruising, in 1957 terms. The B-series gearbox was also used with close-ratio gears but the drum brakes were uprated to 9 inch drums at the front with 8 inch drums at the rear, still using the Minor's master-cylinder-beneath-the-floor set up.

When the Riley One-Point-Five appeared some seven months later, its performance was a revelation! The twin-carburettor 68bhp engine, based on the MG Magnette unit and with larger valves than the

Wolseley/Austin engine, propelled the car to well over eighty miles per hour and required the use of wider front brake linings and drums fitted at the front in order to stop the 21cwt touring car. (Strangely, the brakes used were Girling rather than the Lockheed units used on Morris and Wolseley cars — Len Lord's rationalization plans stopped short of the nuts and bolts, it seems.) With cleaner lines than the Minor, sparkling performance and comfort aplenty, the Riley 'Minor' was a cracker! Unfortunately, the problem of axle tramp was not solved (although the obvious solution, as with the Minor, was to fit telescopic rear shock absorbers) and handling, with extra power and extra weight around, was not up to that of the Minor.

From 1958, the Austin Lancer and Morris Major (both based on the Wolseley 1500) were built in Australia to answer criticisms that the Minor's power was not up to running the longer, straighter Australian roads. The Wolseley 1500, surprisingly enough, was also sold in Australia as an up-market alternative to the Lancer and Major. The following year, however, the Wolseley was dropped and the Austin and Morris cars received an extra 6 inch of body length. Only the original roof panel was retained, every other panel being altered, the new car looking vaguely American and not at all like its forebear, the Minor. In 1962, this car was fitted with the 1622cc B-series engine, using a version modified by the Australian market and produced at BMC Australia and became known as the Morris Major Elite.

It is interesting to note that throughout its lengthy production life, the Minor was only changed in detail, apart from the uprating of its engine in order to (almost) keep up with contemporary trends, but there were so many apparently different cars that were virtually Morris Minors under the skin. They all contain the heart of the Minor and all — apart perhaps from the later Australian cars — can be made structurally sound with the aid of this book.

All Minors and Minor-derived cars, whether a 1948 Series MM, a 1971 Traveller or a Riley 1.5 have that certain 'something', a depth of character shared by no other car. The Minor was a legend in its own time; but the legend lives on!

H1. The engine first used in the Minor was first destined for the pre-war Morris 8, having been 'filched' from Ford by Leonard Lord's team. Spares are not too hard to come by for the engine, although you can't exactly get them from Unipart!

H2. Sitting in an engine bay designed to take a flat-four, the side-valve Morris 8 engine was surrounded with oodles of room. This restored example is showroom-new in appearance.

H3.   Alec Issigonis, the Morris Minor's designer, was said to have believed that the car only looked 'right' in this, its original, headlamps-in-grille form.

H4.   The front seats in early Minors were actually better shaped and more comfortable on a long journey than those in later cars, having a more 'bucket' shaped backrest. Note the very early style of door pull on this convertible.

H5.   Very early convertibles also had removable rear side screens so that, with the hood down, the car became as fully open as any sports car.

H6. Semaphore indicators had become downright dangerous before they were phased out. Nowadays, it's pleasant to see them operate correctly alongside flashing indicators.

H7. Among the rarest of all surviving Minors are these Post Office vans with rubber wings, frog-like headlamps and opening driver's windscreen. Like many other cars in this section, these vans were photographed at a very wet Morris Minor Owners' Club annual rally.

H8. Also relatively unusual is the split-screen Traveller.

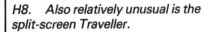

H9. The Morris Minor Traveller is the most versatile of all Minors, although the cost of repairing the woodwork is very high compared with the cost of restoring many other parts of the car.

H10. Morris Minor Pick-ups are worth more than the far more common Vans because they possess the virtues of utility without the noise, smells and untidyness that can be inflicted upon the occupants of a working van with access to the rear.

H11. There were too many changes of dash to picture here but this one is probably the most practicable while a similar-looking dash with a lid over the locker behind the steering wheel was the most awkward to use.

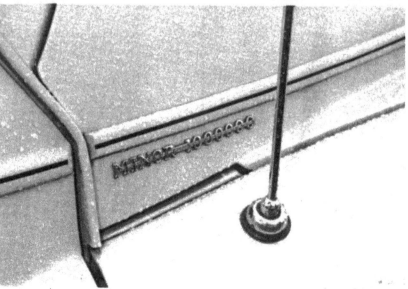

H12. Take a second look at the chrome plated script! The Minor Million was a limited edition run to commemorate the millionth Minor built. Many of the 350-or-so built seem to have survived, complete with their original bright lilac colour scheme!

H13.   Some people will go to incredible lengths to modify their Minor! This owner has gone so far as to squeeze a supercharger under the bonnet!

H14.   This Minor had the chop and ended up as somebody's trailer. Yours could have a better fate if you follow the approach shown in this book!

2 Buying

You might be tempted to think that getting hold of a Morris Minor in good condition would be easy! After all, over 1 ¼ million of the cars were produced (to say nothing of the commercials) and they were built so sturdily that, as everyone knows, Morris Minors go on for ever . . .

Unfortunately, you would be in for a rude awakening! For a start, although vast numbers of Minors were built, production was spread over a very long time, the oldest cars having had twenty-three more years than the newer cars to corrode or crash themselves out of existence. What makes things worse is that most people, when they say they would like to own a Minor, mean they want to own one of the easiest to own nowadays — the 1962-on 1098cc Minors, mostly with the larger type rear lamps. These, however, account for only 20 per cent of all production, which means that there were probably 150,000 post- '63 cars sold in the UK with about 100,000 exported. Of course, the answer may be to turn to one of the more numerous earlier cars (and I would certainly not object to living with a 948cc Minor provided it was for local work); there were, after all, over 500,000 of these cars built.

The second problem will be that it can be extremely difficult to find a really nice Morris Minor at all! *Nothing* goes on for ever, not even the Morris Minor but, in the face of overwhelming odds — ignorant owners; ignorant garages; the ravages of British winters — the Minor could be described as, well, persistent, and certainly more tolerant than many more complex and less soundly designed motor cars. The poor old things will soldier on through the most horrendous abuse, so at least the chances of coming across one are still very high, but the chances of finding one that does not require radical structural work carried out will be very slim indeed. But that's where this book and the unparalleled advice of The Morris Minor Centre comes in!

The existence of The Morris Minor Centre and other specialists with a similar allegiance, coupled with the numbers of Minor enthusiasts who are determined to keep their cars up to scratch, means that parts supply is actually better than for many contemporary cars, and considerably better than just about any Japanese car on British roads and more than a couple of years old! At the same time, parts are incredibly cheap. Anyone who, wistfully remembering the days when you could get drunk on a thrupenny bit, or whatever, thinks otherwise, should just pop down to their local Ford, Volkswagen or Datsun dealer and compare prices of parts and see what I mean! The Morris Minor Centre's supply of parts has been expressly designed with the fact in mind that Morris Minors are now often rusty and deteriorated. This means that it would be hard to imagine any Minor that was beyond restoration; the question becomes one of economic sense. However, Charlie Ware, The Minor Centre's founder has examined the true costs of restoring and running a Minor and concludes that, even allowing for restoration costs, a Minor can be run for a third to a half of the cost of running a comparable new car. This is because new cars loose a fortune in depreciation and tend to have a severely restricted lifespan, whereas Minors are built in such a way that, if repaired properly, they can be made to go on virtually indefinitely. It just takes a shift in the attitude of the owner away from resentment at spending money on repairing an old car — money that will probably not be reflected in the car's value — and towards a view that sees that carrying out repairs to a 'durable

commodity', one that will go on and on, is economically, aesthetically, morally and in every way rationally more sensible than spending money on a new car with in-built obsolescence and a guarantee: the sort of unwritten guarantee that says, 'This car will depreciate so quickly that you will lose a fortune – without even knowing it!'

Two points must be made here. The first relates to the quality of the work carried out on the car. Unfortunately, most ordinary garages just don't understand what should be meant by 'restoration' – and neither, in fact, do most car owners. Folk are often their own worst enemies because they tend to want the cheapest possible job done on their cars, while to meet this demand, most garages have become highly adept (skilful would be too complimentary a word) at cobbling cars together to get you through the next few hundred miles or the next MOT test. Most mechanics know how to cobble Minors together – they've had plenty of practice over the years – but wouldn't actually know how the car should be properly repaired. Even some so-called 'Minor Centres' produce a poor standard of restoration work (although others, by the same token, are vastly superior to the local repairer) which suggests that the owner should do one of two things: have the work done by a trusted restoration-orientated workshop; or the work can be carried out at home over a period of time, developing the skills as required or working alongside a high-class welder, working to a standard rather than a price and following the approach detailed in this book.

The second point regards value. The *only* way of not spending a great deal more on a car than its market value is to do the work yourself. Even then, you can easily spend more than the car is worth, but you should be looking at the value of a Minor perhaps as something of intrinsic worth (beauty is in the eye of the beholder, etc) and most certainly as a sort of investment – an investment in a car

which certainly won't depreciate at anything like the rate of a new car; and investment in a car that can be run incredibly cheaply; and an investment in an attractive motorcar of character that can be made to go on and on and on . . .

Take your pick

Although ostensibly one model of car, the Minor actually consists of a number of models with totally different characters and qualities. If the Wolseleys and Rileys are included in the range then you can see the tremendous contrast in performance between the long-stroke sidevalve MM and the Riley 1.5, its 1500cc engine in an MG state of tune. Then there are the commercials to give carrying capacity aplenty, the Convertible to give infinite stretches of fresh air, and the ultimate in versatility, the Minor Traveller. A good idea of the changes that took place is given in Chapter 1 while the Appendices detail the technical and numerical background to the developments and should be used to check in fine detail a potential purchase's originality. Because all of the cars share the same floorpan and 'chassis', however, it is not unusual to find 'wrong' components fitted. As a result, a number of Series II cars have been fitted with later type front wings, bumper and grille surround, while later, deep type rear wings have frequently been used as replacements for the earlier 'mini-skirt' variety. Engines, gearboxes and differential units are often swapped around with abandon. If you're desperately keen on originality you may be concerned, and avoid problems as a result, but if not . . . beware: some combinations would be terrible! Imagine a Series II 803cc engine used as a replacement for a 1098cc engine (or even one from an A35 van, some of which were of the Mini's 848cc but in-line, of course); the plot would hardly drag itself

down the road! Or what about a late Riley 1.5 differential fitted as a replacement for a standard diff. Even a 1098 is faster in third than in top with this set-up! Or, how about a Riley 1.5 engine and gearbox in an early car with suspect chassis and 7 inch brakes? . . . Ouch! The list of permutations is endless and not always very desirable, so do make sure by studying the specifications given in this book and examining engine and chassis numbers carefully, that you get what you expect.

Assuming that things are as the great Morris Minor maker in the sky intended, you still come back to deciding which Morris Minor to look for. This is perhaps the most enjoyable part of the exercise, giving you all the pleasure of looking through a seed catalogue without yet having the problem of digging the garden. Looking at contemporary road tests will provide a small part of the information you need, but of course the test car will only be judged by the standards of the testers' day, while you might want to know how the car fares today.

This brings us back to the main point. The use to which the car is to be put is the main determinant of, first, which body type to choose and, secondly, the age of the car.

The Minor two-door saloon was made in the greatest numbers and is still the most prolific body style. On earlier cars, with the flat-folding passenger seat backrest, access to the rear seats is excellent while on later cars the fixed backrest seat allows the tubular seat supports to be somewhat obstructive when entering the rear. Incidentally, the fold-flat properties of the earlier seats also make the carrying of long loads easier, since they can extend from boot to front footwell.

As well as having the benefit of better rear access, four-door saloons have more windows to open, since the rear lights on two-door models are fixed. On the other side of the coin are the standard seat belt mounting kits, which on early four-door models are ugly, and

also the fact that there were fewer four-door cars made, hence they are a little more expensive, too.

The Minor Traveller ranks as firm favourite for many owners and in terms of sheer versatility it's easy to see why. With its rear seat in place the car gives little ground to the saloon for family use, except in terms of a slightly harder rear ride and a tendency to rattle more. Renewal of the rear-door rubbers usually cures the latter problem, while the rear seat backrest, and the area around the fixing bolts, can usually be made rattle-free by sliding a piece of rubber tubing over the spring clip under which the fixing bolt is held.

The main disadvantage of the Traveller lies in its very timbering. Because the skeletal wooden structure provides the framework upon which the rear bodywork is based, the soundness of the timer is 'MOTable'; it *does* rot, both deep in its joints and along its length. Also its surface discolours requiring considerable work before the offending parts can be sealed from the elements. However, one can bring and maintain the woodwork on a Traveller to a high standard using 'unskilled' labour, provided that it is sound.

In use, the Minor Traveller is nearly the equal of other, much larger, cars, with a long, flat loading bay available. Even with the rear seat erected the boot space is, of course, excellent. Ventilation on the Traveller is better than that of other closed Minors since both of its rear windows slide open. And for holidays the Traveller is unsurpassable among Minors. Its excellent load carrying capabilities can be augmented by a roof-rack (though note that the rear section of the Traveller roof is aluminium and is susceptible to being dented by roof-rack legs).

So far the choice of Minor has been presented in the light of which would be the most useful. The Minor convertible, however, is for long, hot days and the soft scents of summer. For most other days it is prone to draughts, leaks, flapping and all the other disadvantages of a soft-top car. On the other hand, it is among the most delightful and well loved British cars of all time.

The Tourer hood is fairly easy to fold down and the open car is pleasant to drive. On early Series MM models, the rear side windows were removable, while with windows in position, none of the buffeting from the wind is experienced as suffered by many sports car drivers. Mechanically, and in all the major body and underfloor panels, the Tourer is identical to its sisters. Hoods are still available, so no prospective owner need be scared off on that point.

Well away from the pleasures of the Tourer, however, lie the two Minor 1000 commercials, the Van and the Pick-up. The Van offers the advantage, albeit a dubious one, of having been made for some years after the demise of the Morris 1000 as the Austin 'Minor' van, bearing of course, the 'wrong' badges. Most vans are rather noisy and the Minor Van is no exception. Moreover, its ride, along with that of the Pick-ups, is the hardest of the Minors. The greatest disadvantages are the lack of visibility to the rear quarters and the lower speed limit applying to commercial vehicles in some areas. Moreover, the interior of the Van can become almost unbearable in hot weather, and impossible to heat at the coldest times of the year.

Rear sliding type side windows can be fitted to the Van, and the ventilation problem is then solved. To overcome the British speed limit restriction, however, forward-facing rear seats would also have to be fitted. In theory, the vehicle would then be liable for extra Car Tax, although in practice the Customs and Excise people say that they never charge any duty on vehicles more than six years old, although this is a concession on their part and not a statutory obligation.

In short, the attractions of the Van are that it has the greatest enclosed load-carrying capacity of any Minor, and that it provides the cheapest type — and possibly the newest, in Austin form — of Minor transport.

Cheapness no longer seems to be among the attractions of the Pick-ups, for cult status combined with its great versatility are sending prices higher. Its cab, of course, can remain as cool or as cosy as you like, while the rear loading bed can be used for carrying just about anything. The load can be covered, too, using a canvas tilt. Many Pick-up have been fitted with privately-built bodies, for carrying anything from milk crates to pigs.

So much for having decided *which* model; one is then faced with the equally difficult task of deciding *how old?* Many prospective owners have erred in believing that all Minors, because of the similar appearance, are much the same sort of car to drive whatever their year of manufacture. Nothing could be further from the truth, because as the public's expectations of performance, safety and comfort changed so, at certain stages, was the Minor improved — albeit at a pace which fell increasingly below the rate of improvement of the competition until, at its demise, the Minor was looking a very old-fashioned car indeed. Still, it is those very qualities of 'old-fashionedness' which may appeal to the prospective owner, and the questions which he or she must ask become, 'which qualities?' and 'how old-fashioned?'.

Minor 1000

The most usable, everyday series is the youngest, dating from 1962, when the 1098cc engine was introduced with an improved gearbox and larger front brakes. A higher differential ratio was also fitted so that the increase in the power of the revised engine went mostly towards increasing the vehicle's top speed. In practice, this larger engine works especially well out of town, particularly on hills where the extra torque proves very useful. Many enthusiasts feel that this later engine never runs quite as 'sweetly' as its earlier, smaller kin and that, because of the longer throw of the crank, the bottom-end has a slightly shorter life. Set

against the increased power of the biggest engine, however, these factors are trivial, particularly to anyone using the car every day. A further plus point for the later engine is that it shares many of its components with other BMC and BL A-series engines of the same capacity, which means that the long-term spares situation is rosy.

The only other significant changes to occur after the fitting of the 1098cc engine were, first, the use of a fresh-air heater from April 1963, which was further improved with better performance in October 1964. Unlike the previous recirculatory heater, the fresh-air type is capable of producing just about enough warmth in the coldest weather as well as providing fresh, cold air when required. The second change is the one which externally denotes the modern Minor: the combined round side lamp/flasher unit fitted in June 1963. At the same time the Traveller gained a proper separate amber flasher fitted into the woodwork at the rear.

The pre- 1962/3 Minor 1000s are almost as usable as everyday cars, but bear in mind that parts for the major mechanical components are becoming increasingly difficult to find, although fitting later parts is nearly always possible. None of the later body panels are different, except that the front wings need to be altered slightly where the front sidelights are fitted, but many of the detail fittings are different such as rear sidelight lenses, front seats and so on. For these reasons, the earlier vehicles tend to be cheaper than later models. As a car for local use only, provided that a small stock is maintained of those service parts which are not easy to find, the 1000 produced from 1956 with the 948cc engine, is likely to prove a useful and charming friend. For harder use, realism dictates that the 1098cc model should be sought.

Series II

Earlier still is the Series II with split-windscreen which, perhaps, is an expression of an era of cosy, comfortable self-satisfaction in which post-war parents drove their children to the seaside. It is in connection with this car that the prospective purchaser should heed the warnings about the need to place in context contemporary road tests. At the time, the car was considered to be possessed of satisfactory performance, with a high level of comfort for a car of its type, and road holding that was ahead of its time. Indeed, in 1953, when the Series II was introduced, all of this was true, but for the nineteen-eighties things look very different. The car is simply too slow in traffic. Perhaps you should regard the Series II Minor as a hobby car that is capable of giving regular and reliable *leisure time* service alone.

Spares for Series II cars are difficult, with surprisingly few parts being common to the later cars. Front bumpers, windscreens, bonnet, wings and doors are among the body panels which changed in 1956. Later parts require major surgery to fit, apart from the further difficulties of making them match the *appearance* of the original. The engine, carburettor, gearbox, differential and some of the brake parts were also changed.

Series MM

The same but more so can be said of the earliest Minor, the MM. This used the even less powerful pre-war design of sidevalve engine, and contains a host of different body and mechanical specifications that are peculiar to this series alone. Few would argue that the 'usability' side of the see-saw goes down because of the increasing fragility of elderly parts and shrinking pool of spares, but if motoring of a byegone era appeals, the 'desirability' side rises in direct response. Emphatically not a car in which to commute each day, but equally certainly a fine car to take as a serious restoration project.

Having decided upon the type and age of Minor to be purchased, there still remains one important unanswered question. Should one purchase a roadworthy usable car and put up with the inevitable problems that will become manifest, or buy a car in need of restoration and see it rebuilt to the standards desired? If a rebuild is chosen, would it be wisest to attempt DIY restoration or to have it tackled professionally?

All of this will affect the price of the car. That decision can only be made after honestly appraising the finance, facilities, skills and personal determination available (if a home rebuild is to be contemplated).

Even if you especially enjoy carrying out restoration work – and many people do enjoy that special satisfaction – or if you have ample funds and approve of other people's rebuild standards, it usually pays to spend more time and money initially and find the best car to start with.

One would normally advise against the halfway-house purchase, for by the time all the small faults have been put right that the average older car possesses, a full-scale rebuild could have been undertaken; but with the Minor this advice does not necessarily hold true. It is true of more complex vehicles, such as Jaguars or Rovers, where greater power, weight and mechanical and bodily complexity mean that 'small' jobs, if carried out thoroughly, invariably mushroom into bigger jobs as more wear is found in parts adjacent to those being repaired.

The Minor, however, is so relatively straightforward that by careful buying it should be possible to obtain a reasonably sound, medium-priced vehicle which is roadworthy and usable but whose deterioration could be first halted and then reversed by carrying out a systematic work programme.

Where to look

Not all that long ago, the Minor was one of the staples of the used-car dealer's showrooms; nowadays, the only Minors to appear there are likely to be highly priced 'conversation pieces' designed to

attract the casual looker who may then lose his or her attention to other 'gems' nearby. Nowadays, advertisements in local newspapers and through the pages of the Morris Minor Owners' Club magazine as well as in the 'classic' car journals and local and national advertising magazines are the most usual routes to buying a Minor.

You can go to The Morris Minor Centre, or alternatively one of the other specialists more local to you, where there is always a selection of Minors available. Prices there may be higher than in the local rag (although not in every case), but you will be buying a known quantity from a reputable source. Even the Morris Minor specialist, however, can't magically make a second-hand Minor better than it was without spending a lot of money, so be prepared to only get what you pay for. The important trick is to avoid paying a lot of money for a tarted-up Minor with perfectly smooth glossy paint and a terminally-dangerous underside. In fact, you have to start − quite literally − turning conventional car buying wisdom on its head and, no matter where you are buying from, taking more note of structural soundness than cosmetic appearance.

Bodywork and underframe − in general

One of the main attractions of the Minor is its well-founded reputation of being tough. Most of this sturdiness can be found in the construction of the car's floorpan, one which is not only suitable for the saloon (with its immensely strong roof), the Traveller (with its timber-framed rear), and the convertible (which, while not benefiting from roof rigidity is amply strong enough with little extra strengthening), but was also found suitable for the much heavier Wolseley 1500 and Riley 1.5; a tribute to over-engineering.

Although one rarely, if ever, sees a twisted Minor, its unitary construction has some short-comings, too. There are many mud traps where rot easily forms and severely weakens the body. Where a structure depends upon its very complexity for its strength rather than the raw thickness of metal, any sort of corrosion means trouble.

Rust takes a hold in strangely unpredictable ways. It is impossible, for instance, to say that if W is rusted out, then X, Y and Z will be so, too. The only answer is to check in turn each of the known potential troublespots and be brutally thorough. It is not unknown for a section of chassis rail to appear perfectly sound on the outside, but actually to be paper-thin and totally unsuitable for welding onto.

You may be lucky enough to come across a Minor which has had the entire chassis/floorpan rebuilt but has an extremely tatty body. Unless the car is a Traveller, in which case the woodwork could be very expensive to replace, don't be put off − as long as the price is right of course! The cost of repairing outer body panels is a lot less than rebuilding *properly* a corroded underside.

Using the checklist

This checklist is designed to show step-by-step instructions for virtually all the checks to be made on a car offered for sale. After each check, the fault indicated is shown in brackets, e.g. the instructions, 'Look along wings, door bottoms, wheel arches and sills from the front and rear of the car' is followed by the fault, shown in brackets, as (Ripples indicate filler presence/crash damage. £££). The pound sterling signs require some explanation. They are intended to give a guide to the cost of rectifying the fault. £ indicates that the cost is likely to be less than the cost of a new tyre, £££ stands for the cost of a new set of tyres, or more, while ££

means that the cost is likely to be between the two. The cost guide relates to the cost of the component(s) only, other than in the case of bodywork − allow more if you have the work done for you.

When examining a car you are advised to take this book (or copies of the relevant buying checklists) and a notebook with you. As each item is checked, a record can be kept in the notebook. You may wish to record a running cost total for necessary repairs as faults are discovered − this could be a useful bargaining tool at the end of your examination.

It is strongly recommended that the repair and restoration sections of this book and also the Haynes Morris Minor Owners Workshop Manual are examined so that the checker is fully familiar with every component being examined.

Checking over a prospective purchase not only can but *should* be very time consuming if the right car is to be bought rather than a glossed-over heap of trouble. What follows is an elimination sequence in three separate parts, each one taking longer and being more thorough than the last, this approach having the virtue of saving the purchaser both time and embarrassment. It is always easier to withdraw at an early stage than after an hour spent checking the car over with the aid of the owner's comments and mugs of coffee! Thus Stage A aims to eliminate the obvious 'nails' without having to probe too deeply. Stage B takes matters somewhat further for cars that pass the first stage, while Stage C is the 'dirty hands' stage, the one you don't get into on a snowy February evening unless you are really serious!

Tool box

Old, warm clothes (if the ground is cold). An old mat or board if the ground is wet. A bright torch. A pair of ramps. A small hammer. A

screwdriver or other probe. Copies of the following pages and a notepad. A pencil. A bottle, trolley or scissors jack. Axle stands.

Safety

Safety should be carefully considered and any necessary steps taken. In particular, do not rely on a handbrake holding a car on a slope or ramps. NEVER go under a car supported by a jack only.

Stage A – first impressions

1)   Is the car standing level all the way round? Are door and window frame gaps even? Are bumper gaps even, front and back? (Down at one corner indicates weak springs. £ per spring. Or sagged front suspension due to severe corrosion in crossmember £££ + ; or severe corrosion in rear spring mountings £££ + . Badly fitting bumpers mean light accident damage £ – or is it worse? Doors with poor gaps or which stick out of line at top or bottom indicate: sagged chassis [Tourers especially prone] £££ + ; poorly aligned panels fitted, locking car in distorted position £££ + potential; badly fitted door skin ££. Also check door pillars for rubbing, i.e. door has dropped, hits door pillar before striker plate pulls door up. Worn hinges £. Distortion in body as described above ££).

2)   Look along wings, door bottoms, wheel arches, rear lower body panels (quarter-panels) from front to rear of car. (Ripples indicate filler presence or fibreglass panels £££).

3)   Check quality of chromework especially bumpers (Dents dings and rust ££).

4)   Turn on all lights and indicators and check that they work (Lamps can rust out and later-type lamps are rather expensive £-£££).

5)   'Bounce' each corner of the car (Worn shock absorbers allow the corners to feel springy and bounce up and down. Each damper £).

6)   Examine general condition of interior, at-a-glance (Rips, dirt, parts missing £ to £££ + if parts available).

7)   Check Tourer hoods for rips, clouded or ripped rear screens (New hood £££. Pre-1957 hoods more expensive if originality to be maintained. Replacement rear window ££ by car upholsterer).

8)   Check Traveller woodwork for black stains and softness when pressed with coin, especially beneath side windows, at bottoms of rear pillars and around every joint, as well as in bottom horizontal members (Woodwork replacement is *very* expensive – see Restoration section of this book).

9)   Quality of paintwork. Does it shine when dry? Are there scratches beneath the shine? Is it badly chipped? (Neglect, or poor-quality cover job. Respray £££ +).

10)   Does the seller or his/her surroundings look like those of an enthusiast? Are there any maintenance records? (Poor maintenance £££ + potential).

Stage B – clean hands!

If a car doesn't match up to requirements after Stage A, don't be tempted – reject it! There are always more Minors to be seen. Stage B decreases the risk of making a mistake without even getting your hands too dirty!

Check especially thoroughly for body and chassis corrosion in all the places shown below. Use a magnet to ensure that no filler is present – magnets will only stick to steel. Work carefully and methodically. Where a check point applies to only one model of the car, the model name appears in italics right after the check point number.

Bodywork

1)   Check wrinkled or bent bumper shrouds for accident damage (££ for bumper replacement but a lot more if hidden damage).

2)   *Post-MM cars;* area around headlamp corrodes badly and is often filled to disguise corrosion (New wing ££).

3)   Rear of front wing from top to bottom. Severe corrosion is very common. Line of wing often pushed out of line of door. Bottom of wing frequently adrift (New wing ££ but almost always more corrosion beneath wing).

4)   Open door. Attempt to lift door then lower. Look for movement in hinge pillar (Movement indicates corroded hinge pillar at base £ + but usually involves more corrosion nearby).

5)   Check lower face of door skin and base of door for corrosion (New door ££ + . New door skin £-££).

6)   *Two-door saloons and Tourers;* 'quarter-panels' – body panels in line with the bottoms of the doors, sometimes regarded as a 'rear sill'. Very prone to corrosion (£ + but invariably indicates more extensive corrosion).

7)   *Four-door saloons;* open rear door and examine arched body rocker following curve of rear wheel arch (No repair panels available at time of writing ££).

8)   Check rear wings visually for corrosion. Feel inside flange for corrosion. Shake wing to see if fixing bolts are strongly attached. *Traveller;* the wood around captive nuts rots and allows them to come free. Tricky to repair – usually self-tapping screws or coach screws resorted to. *All saloons and Tourers;* the body flange to which the wing is mounted is prone to corrosion (££ +) as in the wing mounting flange itself (New wing ££). *Commercials;* rear wings are not separate, bolt-on items but are part of the body side-panel. Repairs must be welded and repair panels may be difficult to obtain.

9)   Open the boot lid. Examine the boot lid for corrosion (Replacement ££). Look inside the boot, clearing debris if necessary. Rear of body floor, rear outer corners, rear bumper mounting areas – try lifting and lowering bumper – rear wing mounting areas, all visible and

prone to corrosion (£ to £££, depending on severity). *Traveller;* check rear 'apron' — flat vertical panel beneath doors — for corrosion (Replacement £-££, but tricky if corroded woodwork in that area). *Commercials;* lack of rear bumpers means that rear quarters are prone to light accident damage. Check bottoms of rear doors and bottom of tailgate carefully for corrosion. Replacement could be hard to find!

N.B. Series MM body panels and badges differ in some respects e.g. the bonnet and bonnet badges, from later cars.

The underbody structure of the Minor is so crucial to its overall strength and thus its overall worth that it is sensible to take at least a cursory look at this stage before going any further. If the car is a high-priced car and any of the following areas are severely corroded, forget it or negotiate accordingly. Take a small mat to kneel on and probably a torch. Refer to the restoration sections of this book for pictures and diagrams of how parts *should* look. No £ symbols are given here because when a part is severely corroded it is invariably surrounded by other severely corroded parts also in need of replacement.

10) Look under the front wheel arches (Missing or badly thumped bump stop rubbers and damaged flitch panel indicate severely worn front suspension or collapsed cross member).

11) Look underneath car, in line with rear of front seats. Cross-member should have jacking points attached at ends. Not dire if damage no worse, but cross-member should not show signs of having been repaired with strips of metal and it should be a complete I-section.

12) Examine beneath sill area, front-to-rear. This is often plated over with flat cover sheets, giving very little strength. Should consist of open channel sections.

13) Look closely at front rear-spring hangers. These are often plated over, up to edge of actual spring mounting. Should consist of

mounting shoe clearly fitted beneath floor panel.

14) From inside car, lift carpets at rear and remove rear seat base — it lifts out. Examine area above spring hangers for corrosion or crudely carried out repairs.

15) Looking beneath car again, shine torch on front suspension mounting where it passes/bolts through front chassis leg. If it touches 'floor' at top of box section, box section has corroded and collapsed and requires replacement.

Interior

1) Examine seats and backrests for damage, tears, split seams. Check for rips to rears of front seats, especially in Vans and Travellers. Check that saloon rear seat retaining clips are fitted and usable — visible through boot — and that backrest is *not* screwed permanently to the rear bulkhead (Re-trimming can be *very* expensive, especially if leather faced front seats are fitted).

2) Check dash for correct badges, scratched or painted-over paints, wrong instruments added on (Parts may not be available).

3) *Saloons, Traveller, Commercials;* check condition of headlining (Early cloth headlining will be expensive to repair, later, plastic type may not be available; early Traveller board-type extremely difficult to replicate or repair.

4) *Traveller;* rear seat backs, floor covering, aluminium rubbing strips and wheel arch trim can be badly knocked about (£-£££). *Commercials;* check that heavy objects have not badly dented and damaged body sides (Perhaps £££ for panel beating and repair).

5) Examine door trim (Early trim may be difficult to match, later patterns difficult to replicate, although the Morris Minor Centre's parts list should be studied).

6) Examine carpets for scuffing and general wear (Cheap replacements — £ — are not worth having. ££ for a decent quality set).

7) Quarter-lights and door glass should open and close smoothly but in the case of quarter-lights, not

sloppily, or they will not stay open when on the move (Lubrication or adjustment with, possibly, some replacement of parts £-££).

Mechanical

Ask owner to start engine. Let it idle — thorough warming-up is essential in order to properly test the engine, this will help. Does he/she let it idle on the choke? Harmful practice! A-series engines should not need choke for long (If engine won't idle without choke, could be adjustment required or a more expensive, potentially damaging air leak).

1) Pull and push steering wheel and attempt to lift and lower at right angles to steering column (Clonking indicates wear in column bush, loose column to body connections, loose steering wheel nut, loose column to rack clamp).

2) Open bonnet (Seized if stiff mechanism — lubrication). Check for non-standard air cleaners, rocker cover and engine number (Engines from a wide range of A-series cars can be made to fit and some would not be so desirable! Also, engine may be of dubious quality. Original minor components may be hard to find, especially for early cars).

3) Check engine/engine bay, particularly beneath manifold side of block for general cleanliness and presence of oil (Leaking gaskets, lack of detailed care, leaking tappet chest gaskets. Probably £).

4) Listen to engine (Top end tapping equals tappet wear. Bottom end rumble equals crank wear. Front end tinkle equals timing chain wear. ££, £££ and ££ respectively, but worn engine may require complete overhaul).

5) Is there much corrosion around the battery carrier? (Carelessly spilled electrolyte can damage bulkhead).

STOP ENGINE AND LEAVE TO COOL FOR SUFFICIENT TIME TO CARRY OUT CHECK NO. 10.

6) Remove oil filler cap. Look for yellow or brown slimy sludge or foaming inside cap (Severe bore or valve guide wear ££ to £££).

7) Inspect the radiator for damage or stains that indicate leaks

(Replacement radiator ££ to £££).

8) Examine engine mountings for signs of previous removal. The engine mounts should have nuts and lock washers on all nuts. Rubber mounting brackets should not be under obvious strain or show any sign of having been forced on back-to-front (Previous engine removal is not necessarily a bad thing, but it would be interesting to know why it was undertaken, what had gone wrong and who carried out the work). Note that virtually all Minors will have had their engines removed for one purpose or another by now.

9) Jack both front wheels off the ground together. Turn steering wheel from lock to lock (Roughness or tightspots indicates wear in steering rack. Replacement or overhaul ££).

10) Remove radiator cap SLOWLY with a thick rag. Beware of spurting, scalding water — if water bubbles as cap is first undone, retighten quickly and leave until water is properly cool. (This could indicate a blowing head gasket pressurizing the coolant. Check radiator cap: higher 'poundage' caps are often fitted to prevent leakage from this source. Then look for clues as follows.

Check for orange colour inside cooling system. Check for oil on top of water either in form of droplets or as brown 'gunge'. Remove dipstick and check for water droplets in oil (Orange means rust and a long time since coolant has been changed or topped-up with antifreeze. Poor maintenance — could be £ to £££ + . Oil in water or water on oil dipstick indicates head gasket problems. Probably £££ if head damaged [££ if second — head part used] or if overheating has caused associated problems)

Boot or loadbay inspection

1) Is the spare tyre inflated and does it have a good tread and does the wheel appear serviceable? (Replacement tyre — £, obviously! Replacement wheel £ tu ££).

2) Is the jack available and does it work? (Replacement £).

3) Does the boot/rear door lock work? (Replacement key if right number can be found, or even a replacement lock £).

Road test

If you, the tester, are driving ensure that you have adequate insurance cover. Otherwise carry out as many as possible of the following tests with the owner driving.

N.B. For many of the following checks, specific speeds or speed ranges are suggested. These are generally appropriate for 1098cc and 948cc cars; for 803cc and MM Minors speeds should be reduced with regard to the safe maxima in the gears (see Appendix) and the age of the car. Higher geared Wolseleys and Rileys will be generally capable of higher road speeds without undue engine strain. AT ALL TIMES TAKE CAREFUL NOTE OF ROAD CONDITIONS WHEN CARRYING OUT THESE TESTS.

1) Start up. Does engine turn-over very slowly? (Tired starter motor £. Tired battery £-££. Poor electrical connections — time finding which ones + a little for new battery clamps, perhaps).

2A) Is it difficult to engage first gear? N.B. Pre-1098cc cars often had a 'baulking' first gear when at rest. 1098cc cars ought to go in at first or second attempt (Worn clutch and/or worn gear selector mechanism ££).

2B) Drive off in first gear. Listen for regular cyclic clonking. Repeat test in reverse gear. (Clonking indicates worn first/reverse gears and bearings; a very common problem. ££-£££.)

3) Drive at around 30 mph. Brake steadily to a halt, light pressure on steering wheel. N.B. Try test on several road surfaces to ensure camber on road etc. is not affecting test.

A) Does car 'pull' to one side? (Seized front or rear wheel cylinders. £ each. Failed oil seal behind rear drum brakes £. Oil/grease contamination on front brake drums. £. Worn brake shoes £).

B) Do brakes rub grind or squeal, or go 'on' and 'off' of own accord, especially at lower speed/lower pedal pressure? (Worn brake shoes £. But more if drums ruined. Oval drums £ for re-skimming or more if replacement required).

4) Drive at 25 to 30 mph in 3rd gear. Press then release accelerator four or five times. Listen for transmission 'clonk' (Probably worn universal joint. £. Worn differential ££. Worn halfshaft ££).

5) Drive at 35-40 mph. Lift off accelerator. Listen for differential whine. (Worn differential ££, if severe or unbearably noisy).

6) Accelerate hard in first gear to a high changing-up speed, then lift off throttle. Listen for engine knocking. (Worn engine bearings £££). Also,

7) – does gearbox jump out of gear? (Worn internal selector mechanism £-£££).

8) Drive as in 6/7 above, but lift off in second gear, then third gear then fourth, road conditions permitting. Does gearbox jump out of gear? Try the exercise, as far as is safe and practicable, in reverse gear, particularly (if possible) with pre-1098cc gearboxes. (Jumping out indicates worn selector mechanism £-£££).

9) Drive at around 40 mph in fourth gear. Change into third gear. Does gearbox 'crunch'? (Worn synchromesh £ to ££. Faulty clutch ££).

10) Drive at 25 mph in third gear. Change into second gear. Does gearbox 'crunch'? (Worn synchromesh £-££. Faulty clutch ££).

11) Do front wheels flutter or shake at speed? (Wheels out of balance £. Worn shockers/front suspension ££-£££).

12) Check that road conditions are suitable. With ratchet knob depressed, pull the handbrake on whilst travelling at 20 mph or so. Don't risk a skid! (Car pulls to one side — seized wheel cylinder on opposite side £. Brakes contaminated with oil on opposite side £. N.B. seized rear wheel cylinders are a common problem on Minors).

N.B. In severe winter conditions, particularly in parts of Canada or USA various parts of the handbrake mechanism can freeze simulating other problems.

13) When cornering, does the steering wheel attempt to return to the straight-ahead position when loosed? (If not, tight swivels, probably indicated ££, or stiff and faulty steering rack ££).

14) In second gear at about 20-25 mph accelerate hard, then decelerate hard; don't brake (If car veers to left or right, the rear axle probably is loose on the springs. New U-bolts £. New rear springs ££).

15) At very low speeds, brake and listen for front suspension 'clonks' (Investigate further — see next section on front suspension checks).

16) With the car stationary, operate the brake pedal. Apply light pedal pressure in repeated strokes (If the pedal slowly works its way to the floor, even over a minute, the master cylinder is faulty £-££).

17) Accelerate from low speed in top gear, full throttle. (Pinking/spark knock probably indicates maladjusted timing, poor maintenance and potentially severe long-term damage if engine used hard).

18) Drive car down longish downhill stretch with throttle closed (Pronounced 'snapping' and 'popping' through the exhaust indicates burned out exhaust valves, to which A-series engines are particularly prone. New valve and regrind £. Valve seat inserts fitted by specialist ££).

19) Stop car. Apply parking brake firmly. Engage second gear. Gently let out clutch pedal — but depress again *as soon as car shows any signs of distress* (If car pulls away — worn rear brakes ££. Oil in brake drums £-££. If car remains stationary but engine continues to run, maladjusted or worn clutch ££).

20) Pull away from rest. Does car 'judder'? (Worn or broken engine mountings £. Worn or damaged clutch ££).

21) Brake hard from normal road speed. Don't risk a skid! (Sharp

grating sound from front of engine bay — fan catching on radiator. Broken engine/gearbox tie cable plus soft or broken engine mountings £-££).

Stage C — Dirty hands!

This is the level at which the car — by now being seriously considered — is given the sort of checks that make sure as far as possible that there are no major hidden faults which could still make the purchaser change his or her mind. It might also throw up a few more faults to use as bargaining points with the seller!

While Stage A took a few minutes only and Stage B took quite a while longer, Stage C involves a lot more time, inconvenience and effort, but if you want to be *sure*, it's the most vital stage of all.

Safety

Ensure that the wheels are chocked when using jacks or ramps. NEVER go under a car supported only by a jack.

You should make absolutely certain that every potential corrosion area is examined. They are too numerous to list here in complete detail so refer to the body corrosion problems shown in the chapter on bodywork repair and check again, using a probe such as a screwdriver, the areas mentioned in Stage B, Checks 10-14, 'Bodywork'.

1) Jack up front wheel beneath wishbone, partially compressing front suspension. Spin wheel and listen for roughness in wheel bearing (Imminent wheel bearing failure £).

2) Grip front roadwheel top and bottom — ensure car weight cannot fall onto hand — and rock in the vertical plane (Play indicates: wear in wheel bearing £; wear in suspension swivels or bushes £-££).

3) From beneath car and with a stout lever, attempt to lever both top and bottom swivel trunnions

(Wear in trunnions, means failure is imminent and components must be replaced ££ but Wolseley/Riley parts are hard to find, as are MM parts: both can be fitted with Minor 1000 components with machining, £££).

4) From beneath rear of car, examine rear brake backplates and insides of wheels for oil contamination — compare clues given with earlier brake testing. (Failed oil seal/blocked differential breather £).

5) Closely examine brake lines for corrosion. Look especially hard at points where pipes enter and leave driver's side box-section, where master cylinder is situated (Corroded pipes are dangerous! Pipes inside box section especially prone to neglect. Brake fluid around master cylinder mounting area could indicate failing master cylinder £-££).

6) Lift front carpets and examine inner sills, front of floor and also gearbox cover (Corrosion. Gearbox cover and floor adjacent to rear of cover sometimes butchered during careless engine removal. Screws often missing and/or sheared).

7) Check front and rear apron/beneath boot floor for corrosion and evidence of crude repair. Check chassis legs at front, tops of rear chassis on commercials and rear box-sections on rest of range. Especially examine rear rear-spring shackle areas.

8) Sniff around fuel tank from beneath and look for evidence of fuel staining — dark patches — especially from front of tank and on top of commercial tanks.

9) Inspect the engine for oil leaks. N.B. older A-series engine usually leak some oil from the rear oil seal, which then appears through the drain hole in the bottom of the clutch bellhousing. A non-leaker is rare! Oil should not appear in significant quantities from the rest of the engine, however.

10) Examine the front of the rear axle for oil leakage and oil thrown onto underbody. Slight leakage not uncommon (Heavy leakage suggests faulty seal in nose of differential carrier, clogged vent or

overfilled differential casing £).

11) Grasp each shock absorber linkage in turn and shake it and also look for heavy fluid leakage (Worn bushes, linkages or seals. Shock absorbers £ each).

12) Look for evidence of fresh grease around grease points (Lack of servicing £-£££).

13) Check condition of exhaust system and exhaust mountings (Replacement exhaust system ££).

14) *Riley 1.5 only;* from under the bonnet, grasp the throttle shaft and attempt to shake it at each end (Excessive movement results in an uncontrollable idle and vacuum leaks. Exchange or replacement carbs ££).
All other cars; attempt to shake carb butterfly spindle.

15) Determine how much play exists in clutch linkages (Holes may need welding, redrilling, pins renewing) and side-to-side movement in clutch and brake pedals (Worn bushes – replacement £).

16) Check front chassis legs as carefully as possible for signs of bowing, wrinkling, welded repairs or any other signs of crash damage. Check too, flitch plates and outer panel fit for further clues. If damage is found, check front tyres for uneven wear, indicating an out-of-line car (Tyres unevenly worn by themselves could simply mean worn front suspension, corroded suspension mountings or steering in need of retracking £).

Buying – in conclusion

Having examined a car in this sort of depth, it is likely that the prospective Minor, Riley 1.5 or Wolseley 1500 owner will be confronted with an almost frightening array of faults. The price-check symbols will help in determining the most expensive problems and the following notes will help to provide some sort of perspective to those faults now all too clearly on view – so don't despair yet!

Every car in the Minor range is now 'of a certain age' so you are certain to have come across quite a number of faults in the car you have examined. Decide which faults you can or can't live with either in the long or short term and let the cost of putting them right be the determining factor.

Remember that cosmetics impress the Jones's but that structural strength is far more important – and that body rot and underbody corrosion are far and away the two worst enemies of the whole range, even though the cars were very sturdily designed and built. Any rot should be viewed on the iceberg principle: for every spot of corrosion found on the outside, things are bound to be five or ten times worse on the inside once panels are stripped away.

Don't forget that upholstery can be very expensive to have properly repaired even if, with earlier cars, you can find replacements at all. A Minor with superb interior has got the second most important plus-point in its favour!

All mechanical parts are available for post-Series II cars and will continue to be for some time, partly because so many of the parts were built for so many cars that there are still stocks around but largely because people like The Morris Minor Centre are an absolute godsend! They are BL Heritage-approved suppliers and stock every mechanical part off-the-shelf. Parts that are now obsolete are specially made for the Minor Centre to sell, so the parts situation couldn't be better.

B1. The most popular Minor is the 1098cc – engined car with what seemed at the time to be more up-to-date features. It certainly goes better than the earlier cars (even if its engine isn't as sweet as that of the author's favourite, the 948cc Morris 1000) and it has a fresh-air heater, too, along with 'proper' flashers.

So, to recap on one's order of priorities when buying a Minor, Riley or Wolseley 1500. Of most importance in every case is the underbody area. Second are the outer body panels with interior running them *very* close behind, especially on older cars and Wolseley/Rileys. Bear in mind that outer body panels and especially chrome trim is extremely difficult to find for the B-series engined cars although specialists such as those listed in the 'Clubs and Specialists' section of the Appendices can supply front wings, door skins and an ever-increasing range of outer body components for those cars, too. Lastly comes mechanical components, but do look at the Specification and Production Modifications sections and note that the older the car, the more difficult will the mechanical parts be to find; this point applying especially to 'pure' Morris parts such as the side-valve MM engine and gearbox and the early rear axle.

Happy hunting!

B2.   On the other hand, 'Split-screen' Minors are more of an enthusiast's car, although there is no earthly reason why they shouldn't make an attractive shopping car. Many smaller parts are harder to get hold of, however, although it is still possible to have early mechanical components reconditioned by a high class-engineering specialist. (See 'Suppliers'.)

B3.   How extraordinary that the last of the Minors should be badged as an Austin! Later LCVs (Light Commercial Vehicles) were built as Austins and are not actually called Minors at all − except by just about everyone who comes across them!

B4.   What a pity that you can't tip onto its side every Minor that you might look at with a view to buying. Do your best to examine the underside thoroughly because it's the most critical part of the car. (See 'Bodywork' chapters of this book for all the gory details of what can rot and where).

B5.   This might seem a bit negative, but you can't actually see the sills to check them. Don't be fooled by the kick-plate that covers this area − it's strictly non-structural.

B6.   When a front wing gets to the sticky-tape stage, it's time to replace it! New front and rear wings — indeed just about every body and under-body panel — are available, from the various specialist stockists. Regarding originality of line, quality, and ease of fitting there are many variations, but as a guide the more it costs the better it may be. Ideally, go to a supplier who has been recommended.

B7.   When a car is sold as 'rebuilt', pay close attention to the quality of the underbody, look carefully for the presence of filler (see text) and look for detailing such as the fit of wings and woodwork on Travellers.

B9.   . . . the waistrails which rot primarily because the sliding window drains clog up . . .

B11.   . . . and the rear corner posts. If the wood is soft when pushed with something hard, it is rotten and therefore scrap. Test the rear door joints for soundness by twisting each door to see if they have come at all loose.

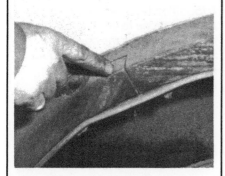

B8.   Ranking alongside underbody repairs as a crucial item is the Traveller's woodwork which is very expensive to have repaired or even to replace yourself. Look closely at the wheelarch joints . . .

B10.   . . . the joints at the ends of the waistrails including the front posts . . .

B12.   A good, original dash layout and interior is another plus-point.

B13. You can re-cover front seats yourself but items like rear seats and headlining are expensive to have repaired and early types are certainly not available.

B14. There's not a lot to go wrong in the boot but check the condition of the spare, the jack and gain an overall impression of care or neglect.

B15. The Traveller's load bay is a lot more prone to being knocked about. As well as the obvious trim surfaces, check the headlining for rips and the seat hinges for breakage or looseness.

B16. If you find yourself a Minor with an engine bay as clean as this, it will be surprising. Make no mistake, restoring an engine bay to new condition is extremely time-consuming.

B17. On a four-door, the wheel arch is a box-section and repays close inspection for the presence of corrosion or filler.

B18. Small items like the correct lamps, badges etc are all available but their cost mounts up if many of them have to be replaced. Make allowances for this.

B19. Check the fit of both front and rear bumpers in this area to see whether any accident damage has distorted them.

B20. Van and Pick-Up side panels are in one piece so any repairs to this area will have to be pieced-in or a complete new side panel found and fitted — not easy!

B21. A Van's rear door pillars are prone to corrosion at their bases. Try lifting an open door and looking for movement. Lack of rear bumpers also leads to minor accident damage here.

Although the Minor was technically obsolete, it was still a remarkable performer for its age. Its demise had been predicted for years and when *Autocar* road tested a 1964 example they had said, 'Back in 1960, when we carried out our full test of a Morris Minor 1000, it would have needed a complete clairvoyant to predict that four years later the car would still be in production and selling well' . . . and indeed, the car was to go on, fundamentally unchanged, for many more years to come. And it is this point — that the car remained unchanged — that must be borne in mind when wondering whether Minor production could or should have been continued.

B22. This is just a part of the Minor Centre's park for 'dead' Minors, plus those awaiting restoration and those awaiting collection. (Note also the Riley 1.5 in the foreground.)

The car to compare it with is probably the VW Beetle which started off by being adventurous in design just as Issigonis wanted the Minor to be but which was a crude and rackety thing by any standards. Ironically, it was the British occupying forces who got Beetle production under way but the car was presented in ways that the Minor was not. First, it was actively *sold* by a management team who went to a lot of trouble to encourage importers, especially in the USA, to *want* the car and to *believe* in it. Secondly, and this dovetails neatly with the first point, customers' needs were listened to and the car built to fit those needs and altered continuously for that purpose throughout its production life. The Minor was just built, and if you wanted it, there it was;'if you didn't like its engine, its seating or its suspension — too bad, it seems! A major difference between the two companies was that for Volkswagen, the Beetle *was* Volkswagen, so it *had* to sell. But for Morris/BMC/BL, the Minor was just a part of a model range.

The Beetle was, fundamentally, a cruder car and yet it outsold the Minor to a ratio of around 20 to 1. That the Minor sold so well and is still so well loved is a great tribute to the original concept and design of a car that may have been underdeveloped but was fundamentally superb.

Improving the Minor — first-hand experience!

For a good many people, there is and never will be anything quite like the Morris Minor. I have owned many examples over the years and used them from everything for a first trip to the South of France to moving house, as well as a reliable and economical way of simply getting to-and-from work, which is something I did before I wrote for a living. As the sort of person who could never leave anything alone, it

quickly dawned upon me that the Minor would benefit hugely from a few simple improvements and this turned into a lengthy quest for the 'perfect' Minor. In its final form, my modified Minor once carried my wife and me over a 500 mile trip broken only for the usual outputs and inputs which, though exhausting, is something that we would not have even contemplated in a standard Minor. (I wouldn't contemplate such a trip in the modified one now, but that's more to do with the onset of grey hairs, I think . . .)

The following list of changes contain the sort of things that BMC could easily have carried out with scarcely any increase in cost, in some cases and could easily be carried out at home.

Each and every Minor owner, without exception, ought to fit radial ply tyres to his or her car. At the expense of a very little more road noise, the car's handling is transformed and the steering immediately starts going where you point it and stops following the directions in which the tarmac was laid! That advice is absolutely categorical, but I would also strongly recommend using 13 inch wheels and tyres, perhaps from an A40 Countryman (they are wider) or from a Sprite or Midget. Unfortunately, Minor hub caps won't fit but you could use 'sculptured' steel wheels (which don't look at all original), or you could try to get hold of a set of plain Austin 'Minor' van hubcaps or equally plain early MG Midget hubcaps which would not look as out of place as 'Austin' hub caps on a Minor! These smaller wheels lower the car's effective gearing so increasing acceleration and, on the 1098cc cars, top speed as well at the expense of some noise because the engine turns over more quickly, but they lower the Minor's centre of gravity which makes its cornering even better and cuts down the amount of unsprung weight on the rear axle which, combined with the softer radial ply tyres could well solve all the axle-tramp problems of a car with standard engine.

Whilst not such a simple modification, the fitting of better seats would be high on the priority of anyone who has to use their Minor for long journeys. The Morris Minor Centre in Bath can supply specially adapted reclining Metro seats to fit the Minor, which are a huge improvement. I fitted a pair of reclining, all leather, all-singing, all-dancing Rover 2000 seats to mine with a very simple, specially made-up subframe. They fit a treat and hold you in luxury – as long as you don't want to get granny or a long-legged friend in the back!

On the basis that you don't buy a Minor in which to win races (I fitted a 1275cc Sprite engine and gearbox to mine: an easy conversion, but many of today's economy cars are not much slower), the next things to change are the front brakes and shock absorbers. Companies like The Minor Centre and Spridgebits (who can supply all the larger engine/smaller wheel and other ex-Sprite and Midget goodies mentioned here) sell front disc brake conversion sets which really make a big difference to the Minor's power, while conversion to telescopic shock absorbers, especially of the adjustable type, make the suspension and handling so much more modern.

Of course, you can go on with an all-synchro gearbox, better soundproofing, an improved cylinder head and electronic ignition – and you end up with a Minor that carried all the virtues of the original car with so many of the vices ironed out – the car, in fact, that BL should have produced as a 'world car' competitor to the Beetle.

Improving the Minor – The Minor Centre way

The Bath Morris Minor Centre has been developing a Minor for the nineteen-eighties. Over the last year a programme of research and

development has been contracted out to an engineering development company. This programme has resulted in a series of engineering improvements being designed which give the Minor a road performance more suitable for present day road conditions. The changes introduced have been engineered to a high specification. The modifications are in no sense simply bolt-on parts. The vehicle chassis requires modification for additional load-carrying points for the re-engineered suspension system and the entire running gear is replaced with current specification components.

The New Minor has a number of different specifications designed to offer the motorist a wide choice of economy and performance options.

Brakes and suspension

Anyone who drives a Minor in today's traffic conditions quickly becomes aware of its limited braking performance. To give the vehicle an up-to-date safety specification the braking system has been completely revised. The front being equipped with 9.75 inch disc brakes and the rear drums increased from 7 inch to 8 inch. A matched brake servo operating from the original underfloor master cylinder gives a sensitive and immensely powerful braking performance. Clearly, the loads generated by this system would create considerable problems for the original wheel/tyre and suspension arrangements. The new specification includes improved wheel hub and bearing components. Telescopic gas-filled dampers replace the rather ineffective lever arm originals. The rear axle location has been dramatically improved by radius arm and panhard rod fittings.

Further improvements have been made to the quality of ride by changes to the front and rear spring rates, which gives a reduction in fore and aft pitching, particularly on the Traveller. An anti-roll bar has been utilized in order to limit front roll angles. The superior characteristics of the new

suspension geometry allow softer springing to be used with no loss in handling and cornering performance. The whole suspension package gives a ride and handling performance comparable to many modern small rear wheel drive cars. The Minor can be now driven at today's traffic speeds with confidence and can be a delight to drive.

Engine and Transmission

To complement the modernized brakes and suspension there are available a number of engine and transmission options.

1. 1098cc enhancement package, comprising: Modified cylinder head, camshaft, carburettor, inlet and exhaust manifolds, inlet filter.
2. 1275cc replacement unit, standard.
3. 1275cc replacement unit with power increased to 80 bhp.
4. 1275 cc replacement unit fully blueprinted for maximum engine life or high power modifications.
5. 1275cc replacement unit with economy modification package.

The above engine options require improved transmission systems to cope with their extra power. Two stronger specification manual gearbox types are available plus an automatic transmission unit. The ride and handling package includes a stronger rear axle capable of handling the higher power engine options. The transmission and engine packages are complete with fitting kits for immediate installation.

Interior

Also available is a trim package giving a completely revised standard of passenger comfort. Included are rake adjustable front seats and inertia reel seat belts. The new trim is available in a range of traditional and modern fabrics and colours.

Electrical

Two speed wiper kits are available. Under development is a more powerful fresh air heater system. An alternator kit is provided with the 1275cc engine kits.

IM1. The 'thoroughly modern Minor's' brakes and suspension have been improved with better safety and comfort in mind. You can buy whichever parts of the package you want for your own Minor, although front disc brakes may unbalance the car's braking system and shouldn't be fitted in isolation.

IM2. A choice of improved engine specs. are available, taking advantage of Austin-Rover-type improvements to their 'A + ' range of engines and giving more power and economy from the smaller unit with the option of a fully-sorted 1275cc engine for those who want to travel at modern-day cruising speeds.

IM3. The Minor Centre's new interior trim packages have tackled and solved one of the biggest problems faced by Minor owners: how to get comfortable on a long journey. The new reclining, tilting seats, based on A-R seats are light years away from the old Minor seats.

Classic car insurance

If you own a 'classic' Morris Minor, you can save money and ensure that you aren't caught in the 'old-car-not-worth much' insurance trap. Classic car insurance is usually cheaper than private motor insurance. This is because classic vehicles are generally used less than the main family vehicle and with extra care, making them a good risk as the likelihood of a claim is lower.

Naturally enough, most insurance companies will set some restrictions to qualify for this. Models considered to be 'classics', are usually supported by an owners club. In addition, insurers specify that the car must be above a certain age, in most cases 15 years old. In addition, the car must not be the main vehicle or be used for more than a specified annual mileage. To an extent you can choose the mileage that suits you, but the lower this is the lower the premium.

Above all, there is a cardinal rule that must be remembered when insuring your 'classic' Morris Minor. Make sure you can agree the value of your vehicle with your insurer. It's the only way to protect your investment, should the worst come to the worst.

One thing is for sure. If your vehicle is eligible, you really should consider an agreed value classic car insurance policy.

UK tax exemption
Cars built before 1 January 1973 are exempt for vehicle excise duty ('car tax'). The important point here, especially for cars first registered in early '73 or later imports, is that the relevant date is the build date, not the date of first registration. If you have any queries you can contact the Morris Minor Owners' Club who should be able to help you find the evidence you will need to claim tax exemption from your local Driver Vehicle Licensing Centre.

Spare parts availability

There can be few cars, old or new, with a better source of spares than the Morris Minor! Many Japanese cars, Fords and discontinued models of Austin-Rover Group cars have presented enormous difficulties with parts availability even for cars which are just a few years old, so it comes as a pleasant surprise to many owners new to Minor ownership to find that there is virtually nothing, down to the smallest nut and bolt, that can't be bought for the car.

While The Morris Minor Centre, with its A-R connections and permission to use original drawings and specifications, is undoubtedly the business which has invested most time, money and energy in developing the new manufacture of Minor spares, there are many other sources, each of which can supply various Minor parts. Most mechanical parts can still be bought from motor factors, mainly because many of them were common to so many other cars as well. As far as is known, all of the leading makes of piston or bearing manufacturer's parts are every bit as good as (and often no cheaper than) Unipart or Minor Centre parts, but it does pay to buy the best when it comes to brake components and also oil filters. These mundane items can make a very big difference to an engine's longevity so it's not worth risking the use of inferior filters which may not do the job as well as those costing a tiny amount more.

It is in the area of body panels that some of the biggest pitfalls lie when it comes to trying to save money. There are two alternatives to Unipart or Minor Centre body panels (although Unipart don't market the full range of repair and restoration panels developed by The Minor Centre from the original specs.) One is to fit cheap so-called 'pattern' panels where these are available. These panels have mainly been developed for the repairer who wants the quickest way of fitting a cover-up job that will look good under paint long enough for him to sell the car and avoid any immediate comeback from the customer. They are cheap and, in the author's opinion, very nasty as far as the serious restorer is concerned. They are designed in many cases to go over the top of existing rust and the crude imperfections in shape are intended to be compensated for with liberal applications of filler. They almost always take a good deal longer to fit than 'proper' panels and so, if you're paying someone for their time they're usually more expensive to use in the long run. Very occasionally, 'pattern' panels will consist of manufacturer's rejects or copies made overseas of the original item and these will sometimes be of slightly better quality than cover-up panels, but if you look at the difference in cost as a proportion of the finished value of the car, the difference will be very small indeed and not worth worrying about.

The other alternative is to use fibreglass front or rear wings. They are certainly cheaper than steel wings but they are always an absolute pain to fit properly and, worse still, the stigma attached to them means that the value of the car will be quite severely reduced. They are certainly not worth considering as part of a serious restoration project except in perhaps one or two specific circumstances. Some people consider their Minor to be no more than a workhorse, its intrinsic value being in how well it can do its job. As long as they have no intention of selling the car and as long as they remember that to remove the old

wings is going to involve just as much work and welding as if steel wings are being fitted, then they may want to put up with the extra effort involved in fitting fibreglass wings accurately. The other circumstances in which someone may consider fitting a fibreglass wing would be if the car is being subjected to a long-term restoration in which the underside of the car is being attended to first and the top-side patched up until time and finances permit an extension of the work. Then, if a second-hand fibreglass wing becomes available for next-to-nothing and the old wing is beyond being refabricated with a fibreglass kit, then why not . . . Do buy the best fibreglass wings available if you must use them as cheap ones are usually badly rippled, which looks dreadful after the car has been painted, and they crack and break easily in use. The thickness of the panel is a good guide.

Apart from Traveller woodwork, every part of the Minor can be bought at very reasonable cost and certainly for less than those of the great majority of new cars. Buy well, and you'll have little trouble and low cost in keeping your Minor on the road.

3 Bodywork

One of the simplest cars to restore

The Minor has been described as 'a big mobile Meccano kit' and while that might be stretching the point a little bit, it really must be one of the simplest cars to restore of all time, with the proviso that you first go to the trouble to understand how the floorpan panels fit together. It has several other big advantages for the home restorer too: virtually every part is available, from the smallest clip to a complete set of body panels, from the Minor Centre in Bath (while for Wolseley and Rileys the situation is not quite as good but even so, an excellent range is available); there were very few modification or option extras, so there are no complications whatever to worry about and certainly no need for specialist tools; the Minor is small enough to be worked upon in the average garage.

Also, the Minor can be made to go on 'for ever' if it is repaired properly and will give far less costly motoring than in any modern, depreciating motor car. All of this makes the 'Bodywork' section of

this book potentially the most useful to the home restorer, especially since much of the information it contains can be found nowhere else.

The Minor was one of Morris' first ever unitary construction cars, that is to say, the strength of the vehicle depends on the whole structure rather than most of the strength being contained in a chassis with outer body panels doing little more than clothing the skeleton. On the other hand, the Minor was designed in a sufficiently distant age for some of the qualities of a chassis to have been in-built giving the best of both worlds, such as substantial structural components that can be split up into recognizable areas or sub-assemblies combined with the extra stiffness and space-saving qualities of a chassisless car.

The Morris Minor's structure means that, if you wish to restore a Minor with a view to keeping it for many a long year (and with a view to making the invariably expensive business of restoration sensibly cost effective) you really need to proceed in the correct order, especially if you're not able to do all of the work in one go. It's the most natural temptation in the world to want to

make your Minor look pretty as a first priority, but if you're interested in making it last, you'll have to forget looks to start off with and concentrate on structure.

BOD1. This is a pretty extreme example of not worrying too much about how a car looks! This punk 4-door Minor had been made as sound as new underneath, leaving no money for new wings 'n' things. The old ones were patched back on 'just for now' until new ones could be afforded.

That's why the bodywork section of this book starts by telling you how to fix the most unglamorous, totally unseen, but absolutely vital, structure of the car. The trouble is that the neighbours will never know how much you've

spent — except that your Minor will still be going when the Jones' Minor has collapsed inside shining paintwork — followed by their Metro and their year-2001 fuel-efficient Super Bubble De-luxe. But seriously, the only way to make a Minor last is to ensure that the underbody, the part which includes chassis-type structures, is repaired thoroughly before the outer panels are repaired.

BOD2.   In order to follow this section of the book, you'll have to get used to seeing a Minor from a somewhat unusual angle! To the left of this picture is the rear-axle and suspension, at the other end of the car are the main 'chassis' legs linked by the gearbox cross-member while towards the front end of the propshaft is the main structural cross-member.

BOD3.   The roll-over cage which the Minor Centre uses (and which can, it seems, be purchased direct from them) has to be bolted securely to the wheel hubs after jacking up one side of the vehicle and removing the wheels. The battery has first to be removed, of course, to avoid battery spillage and it also pays to drain out the engine oil and coolant. It may also pay to drain rear-axle oil because it is all too easy for an oil seal to leak oil into the lower brake drum.

BOD4.   After lifting the other side of the car as far as possible with a jack, four men can lift it . . .

BOD5. . . . onto the roll cage, making certain of course that there is plenty of room for the roof of the car. The whole thing can then be propped up in position with the supports provided. The access that this gives when working on the underside of the car could not be bettered and it's so much safer and less tiring than working overhead. If you have to work beneath the car, don't worry: the procedures are still exactly those described here.

Hints, tips and equipment

More and more DIY restorers and enthusiasts are discovering that doing their own welding not only saves them a great deal of money, it also gives them a great deal of satisfaction. Of course, no one can expect to pick up a piece of welding equipment for the first time and make a perfect weld, but there are welding sets that make life so much easier for the DIY-er. Those recommended here are not necessarily the cheapest on the market but they are considered by the author to be the best having been used extensively by him and having been built for light professional use rather than down to an 'occasional use' standard.

And, of course, the home restorer has to invest in a certain amount of other equipment, too, although most people carrying out a full-scale project will already have acquired much of it. Those who have to buy gear from scratch can console themselves with the knowledge that the equipment they buy should cost far less than the labour costs of a rebuild plus the fact that they will still own the equipment for future use. Hand tools receive the largest amount of use and it is always well worth investing in the best that is around, because poor tools make a good job well-nigh impossible. Sykes-Pickavant produce a huge range of bodyshop panel work tools and are developing an increased range at lower cost suitable for the DIY repair/restorer. An electric drill is invaluable, of course, but so is a mini-grinder which can be useful at almost every stage for cutting out rusty metal, linishing paint and surface rust away from weld surfaces, dressing welds and dressing the edges of repair panels.

With these basics plus the more obvious hammer, bolster chisel, screwdrivers and spanners, as well as a means of cutting out sheet steel (a good pair of universal tin snips will do for a start) the first-timer could make a start. He or she, would have to fit panels together with self-tapping screws and/or clamps until a 'mobile welder' could be dragged out of Yellow Pages, or the bodyshell trailered to professional premises. Several such visits would be necessary as some panels have to be 'closed-off' before others can be welded into place, but the procedure is not impossible. If restoration is to be taken seriously, it will be necessary to learn to weld at some time or other. It is possible to hire arc welding equipment in most large towns, although this type of welding equipment is considered to be too fierce for outer body panels by even the most experienced hands. For work on 'chassis' members and tack-welding inner panels or door skins, arc-welding can be acceptable. Arc-brazing, which is more versatile but less strong, can also be carried out with an arc welder with the addition of the appropriate accessory.

In the UK most Technical Colleges and Evening Institutes run evening classes where beginners can learn the rudiments of gas or arc welding. Gas welding is far more versatile than arc welding at least as far as car bodywork is concerned, but gas bottles are more difficult and more expensive to obtain and are far less safe to store and use. A company called Murex, owned by the Scandinavian welding rod firm ESAB, now market a range of products including 'Portapack' (nothing to do with the author!) welding kits. These are small-scale oxyacetylene welding kits which the user buys and then rents the mini cylinders for a renewable seven year period, the cylinders being exchangeable at a BOC centre in the normal way. There are a number of other independent concerns producing cheaper alternatives, the foremost among them being The Welding Centre. Their products consist of excellent quality welding and cutting torches run from a replenishable oxygen cylinder and a discardable container of Mapp gas which is almost as hot as acetylene but has none of the storage risks.

It is worth pointing out that there are a number of manufacturers such as Melbros, and Saltofix making repair panels for the repair trade, through to

Austin-Rover and the Morris Minor Centre in Bath who have parts made to original specifications. In the author's view, the dearer original or original-type parts are a thousand times more worthwhile than fit-where-they-touch cheap-jack repair panels which can treble the time even a skilled repairer takes to fit them and even then end up not being dimensionally spot-on. For ease and quality of fit, it pays to stick with high quality when working on the underside of the car and it pays not to cut away too many panels at once and so lose the structural rigidity of the car. Fit panels to a small area at a time and constantly check for dimensional accuracy.

BOD6. The Welding Centre produce a fully portable gas welding set which looks and feels more like a professional welding set than any of the DIY sets on offer. When used with a cylinder of Mapp gas (bought from many DIY centres) it gives a flame which is very nearly as hot as an acetylene flame. The only drawback is that the torch controls are a bit sensitive and also running costs are higher than for a full scale set, although the advantages of portability and lower purchase cost can more than balance this out.

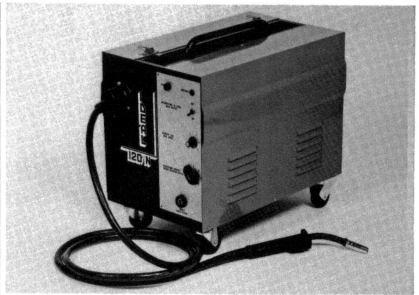

BOD7. MIG welding is, as far as both DIY enthusiast and full professional are concerned, simply the finest type of welding there is. Both the SIP Ideal 120N and its bigger brother the 150 are as easy to use as drawing a slow line with a felt tipped pen — well almost! As well as being the most straightforward form of welding for the beginner to use, it is also more economical to run than gas welding and it creates far less distortion. It can also be used for a form of spot welding. Minus points are that it can't be used for heating or bending in the way that gas can and it needs an Argon bottle (Air Products or BOC) to accompany it.

BOD8. Spot welders work by passing a current through two overlapping pieces of metal, the heat formed actually fusing them together. The only material consumed is electric current. You can reach round obstructions with the spot-welder by using a set of extension arms like these available from the SIP Spotmatic spot welder.

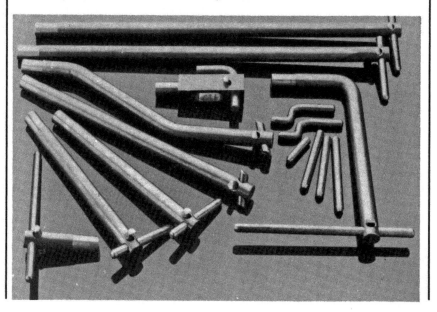

BOD9. Right down the price scale is the arc welder set which can be bought through national ads and DIY centres at very moderate cost. You have to be a real dab hand to be able to weld thin metals with an arc welder and, indeed, the conventional wisdom is that you can't do it. Actually, you can sometimes just get away with it if you are extremely careful and just a little accomplished, DC arc welders being easier to handle with thin metals than AC. A carbon arc brazing kit makes working with thinner metals far, far easier, although you are of course restricted to brazing with this part of the kit.

BOD10. The Portapack, available jointly from BOC (who supply the gas) and Murex (who provide the hardware) is a fully professional standard of kit available to the DIY user. Portapack presents a convenient source of gas and absolutely first-rate equipment, albeit at a price that reflects such excellence,

BOD11. This is one of BOC's many Cylinder Centres where Portapack cylinders can be changed when they have expired. (Find your local centre in the telephone directory.) Portapacks can be purchased there or at many motor factors.

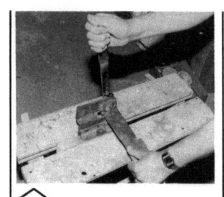

⬆

BOD12.   This tool, made by Sykes-Pickavant, is terrific for cutting out sheet steel. Taking up far less room than a guillotine, it can also cut slight curves, and consists of upper and lower cutting wheels which slice through the sheet while pulling it through the machine.

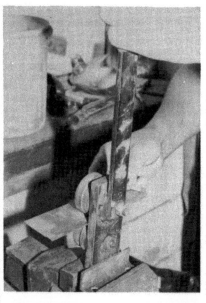

BOD13.   This is another Sykes-Pickavant tool and this is really invaluable for the home restorer. It pulls the edge of the sheet along between two rollers which form a 'set' or a shoulder in the edge of the steel. This allows you to join two flat pieces of metal with all the smoothness of a butt joint but with all the strength and ease of welding of a lap-joint. Wonderful!

BOD14.   Although a little more expensive, the Sykes-Pickavant sheet metal folder is the only way to create perfectly formed folds in sheet steel. It forms very accurate, very crisp folds and even pulls any light wrinkles out of the sheet while it does it.

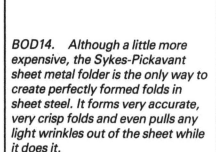

Tool box

At the start of every section, a 'Tool Box' section appears, listing most of the tools and equipment needed to ebable you to carry out the work. No list of 'essential' workshop tools is presented here but simply the advice that is is safer and cheaper in the long run to always buy (or hire) the best tools available.

Safety

At the start of every section is a 'Safety' note. Naturally, safety is the responsibility of each individual restorer or repairer and no responsibility for the effectiveness or otherwise of advice given here nor for any omissions can be accepted by the author – 'Safety' notes are intended to include some useful tips and no more. Some further useful information on workshop practice and general safety measures is given as an appendix – you are strongly advised to read this appendix before starting any of the tasks detailed in this book.

BOD15.   Always have a fire extinguisher close to hand when

⬆

carrying out welding. Small 'toy' extinguishers sold to clip inside the car are not much use at all – go for a full-sized model – it can be a remarkably cheap form of insurance!

BOD16. *A small but useful tip: always bend over the ends of gas welding rods. Then you know which is the 'hot' end and you also reduce the risk of eye damage from the end of the rod.*

Stripdown and examination

Before attempting to carry out any major bodywork repairs, all or part of the bodyshell will need to be stripped of its lights, trim and ancillaries. Removal is a common-sense procedure and should be carried out with reference to the relevant sections of this book. Be sure to have sufficient storage space available and store large components logically in cardboard boxes with smaller trim items being placed in labelled plastic bags. Often, stray nuts and washers are best stored by fitting them temporarily back on to the component from which they came. At the time of taking parts off, it may seem as though you couldn't possibly forget where various bits and pieces belong but it won't be quite like that in a few days or weeks time! Discipline yourself to thoroughly label components as they are removed and tag wires with pieces of masking tape which can then be written upon to give positive identification.

Before starting work, store any glass under cover and mask off any glass, including the interior mirror and gauges which remains in the car. The sparks from a mini-grinder will embed themselves in any glass they hit and be impossible to remove

This section shows how to repair all of the major sections but there will inevitably be small areas of additional rust. Then a patch repair will have to be carried out. In general, the techniques shown here under sections such as that on 'Rear wheel arch patch repair' can be applied to any area. For more specific information on techniques and the full range of body repair and paint systems, see Haynes' *The Car Body Repair Manual* by the same author.

Tool box

Axle stands or ramps; a thin-bladed screwdriver; eye protection; paint stripper, rubber gloves and a scraper; notepad; bags and boxes for strong nuts, screws and small fittings etc; a range of spanners and screwdrivers including an impact screwdriver; releasing fluid and a source of heat for freeing stubborn threads.

Safety

Never use a flame near the fuel tank or fuel lines. Paint stripper is damaging to the skin and eyes – read instructions before use and wear gloves and goggles and protective overalls. Ensure that the car is firmly supported when lifted off the ground – a jack is NOT safe enough. Wear goggles when 'poking' beneath the car and beware of rusty, jagged edges.

The first task in carrying out a restoration of any size is to go round the car and methodically examine it, taking notes of all the problem areas.

Of course, your instincts tell you to make a start, to strip bits off the car straightaway. Once begun, this idea can be so infectious that you can lose yourself in a haze of releasing fluid fumes and rust dust, the excitement overcoming you until you reach the point of no return – and it's past closing time! Once graceful lines are now a tangled heap of metal on the floor and you haven't a hope in hell of remembering where all the bits came from. Perhaps the reader might see something of an exaggeration in this – but beware: it's not so far from the truth!

The Morris Minor Centre publish check-point diagrams, like the one shown here for the Traveller. You can use it to identify the problem areas with your car's structure, adapting the drawings of the rear of the car to suit the type of car you own.

Figure 1. Bodywork check-point diagrams (Courtesy Morris Minor Centre)

1. **1A.** Check for corrosion on shoulder of wing and around headlamp.
2. On late models remove side light/indicator lens and check base.
3. Condition of grille, grille surround and chrome finishes.
4. Condition of chrome bumper blade, valance and over-riders.

1. Shade 'soft' areas of woodwork in red. Discoloured areas of woodwork shade in black.
2. Condition of chrome bumper blades.

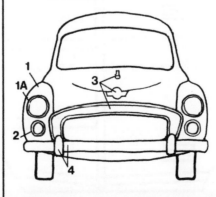

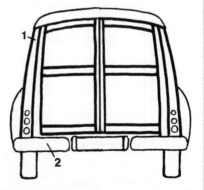

(Figure 1. Continued on next page)

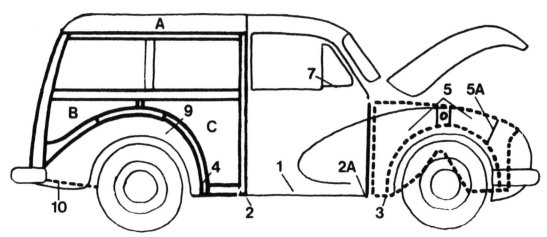

1. Bottom of front door.

2. **2A.** Open door and check bottom of shut pillar (**2**) and hinge pillar (**2A**).

3. Wheel arch rise, behind front wing (tap with hammer).

4. Wheel arch rise, behind rear wing (tap with hammer).

5. **5A.** Lift bonnet and check this area and this seam (**5A**)

6. Check for flaking paint on aluminium panels. A,B & C.

7. Check for interior split below quarter light.

8. Shade 'soft' areas of woodwork in red. Discoloured areas of woodwork shade in black.

9. Check for corrosion on rear wing.

10. Check area above rear spring hanger.

Nearside – as above.

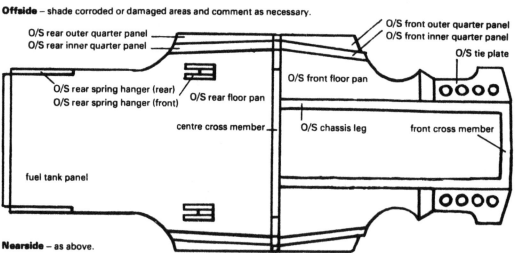

O/S rear outer quarter panel
O/S rear inner quarter panel
O/S front outer quarter panel
O/S front inner quarter panel
O/S tie plate
O/S rear spring hanger (rear)
O/S rear spring hanger (front)
O/S rear floor pan
O/S front floor pan
centre cross member
O/S chassis leg
front cross member
fuel tank panel

Nearside – as above.

Ch 3 Bodywork, part II: chassis and floorpan repairs

This part of the Chapter deals with the sort of underbody and structural areas that you are advised to check most thoroughly when buying a car, because they provide most of its strength. When restoring a car, these areas should be tackled first. 'Tool box' and 'Safety' notes should be read carefully along with the safety notes in the appendix; they apply, in the main, to the whole of this part of the 'Bodywork' Chapter.

Tool box

Sharp, thin-bladed bolster chisel; air chisel or similar mini-grinder; goggles; electric drill and bits; variety of welder's clamps and/or self-tapping screws; MIG or oxy-acetylene welding equipment; engineer's hammer; impact drive screwdriver; basic set of spanners and screwdrivers; a large and a medium sized lever; releasing fluid; paint and zinc-rich primer.

Safety

Beware of sparks from the grinder and hot metal when cutting away. Wear goggles and thick industrial-type gloves. Ensure that the car is securely raised off the ground in such a way that
a)   It cannot topple onto anyone beneath it, bearing in mind the amount of force that will be applied to it, and
b)   it will not twist or distort as old structural panels are cut out. Take all the usual precautions when welding — see appendix at the back of this book and contact your supplier for specific safety information. You should seek training in welding skills before tackling oxy-acetylene welding; follow the maker's safety instructions carefully before carrying out electric-arc welding of any kind. Wear goggles when working beneath the car.

Fuel Tank Removal

You may notice from many of the pictures in this book that the Morris Minor Centre do not consider it necessary to remove the fuel tank from a car whilst working on the car. But remember that home restorers will be working under far less tightly controlled conditions and so it must be considered essential for the fuel tank to be removed to prevent the risk of a fuel tank explosion.

If the fuel tank is to be stored for any length of time, have it steam cleaned to remove all traces of petrol and petrol vapour; it is the vapour from petrol that ignites and explodes so simply draining the petrol out is not enough. Moreover, in time, sediment is prone to collecting at the base of the tank and this is likely to find its way into the carburettor, especially after the tank has been disturbed. Having the tank steam cleaned is an excellent way of removing the sediment; or the tank could be vigorously flushed out with a hose — but be sure to dry it thoroughly before refitting.

Tool box

Open-ended spanners for tank removal; cross-point screwdriver/impact driver; releasing fluid; ratchet spanners and a power drill for removing rusty nuts; large safe containers for catching and storing petrol drained from the tank.

Safety

Take note of information in the text and appendices on safety hazards. NEVER drain petrol over a pit nor anywhere a spark could ignite the vapour, e.g. near a central heating boiler — outdoors is best. For obvious reasons, attempting to weld a fuel tank can be lethal and is a task which should always be left to specialists.

1)   Remove the ½ inch hexagon head drain plug from the tank and drain the petrol. Replace the plug when the tank is empty.
2)   Undo the $^5/_{16}$ inch union nut holding the petrol pipe to the tank (you may need to soak it in releasing fluid and/or to grip *carefully* the pipe with a self-grip wrench. The pipe is prone to shearing as the union is undone).
3)   Take out the luggage compartment floor after unscrewing the retaining screws.
4)   Remove the filler pipe cover (Traveller), slacken the filler pipe hose clips and remove the pipe. Disconnect the battery terminals to prevent sparking and disconnect the petrol gauge wire from the tank.
5)   Remove the tank securing the screws and lift out the tank, taking care not to damage the packing strip beneath the flange.

When replacing the tank, you may have to reseal with a suitable mastic the rubber grommet on the filler pipe and the packing strip and check also that the petrol pipe and drain plug are properly seated with no trace of petrol 'weeping'.

Gearbox tunnel cowl removal

GTC1.   At best, removal of the gearbox tunnel cowl is a wrist-achingly slow job because something like 32 machine screws have to be unscrewed. In practice, the problem is usually much worse. In many cases, the screws lock solid into position in which case you have

a number of options. You can try cleaning out the head of the screw and using a screwdriver with a really good point; you can tap the head of the screwdriver sharply with a hammer to try shocking the screw free (you can try turning at the same time with a self-grip wrench locked onto the shank of the screwdriver); you can turn to an impact screwdriver which actually stands a far better chance of freeing the screw; you can crawl underneath and get some heat onto the captive nut (but watch out for the fire risk around petrol pipes, underseal and carpets); and if all else fails, you will have to drill out the machine screw, taking care not to damage the threads in the captive nut and, if necessary, re-tap the nut.

Good luck!

Front chassis leg renewal

FCL1. The Minor's front chassis leg is frequently patched and then patched over patches well beyond its safe working life. (Courtesy Morris Minor Centre)

It is a crucial structural member since the whole of the front suspension is mounted through a tube in the chassis leg. Part- and full-length replacements are available. Driver's side chassis legs are often sound around the area of the brake master cylinder because of brake fluid leakage! See Chapter 5, 'Front suspension overhaul' for details of how to dismantle the front suspension in preparation for removing the bottom suspension arm.

FCL2. One of the author's Minor's chassis legs rotted out here even though the paint on the outside was still shiny! The only way to check is by tapping firmly with a hammer. Remember that all these shots were taken with the car on its side! Refer to Figure 2 for further guidance.

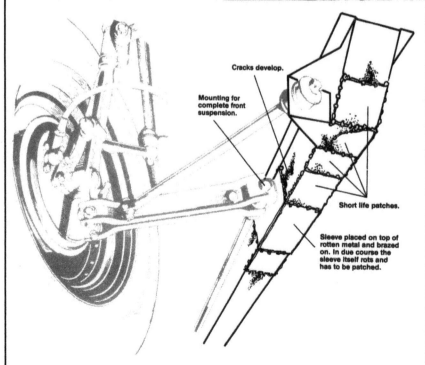

Cracks develop.

Mounting for complete front suspension.

Short life patches.

Sleeve placed on top of rotten metal and brazed on. In due course the sleeve itself rots and has to be patched.

FCL3. The tie-rod is removed from the chassis by undoing the nut here. Reassemble all washers and rubbers back onto the tie-rod after removing the other end.

FCL4.   Use a pair of spanners to undo the bolt holding the rearmost end of the tie-rod to the mounting fork.

FCL6.   The same tool is shown here removing a nut from one end of the fulcrum pin . . .

FCL8.   A further bolt holds the two halves of the suspension arm together and is removed as shown. (There is no need to use the long socket extension shown here!)

FCL5.   Now use a rod or pin inserted into the holes in the fork to stop it turning while the mounting nut is removed from the other side. (Shown here is an air-driven spanner wrench, used in the Morris Minor Centre's workshop.)

FCL7.   . . . followed by the other end.

FCL9.   Finally, the inner fulcrum pin nut and washers shown here are removed . . .

FCL10.   . . . and the front half of the suspension arm lifted, tapped or levered carefully away. It is not under any tension provided that the top arm has been disconnected — see Chapter 5, 'Front suspension overhaul' for details.

FCL11.   While supporting the front hub/brake assembly with one hand, the rearmost half of the suspension arm can be tapped off the top fulcrum pin.

FCL12.   This leaves the assembly free, so prop it up (or out, if the car is still the 'right' way up) as shown in FCL16.

FCL13.   Now tap the suspension arm back along the torsion bar far enough to clear the eyebolt and fulcrum pin, but NOT off the splines on the torsion car, or the correct suspension setting will be lost.

FCL14.   The eye-bolt is held through the chassis: remove the nut and washers . . .

FCL15.   . . . and lever the eye-bolt loose in its tube.

FCL16.   Then turn it to clear the torsion bar.

FCL17.   If you have to repair the cross-member, too, you can now remove the whole torsion bar. (See section on Front Floor and Cross-member repair.) If not, refer to FCL19.

FCL18.   The eye-bolt can be lifted or tapped and levered out of the chassis leg and put to one side for later use.

FCL19. Now for the good news! If the torsion bar can be left mounted on the cross-member, simply disconnect the tie-rod, as shown, undo the eye-bolt and lever the torsion bar upwards propping it out of the way with a block of wood, as shown.

FCL20. You can replace either a half-chassis leg or, if the whole thing has corroded, you can fit one that goes right the way back to the cross-member. If you replace the driver's side leg, you will have to remove the master cylinder — see Chapter 5, photo BS12 for details. You will also have to remove the clutch release assembly (see Chapter 5, Engine and gearbox removal sections) and the engine mounting tower-to-chassis bolts.

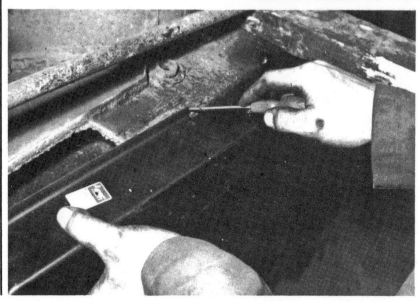

FCL21. Paul Bidgood, fitting this panel at the Morris Minor Centre, cut away the old corroded member with any oxy-acetylene cutter, leaving more metal in place than he would finally want. The half-length repair panel has a generous reduced-size flange on the end which is sleeved into the sound panel. Paul felt that he didn't need all of this so he cut some of it away.

FCL22.   Then he offered it up and accurately marked where to make a final cut in the existing panel.

FCL23.   Paul then cleaned up the existing panels with the mini-grinder to remove all traces of the old flanges and so that he could weld to clean metal.

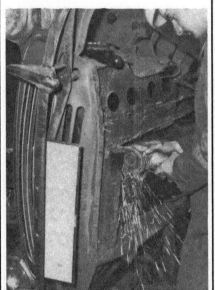

FCL24.   Major alignment points for the new panel are the engine mounting tower bolts . . .

FCL25.   . . . and the eye-bolt mounting hole. Check its position by measuring from the cross-member and comparing it with the other side of the car.

FCL26.   Paul used new bolts through to the outer . . .

FCL27. . . . and inner engine mounting bolts. Note how the flap of metal from the small cross-member that lives beneath the radiator has been retained and bent out of the way.

FCL28. Then, being a careful sort of chap, Paul made a final, careful, visual check that the outer and bottom faces of the member were exactly in line with the sound half of the old one. A complete member would have to be measured with care for being parallel with the other side and it would also be essential that no other panels were removed at the same time, or the bodyshell might twist. If there is any question of this happening have the car checked on a jig by a specialist.

FCL29. Paul chose to gas weld all the flanges and to MIG the ends in place.

FCL30. Then he showed how he ensures that the front cross-member is welded neatly in place. First, he drives a piece of flat steel beneath the flap, as shown.

FCL31 Paul taps the flap over, onto his piece of flat steel, pushing it down as he goes.

FCL32. When the flat of steel is level with the bottom face of the chassis rail, he dresses any distortions out of the sides of the cross-member, caused by cutting the old panel out . . .

FCL33. . . . followed by tapping the flap down and MIG welding it in place.

Hinge pillar/flitch panel/ tie plate

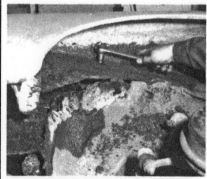

HP1. Obviously, the front wing has to be removed in order to gain access to the hinge pillar or flitch plate. See 'Front wing removal' section for details.

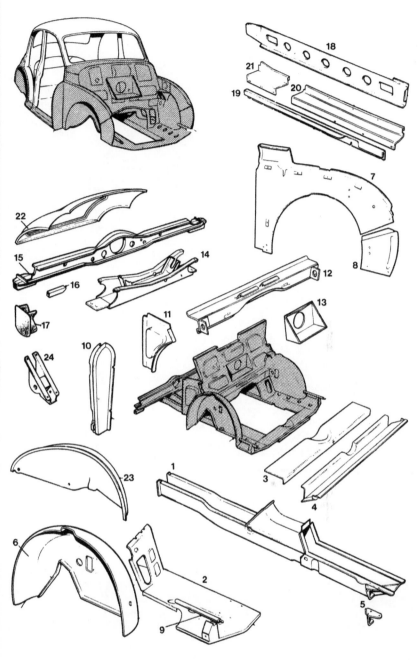

Figure 2. Body panel assemblies. (Courtesy Morris Minor Centre)

1 RH Chassis leg	8 Flitch extension	16 Jacking bracket
2 RH Tie plate	9 Bumper mount	17 Rubber
3 Upper front cross-member plate	10 Hinge pillar (A-post)	18 Sill boxing plate
4 Front cross-member	11 Inner panel	19 Sill finisher
5 Tie bar bracket	12 Cross-member	20 Front kickplate
6 RH front wheel arch	13 Battery box	21 Rear kickplate (4-door)
7 RH front wheel arch panel (flitch plate)	14 Engine mounting cross-member	22 Boot closing panel
	15 Centre cross-member	23 RH rear wheel arch

HP2. On the other hand if only a small, localized repair or a temporary one is necessary, you can get away with unbolting only the rearmost mountings, leaving the trickier grille bolts and wiring in place and propping the wing clear.

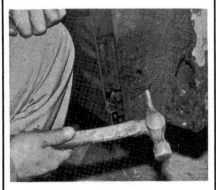

HP3. Tap the hinge pillar shroud and lower flitch panel with an inquisitive hammer in order to search out corrosion . . .

HP4. . . . and continue these investigations around the top of the same area.

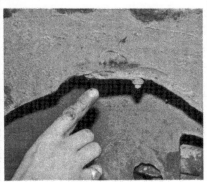

HP5. Look further forwards along the flitch plate, especially above the bump stop, (where the rubber is so often missing as in this case) because weak suspension and weak metal often allow the bump stop to be bashed upwards into the flitch.

HP6. This is a case of really severe rot in the whole floor, hinge pillar and flitch panel area and is a prime example of support being required before any further cutting away is carried out (See 'Sill replacement' for details).

HP7. It was necessary to use a flitch rear-half repair panel which in the Morris Minor Centre version comes with the hinge pillar cover ready welded to the flitch.

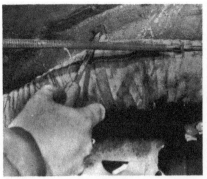

HP8. When carrying out your own flitch panel repair, remember to strip out any fixtures and fittings from the insides of the flitch panel, such as the heater trunking shown here,

HP9. Then cut out as much or as little as is necessary – but DO go well beyond the area of the rot. Here an angle grinder with special thin cutting disc is being used to cut cleanly through the existing metal.

HP10. If possible, leave the threaded wing mounting plate in place and take the chance to clean out the thread with an appropriate size of tap or at least a bolt with a saw cut down ½ inch (1cm) of its end, lengthwise.

HP11. Where a small patch repair will suffice, make it up in two sections rather than one folded section so that you can weld the flat piece shown up to the hinge pillar itself before closing off with another plate.

HP12. At the other end of the scale, this is an instance where both the flitch and the inner panel have rotted out. The first job here, after linishing off all the surface rust with the angle grinder, of course, is to plate the inner panel.

HP13. Before offering up the replacement flitch panel, it is important to remember to weld nuts onto the reverse of the flitch where captive nuts originally fitted. Do so by fitting two nuts and a bolt to obtain the correct position, then screw out the bolt after the nut has been welded in (and after it has cooled down!)

HP14. If the hinge pillar is 'tied' into place — and it's the wrong place — you've got trouble! In this shot, a professional hydraulic ram is being used to push the hinge pillar into place while the flitch repairs are tack welded. The door shut is then tried and any further adjustments made before final welding takes place. With the car in its normal position it is particularly important to ensure that no sagging takes place — see 'Sill replacement' section for details.

HP15. And this is a flitch repair section being fitted and bolted up into place through some of the wing mounting holes, before being welded in all round.

HP16. Meanwhile, back on a car where only localised repairs were necessary, steps are being taken to hold back future corrosion by painting the whole area with a tough type of paint, such as 'Hammerite'.

HP17. When Practical Classics magazine rebuilt their Minor, they found it necessary to replace the whole flitch panel but the principles of fitting it are exactly the same as those shown here; support the front corner of the car to prevent any dropping when the old panel is cut away.

HP18. The tie-plate is available as a replacement panel, its cutting out and 'stitching' in being a relatively straightforward matter. It cannot be overemphasized that each of these important structural panels should be replaced one at a time so that maximum strength is left in the bodyshell and so that there is, in each case, a good set of reference points for fitting each new panel in turn.

Front floor and cross-member repair

Some reference to repairs in this area is made in the section on 'Sill replacement' and in cases where the torsion bar is to be removed from the front suspension, for any reason, see 'Front chassis leg renewal'.

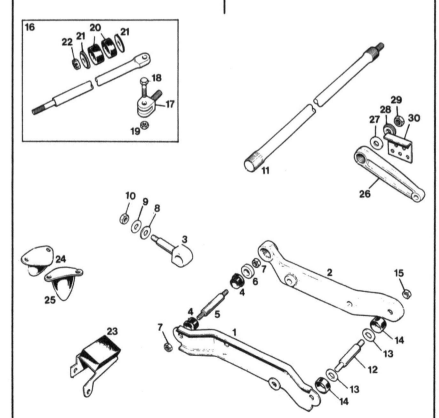

Figure 3. Components of the front suspension. Main part numbers are: Torsion bar 11, Torsion bar lever 26, Adjuster plate 30; for other parts, see 'Front chassis leg renewal' photo sequence. (Courtesy Morris Minor Centre)

FF1.   Begin by removing the torsion bar lever from the cross-member. Undo the torsion bar nut (in this picture an air driven spanner wrench is used) . . .

FF3.   Next, take nut and washers from the bolt holding the torsion bar lever in place . . .

FF5.   If you are working alone, pull the bolt out with the bar as shown but be prepared to replace the bolt if the threads are damaged.

FF2.   . . . and remove and retain the nut and special washer.

FF4.   . . . lever against the spring of the torsion bar with a stout bar in order to take pressure off the bolt and tap it through as far as possible. If you are working with an assistant, drift the bolt out whilst the lever is held against the spring.

FF6.   Retrieve the adjuster plate and washer (Figure 3, 30 and 27) and save for later. The different hole positions in the adjuster plate allow the selection of slightly different suspension height positions so that the suspension can be accurately 'trimmed'. The hole in the cross-member is in fact slotted, positive location being made by the adjuster plate. Mr. Issigonis, you're a genius!

FF7.   Now, before tearing into the old panel work with a cutting flame, disconnect the wiring or petrol pipe clips that run down whichever side of the transmission tunnel you will be working on and tie wires or pipe well back and out of harm's way.

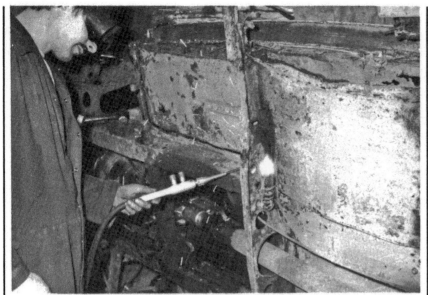

FF8.   Cutting off the old cross-member tight against the old floor is a simple matter but if the floor is not to be replaced (unlikely!) or if it is to be patched in this area (only if the rest of the floor is very sound — unlikely again!) grind back to a smooth clean surface.

FF9.   On this car, the rear floor had been fitted before the shot of the cut-away cross-member could be obtained. They work fast down in Bath!

FF10.   Here, Mark offers up a complete new front floor after the old one has been cut away and the remaining panel edges linished clean of paint and rust.

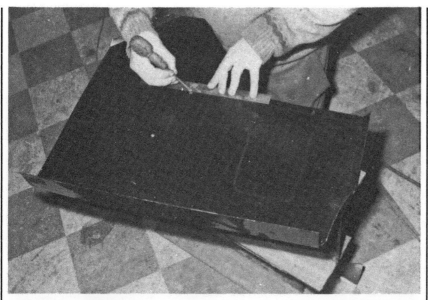

FF11. Morris Minor Centre floorpans are fairly generous in size, leaving you to cut off any surplus; in general, leave areas of sound metal in the car if possible.

FF12. And in this shot a full length floor has had to be fitted. As you can see, the entire sill area has been cut away too — not recommended by this writer for home restorers! Stick to cutting away the bare minimum because you're not likely to have the expertise to overcome any major distortion problems; replace the floor, if necessary, half at a time, front and rear. See section on 'Rear-spring front hanger and rear floor' for more details on floor fitting.

FF13. Replacement floors do not have seat mounting brackets built into them. Carefully measure their position on the old floor, cut them out of the old floor and weld them to the new, not forgetting to drill generous clearance holes for all four mounting bolts and tapping out each of the threads.

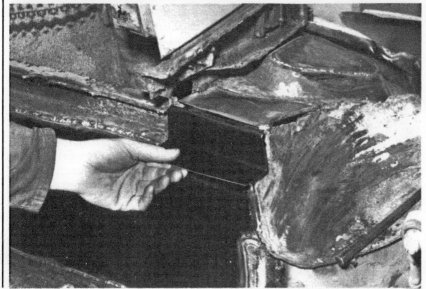

FF14. If the floor is rotten, surrounding areas are likely to be rotten, too. See sections on repairing sills and hinge pillar/flitch plate for more details. Here a new section of the sill box section is being let in.

FF15. Linish paint from the floor and cross-member and offer up the replacement cross-member. It is crucial that the jacking point end of the cross-member sits beneath the bottom of the sill in order to support it. In exceptional cases, an extension may have to be fabricated from mild steel to enable it to do so.

FF16. Bolt the torsion bar assembly back onto the new cross-member before fitting it. Then the whole assembly can be levered back into position. A friend's assistance is crucial here and very great care must be taken to prevent the lever from slipping and the cross-member jumping back and causing damage or injury. If the car is repaired in the 'upright' position, the assembly could be pushed back into place with a trolley jack.

FF17. With the assembly held closely in place, the cross-member must be very accurately located . . .

FF18. Remembering the location of the aforementioned sill, it can be levered into position before

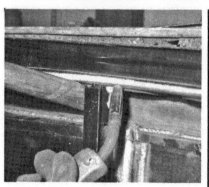

welding the cross-member to it. The jacking point is a separate structure and it is usually recommended that you do not fit it or, at least, that you do not use it because in time it can become structurally unsound and therefore unsafe.

Rear floor repair

Experts at the Morris Minor Centre will sometimes fit a full sill and front-to rear floor replacement on one go. In general, that's not such a good idea for the home restorer who ought to be content to work within his own resources, rather than risk a major disaster! When front and rear floor pans are fitted separately and the cross-member is also cut away, it will be found that there is a gap between the two floor sections which are made to butt up against the cross-member. In this case, be prepared to weld a bridging plate of

around 18 gauge across the gap between floorpans.

It is not advisable to remove either front or rear floorpans *and* the sill at the same time unless there is no alternative and care must always be taken to support the vehicle so that it does not sag out of alignment.

RF1.   This is the rear floor pan repair, including the sill inner box-section wall and the rear support panel, which fits beneath the rear seat, both of which are inclined to rot along with the outer edges of the floor. Note the comments on 'Front floor repair' regarding the need to move wiring and the petrol pipe from the transmission tunnel.

RF2.   This is actually a section of front floor being cut out, but the principle is exactly the same: mark out the extent of the repair panel to be used, remembering to leave an inch or so of overlap between original and repair panels. Here, Alan Jeffrey, the Morris Minor Centre's welding workshop foreman, has fitted the rear floor before cutting out the front. Which ever you do first depends on the job and your personal preference.

RF3.   Alan has cut the rear floor away on this car and the completely rotten cross-member, too. (See appropriate section for details.) Note that he is wearing a heavy-duty 'industrial' leather glove as proof against burns from hot metal.

RF4.   All too often, Minor floors have been patched with overlays placed over corrosion above and beneath; you'll have to cut them off patiently one at a time. Alan's using an ordinary welding torch for cutting, with a largish nozzle and the oxygen turned up high, but you are recommended to use the correct type of cutting attachment to reduce the risk of dangerous blow-back.

RF5.   The front inboard corner of the rear floor is a strong, dished member. It is not usually corroded so leave as much of it as possible in place and cut the repair panel to fit.

RF6.   With the old floor cut away, offer up the new one from the inside and mark out any cutting down that may be necessary.

RF7.   Trim the floorpan with tin snips . . .

RF8.   . . . then clamp it in place and tack weld all the way around . . .

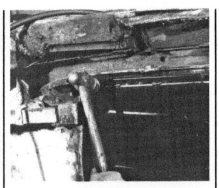

RF9.   . . . tapping the floorpan and the edge of the old floor tightly together inside and out.

RF10.   Then weld in a continuous seam both inside and outside the overlap. Weld for around 6-8 inches (100-125mm) in a run, then transfer to another side of the floor so that there is not too much distortion-inducing heat concentrated in one area at a time.

RF11.   The cleanliness of these welds demonstrates one of the major advantages of MIG welding. It is essential to clean up the old metal so that no contamination gets into the weld. Note that, even though the spring hanger is also to be replaced, it has not yet been cut out.

RF12.   The outer floor panel, shown here, closes off the bottom of the sill. Make sure that you weld the floor/inner sill panel before attempting to fit it.

RF13.   Also, if you're replacing the spring hanger, do it before fitting the outer floor panel. Grind off any welds which prevent it lying flat on the new floor pan, seam weld it along its inner edge . . .

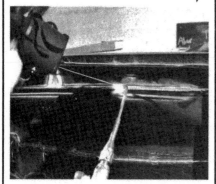

RF14.   . . . then weld the flanges shown with the spot welder in a continuous, watertight seam. Gas gives the neatest results in this kind of weld.

Rear-spring, rear mounting and chassis rail

A box-section snakes its way inside the rear wheel arch giving support to the rear of the car and providing a mounting point for the rear of the spring. Here's how to rebuild the box section and the bump stop buffer at the top of the arch.

Note the comments on fuel tank removal (*strongly recommended*) at the start of Part III of Chapter 3.

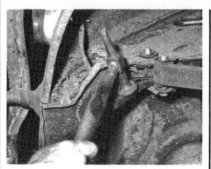

RSH1.   Undo the two nuts and washers holding the shackle pins in place, remove the outer shackle plate, then knock out the inner plate – with-pins. Here a bar is held against the inner plate and hit with a hammer; to hit the threaded pins is certainly to damage them.

RSH2.   After removing the rubbers, the condition of the mounting area can more easily be seen.

RSH3.   Often, underseal conceals the true nature of the steel; heat it gently and scrape it off then check out the whole panel properly.

RSH4.   On this car, the inner side of the rear of the box-section had rotted. Here an inner repair section is being offered up.

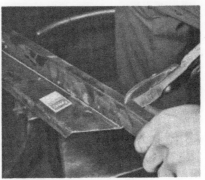

RSH5.   You can see that this repair section provides a new inner wall and base for the box-section but the flange shown may need to be split so that the repair panel can be bent to fit the shape of the original.

RSH6.   As always, the surface of the metal where the weld is to be made must be ground back to shiny metal as should that of any steel that will be hidden. Any untidyness from the cutting-out process should be attended to at the same time.

RSH7.   Corrosion has occurred differently here: the inner wall has remained sound and the corroded outer wall has been cut away leaving the rearmost reinforcing section in place along with the shock absorber mounting. A repair panel is being offered up here for the outer part of the boot floor.

RSH8.   And here, the boot floor repair has been neatly MIG welded into place.

RSH9.   The outer wall comes as a strongly made repair section, too. It is clamped onto the inner wall flange . . .

RSH10.   . . . and MIG welded in place with a continuous seam weld all the way round.

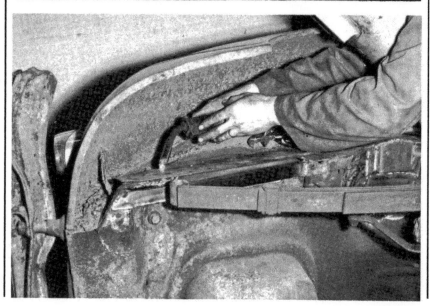

RSH11. At the Morris Minor Centre, they like to gas-cut a recess in the flange near the spring shackle, as shown and re-seam weld.

RSH12. This is a different car again, but the principle remains the same for all. The box section above the axle (amd remember, once again, that the car is on its side) has been cut away and a start is made in re-making the bump-stop buffer.

RSH13. The outer edge is seam welded and then the inner edge hammered carefully to the curve of the panel, as shown.

RSH14. A piece of thick plate, with a narrow distance piece at each end to support the plate a little way away from the box section, is welded on. Then the outer and bottom walls of the box section could be made up and fitted. No repair panels are currently available.

RSH15. In this case, the box-section base was fairly sound and so the bump-stop buffer was made up and fitted before cutting away the corrosion from the outer wall — it just goes to show that the order of work you follow in this area depends on your preference and the nature of the problem.

RSH16. Where the side wall of the box-section goes past the bump stop buffer, it should be taken over its edge as shown, and seam welded in place.

RSH17. The inner wheel arch is also prone to rot, especially in its rear lower corner, which happens to be a rather tricky shape. Here a repair panel is being trimmed to fit . . .

RSH18. . . . neatly around the repaired box-section area beneath it. The wheelarch rot above, on the Traveller shown here, can be repaired with repair panels cut from flat steel sheet.

RSH19. Finally, of course, the shackle pins and plates are refitted, preferably with new rubbers, and the repair is painted.

Rear-spring front mounting renewal

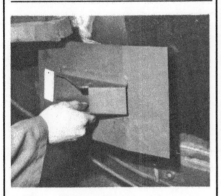

FRS1. The spring mounting 'shoe' comes complete with a plate to cover the surrounding area most likely to corrode.

FRS2. Detach the spring from the mounting (see later part of this section for details) and measure with great accuracy a set distance from the centre of the mounting hole and mark a point on the floor. (Note the measurement you have chosen!)

FRS3. Make another measurement 'sideways', marking, of course, a part of the panel that is not going to be cut out, and again noting the measurement. These datum points enable you to locate the new panel exactly.

FRS4. Cut out the old spring hanger after referring to the new panel and leave half an inch or so overlap.

FRS5. Take away the old mounting point . . .

FRS6. . . . and clean up any rough edges, using the mini grinder. Also clean off any paint or underseal around the area of the weld.

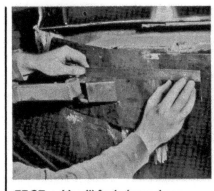

FRS7. You'll feel pleased you didn't lose those measurements, because now, the new panel can be exactly located in place. Be sure that the actual mounting sides are parallel to those on the other side.

FRS9. Fit the mounting plate to the inner face of the spring mounting shoe before attempting to fit the spring (See Figure 11, 24, 25 and 26 under 'Rear suspension').

FRS11. The rubber bushes are freer and ease spring fitting if they are assembled with hand cleaner, petroleum jelly or some other non-grease lubricant.

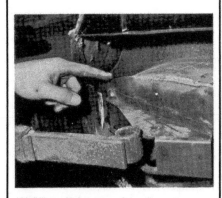

FRS8. If the rear floor has also been cut away, shape the rear of the repair panel to fit the edge of the (normally hidden) box section and weld all the way along it.

FRS10. And this is how the pin and rubber bushes go together (See Figure 11, 21 and 23).

FRS12. Push each bush into the spring eye, from one side . . .

FRS13. . . . and 'encourage' the shoe sides to open up a little and allow the spring bushes to slide in, using a stout lever.

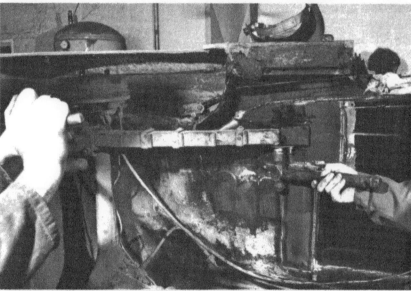

FRS14.   Then insert the pin from the side on which the plate has been mounted.

FRS15.   You really need an extra pair of strong arms, a stout lever and a jolly good shove against the axle to compress the spring and take the pressure off the shackle pin which can be tapped into place. Be careful not to damage the thread on the end of the pin as it comes through.

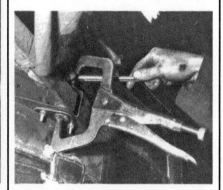

FRS16.   Note how the pin seats up against the mounting plate. You will very likely have to push the sides of the mounting shoe together to enable the nut to 'bite' onto the thread of the shackle pin.

FRS17.   A note regarding the use of van-type rear springs. They can be used (although they give an unnecessarily harsh ride), but the van rubber bushes must be fitted. Inside them, to reduce their effective diameter to that of the shackle pin, you can use standard rubber bushes with their shoulders cut off, pushed inside the van rubbers.

Sill area repair

A Morris Minor's sills are just as vital to its strength as those of any other car but in many ways they are like no other at all! For a start, they're normally invisible, the bit that most people think of as the sill being no more than a decorative cover plate. What makes things worse for the repairer is that working out how this area goes together is probably more difficult than in any other part of the whole car. If you are removing sills and other structural members, and body distortion is likely to be a problem, have the body checked for alignment on a jig by a specialist.

S1.   The sill outer panel (Figure 2, 20) clips over the top of the sill (hidden) and is held down with the line of bolts shown here. The bolts themselves are hidden by the sill finisher (Figure 2, 19) shown in S2.

S2.   Back to the car-on-side: unfortunately, over enthusiastic 'bodgers' sometimes weld the whole lot together instead of getting inside and properly repairing the sills. This type of repair has to be cut away.

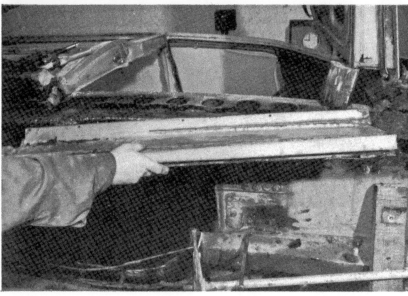

S3.   Then the finisher can be lifted away . . .

S4.   . . . followed by the cover plate.

S5.   Beneath the sill area is the floor side extension panel — or at least should be! In most cases, this area is 'botched' with overlays — flat pieces of steel welded straight over the problem area, and when these rot out they are frequently 'repaired' with more overlays on top, doing nothing for the car's inherent strength but simply covering up the problems so that the car can be given an 'MOT' certificate.

S6.   Behind it all is the sill proper, or sill boxing plate, as it's called in the manual. Just cut all the way along, level with the tops of the holes, as shown.

S7.   Here an air chisel is being used to slice apart the joint between the sill plate and the flange on the box section behind it. An alternative would be to ignore S6, drill through the sill side of the spot welds holding the two pieces together and split them with a hand-held chisel.

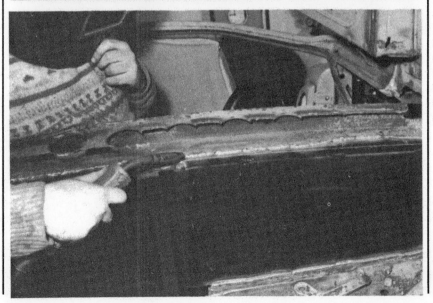

S8.   On this particular car, a new front floor has been let in. If new floors are needed, it is best to replace them one at a time before cutting the sill away but to weld up the floor-to-box-section joint after the sill is removed.

79

S9. The new sill boxing plate is offered up, after cleaning up the existing flanges, and also the painted surfaces, to be joined together, using the mini-grinder.

S10. The rear end of the boxing plate can be trimmed to suit whatever length you need. This two-door car had its rear quarter-panel (sort of, the rear sill) cut away, so you can see how much was needed here.

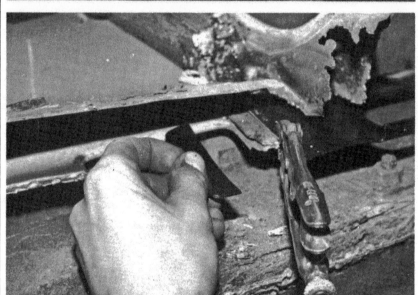

S11. You frequently find that a rotten sill leads to a rotten hinge pillar, especially at the base. It pays to cut away corrosion from this area before fitting any other new panels other than the sill boxing plate.

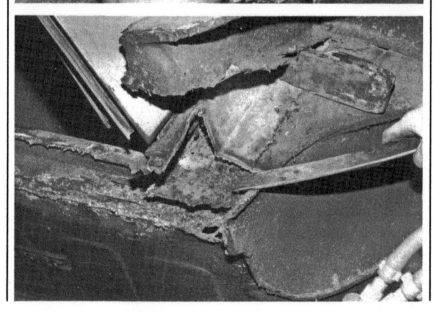

S12.   A piece of angle of suitable size but deliberately over-length was made up to extend the hinge pillar down to where it went before it rotted away.

S13.   It was then tack-welded in place with the MIG.

S15.   Now that there are things to weld to, push and cajole the boxing plate into place and clamp it with a line of self-grip wrenches.

S16.   Then tack the panel to the inner flange every couple of inches using an oxy-acetylene torch and rod.

S14.   A word of warning here regarding cars with a severely corroded sill, hinge pillar and front floor. There is a severe risk that the correct shape of the car will be lost as the old metal is removed, then the wrong shape locked in when the new panels are fitted. If the car is on its side, support the door pillar just beneath the dash, so that it can't drop inwards, if it is upright, support it along the length of the car just inboard from the sill with a very stout piece of timber and axle stands plus jack(s) as required. Use the door as a template and ensure that door gaps stay constant, that the latches line up as it is open and closed and that there is no sagging in any direction.

S17.   Next, go all the way along the joint without a rod, flowing both pieces together in a neat, smooth weld. You could use MIG but some grinding would be required, or MIG-spot or ordinary spot welding, as the manufacturers did it. Seam welds are strongest, however.

S18. Next, the floor side extension is offered up. Its inner flange butts against the sill boxing plate just fitted.

S19. Its two outer ends are fitted to the hinge pillar (A-post) and door shut pillar (B-post). As you will recall, they were suffering from an absence of sound metal; the B-post is shown here with an extension similar in principle to the one on the A-post, being clamped onto the floor extension plate. ⇨

S20. Now here's a crucial part of the operation. Before welding the floor extension in place, offer up the finisher panel and check it for accuracy of alignment with the door when it is held tight against the floor extension outer flange – but remember that it will be pushed very slightly outwards by the thickness of the metal in the outer panel (or kick plate) when fitted properly.

S21. Clamp the finisher rail on, then manipulate the whole thing, sill boxing plate bottom included, to get an accurate fit.

S22. If necessary, lever the sill components into the right position while tack welding them in place. (Here, a headshield becomes vital!)

S23. With everything tacked into place, seam weld every joint of the structure together for better-than-new strength.

S24. The A-post and B-post structures can now be built up with the aid of some creative tin-snipping!

S25. Morris Travellers present their own problems here as part of the B-post structure is hidden by the timber.

S26. All you can do, without removing woodwork, is to let-in and

weld in pieces as far as you can see and reach, after removing as much corroded metal as possible. This area can then be repaired properly later on when the woodwork is replaced.

S27. Patch repairs can be carried out on the floor, as necessary . . .

S28. . . . and there are repair panels available to complete the outer area between floor and floor side-extension, as well as the panel that fits beneath the Traveller woodwork, as on the left of this shot.

S29. If you have found considerable corrosion in the sill and door post area, you can expect other, adjacent areas to have corroded, too. See appropriate sections for repair details but allow time and funds for the whole job.

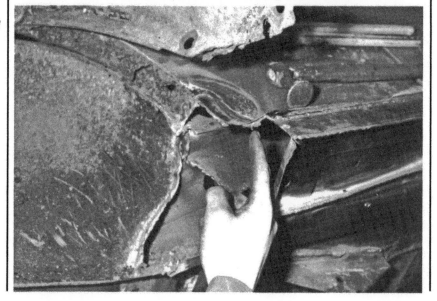

S30. You can now fit the sill kick plate into place. You may have to trim the end to obtain a good fit.

S31. It is held in place with a bolt, large flat washer and a nut and spring washer on the inside of the floor extension plate. Use bright zinc-plated bolts in all body mountings for rust resistance.

S32. Depending on where the cross-member/jacking point was fitted, you may have to make a small cut-out in this panel to clear the jacking point.

S33. Check with the door closed that the plate is properly aligned, then slacken the mounting bolts.

S34. This is to enable the finisher rail, which shares the same bolts, to be fitted up permanently.

S35. The finisher has slots which slide over the mounting bolts. If it can be fitted accurately as is, then that's fine, but if you find that more adjustment is needed, you may have to open the slots out a little.

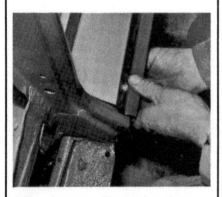

S36. Here the finisher is being pushed over the shank of the bolt, the bolt head and large washer hidden from view.

S37. Then it's a matter of adjusting, tightening, loosening, readjusting until the finisher lines up with the door well-nigh perfectly.

S38. The Morris Minor Centre recommend spraying rustproofer into enclosed box-sections such as these. Since you have the time allowed by a home rebuild, you can take the trouble to paint the inside of the sill with a zinc-rich paint before *closing it off*. Remember, though, that the finish will be burnt off locally if welding is required subsequently during assembly.

Traveller boot floor repair

Two points worth bearing in mind here are a) that the rear of the Traveller is structurally supported by woodwork and that in the area shown here, timber lies next to steel which means that rotten timber may need to be replaced; and b) that The Morris Minor Centre does not feel the need to remove the fuel tank when working in this area. The home restorer is STRONGLY recommended to remove the fuel tank before welding in this area as described at the beginning of Part III of Chapter 3.

BF1. Be sure, when cutting the old rear panels away, to leave the mountings at each end intact. (Remember that this car has been tipped onto its side. This is a view of the left-hand mounting viewed from beneath.)

BF2. Also leave in place this strangely shaped reinforcement strap which includes the spare wheel mounting bolt thread.

BF3. Here, a new rear panel is being offered up to the car . . .

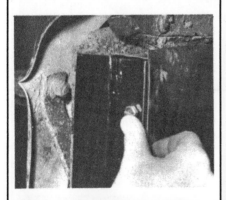

BF4. . . . and, after any under-woodwork and hidden steel has been painted (the author strongly recommends several coats of well-stirred aluminium paint for both), the panel can be bolted up.

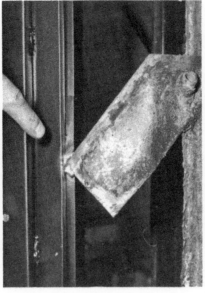

BF5. Then the reinforcement strip can be tack-welded into place . . .

BF6. . . . and repair panels made for the rear boot floor, in two easy-to-handle halves.

BF7. After neatly welding each of the repair panels in place . . .

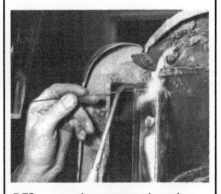

BF8. . . . the rear panel can be seam welded to the wheel arch repair mentioned in the previous section.

Van/Pick-Up body mountings

You can unbolt and remove the whole of an LCV's (Light Commercial Vehicle) body, the whole thing being mounted on a chassis which is similar to but not identical to the Saloon's at the front but totally different at the back.

VP1. This is a view of the Van/Pick-Up chassis looking back from beneath the engine. The chassis rails themselves are corrosion-prone but they cannot be properly repaired without taking off the body.

VP2. One instance of how the LCVs differ from the passenger vehicles is in this cross-member end which is cut off short with no jacking point.

VP4. At the front, the cab is also bolted to the chassis, unlike that of the passenger vehicles. It's bolted in the area of the front valance . . .

VP6. Major body-mounting plates are found further back again near the exhaust mounting, with one bolt on the outside of the chassis . . .

VP3. The rear body of the Van is bolted to the rear of the cab with a ring of bolts all the way around.

VP5. . . . and behind the steering rack, in the area of the torsion bar.

VP7. . . . and two in the adjacent area on the inside of the chassis.

VP8. It's easy to miss this bolt, recessed cunningly near the top shock absorber mountings (note the inherently superior telescopic shock absorbers used as standard on LCVs).

VP9. While at the very rear, another bolt inside the open rear end of the chassis secures the rear of the body. You're ready for lift-off and the most useful degree imaginable of access to chassis repairs, making the LCVs even simpler in this respect than passenger vehicles to restore.

Rear Wing Repair

The LCV's rear wings are part of the side-panel, so if they rot out because of an accumulation of mud on the inner lip, they can be hard to repair, especially since there are apparently no repair sections available. Here's how to make your own very simply. Cut out a piece of at-least- ½-inch plywood to the exact curvature of the wheel arch. Next, cut a crescent of steel, again to the exact curvature of the wheel arch, but with the inner curve set about ⅝ inch further in. Clamp the steel to the plywood so that the inner curve of the steel overlaps the ply by its ⅝ inch overlap and simply tap the excess over to form a flange, but only to 90 degrees, of course. When completed, you've got yourself a rear wing repair section!

Ch 3 Bodywork, part III: panel, wing and door repair

This part of the 'Bodywork' Chapter covers what can be described as 'upper body panels and superstructure'. Many of the techniques employed are those already adopted for repair of the underbody and chassis area. Before starting a repair job in any Section in this Chapter, take note of the 'tool box' and 'safety' details below.

Tool Box

Sharp, thin-bladed bolster chisel; non-distorting panel cutter such as a power driven 'nibbler', a hand-operated cutter such as the Monodex or a jig saw; panel beating tools; variety of welder's clamps; MIG or oxy-acetylene welding equipment; spray equipment (see first part of this chapter); basic set of spanners and screwdrivers; tin snips; a sheet of 20 gauge (or metric equivalent) steel sheet metal; respirator; goggles.

Safety

Take all the usual precautions when welding – see appendix at the back of this book and contact your supplier for specific safety information. Sharp edges and slivers of metal are a panel-beater's hazard – wear thick industrial-type gloves. Wear goggles when using the mini-grinder and when working beneath the car.
    ***Never* spray paint without wearing an efficient respirator and note that atomized paint in the air is highly flammable, as is thinners of course.**

Front wing and grille panel renewal

Behind most rusty outer panels are rusty inner panels, so be prepared to have to carry out some welding

when a rusty front wing is removed. New front wings are freely available, in both the original steel and in glass-fibre. There seems little point in using glass-fibre items; they are only marginally cheaper, they don't have the original's strength, they won't hold a good paint finish for long — and they are not original!

FW1.   The biggest pain can be removal of the old wing. Don't fiddle around with rusted bolts – cut the wing off and lift it away because it's scrap anyway. Access to the bolts will be hugely improved, but you will still probably have to do some drilling out and replacements of captive nuts with the standard item. Watch out for those sharp edges!

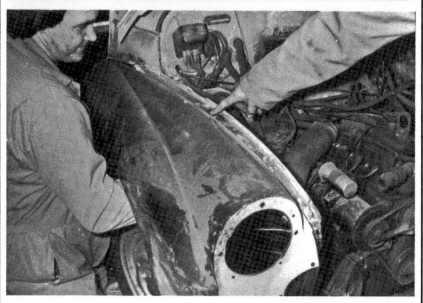

FW2.   If you do need to remove a good wing, you'll just have to grope! Bolts are fitted around the rear, top and front edges of the wing and all are found(?) beneath the wing.

FW3. Hints 'n' tips department — if the old wing is being removed as part of a large-scale rebuild with parts being stored everywhere, cut off the light units as-a-piece, too. If a wing mirror is to be saved cut that out; it makes access to the mounting nut far easier.

FW4. This shot illustrates the mounting holes inside the wing flange. Underseal or paint the inside of the wing, and give several coats of top-coat to the flanges for protection before fitting.

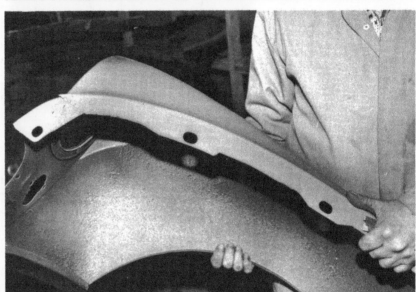

FW5. The wing is carefully offered up and 'hung' loosely on the mounting bolts . . .

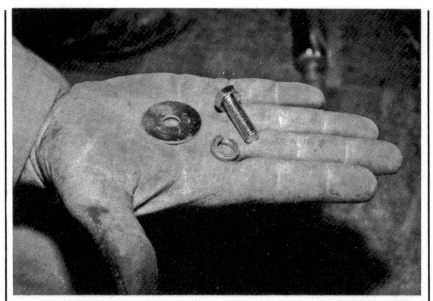

FW6. . . . using rust-resistant BZP (bright zinc plated) bolts, spring washers and large flat washers.

FW7. At the front of the wing there are three skinny studs held in the chrome trim which pass through both front panel and wing. If you hope to save them when removing the wing, you'll need heat on the nuts and lots of luck. It's best to budget for new chrome strips.

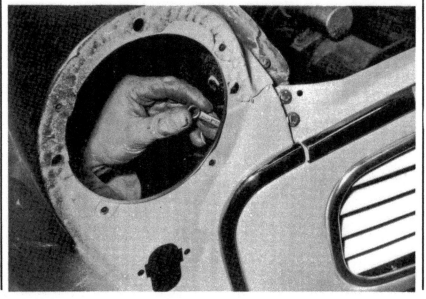

FW8. Once again, access is from beneath the wing.

FW9.	At the rear of the wing, another line of bolts passes through the vertical flange.

FW10.	Note the size of the mounting holes — they allow plenty of adjustment. Tighten up the bolts so that the wing will just *move* but will hold its position.

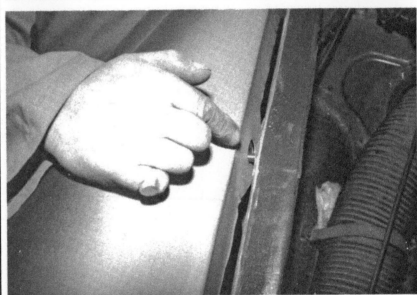

FW11.	An important point to watch is that the curve of the wing is at the same height as the curvature of the door and that the wing-door gap is even.

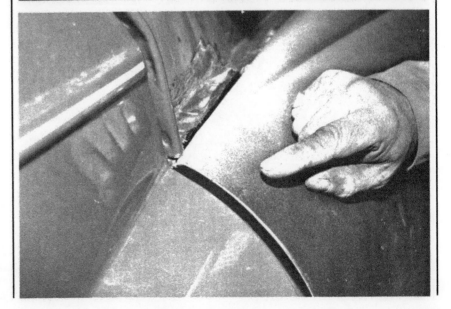

FW12. The gap at the bottom can be opened up by levering against the sill finisher then tightening a bolt or two.

FW13. You may have to apply carefully even more pressure by using a trolley jack, cushioned by a wooden block, beneath the front of the wing. Don't break anything!

FW14. Only very early cars had a piping strip between wing and flitch. Always apply a good quality seam sealer in the joint before it is closed up.

FW15. The grille and bumper assembly is shown here (but see the appropriate section for fitting the latter) and you can see the front structure, ahead of the engine, to which the base of the grille is bolted.

FW16. Between grille and wing goes this rubber gasket.

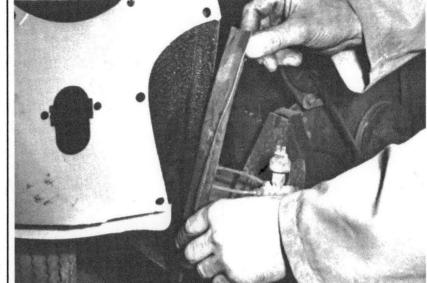

FW17. First offer up the grille with one bolt in each of the top corners.

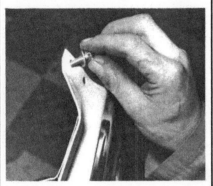

FW18. Fit it in place and ensure that everything is where it should be.

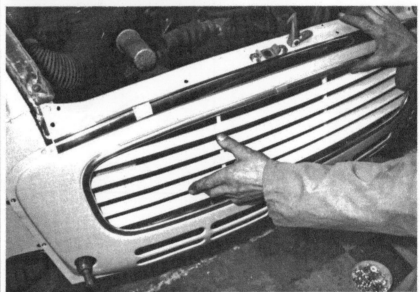

FW19. Bolt the grille panel to the wing as shown in FW7 and FW8.

FW20.   If a new inner panel has been fitted, you may have to drill holes for the bottom line of mounting bolts, otherwise use existing holes, of course.

Figure 4.   The bonnet lock components fitted to the grille panel. Items 14-19 inclusive comprise the primary catch mechanism. Items 20-22 inclusive comprise the safety catch mechanism. (Courtesy Morris Minor Centre)

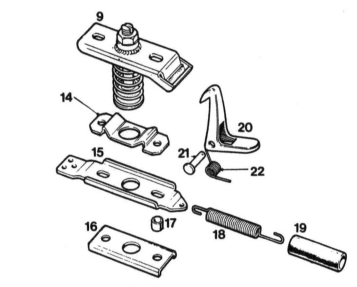

Rear wing renewal

This section shows how to take off an old rear wing and immediately fit a replacement item. In practice there will probably be some remedial work needed to the wing arch. See the following section for details. The comments about glass-fibre replacement front wings apply equally here.

Traveller

RWR1.   There's one way of getting an old Traveller wing off that you won't find in a normal manual – give it a tug! But be careful because if the bottom rear bolt holds, you could split the wood.

RWR2. In any case you may not be able to shift it that way. Then chisel the thing off (this picture shows a power chisel being used) but beware those sharp edges.

RWR3. Take off the scrap wing leaving an inch or so still in place.

RWR4. You almost certainly won't be able to use the original bolts which screw into inserts in the timber. They may knock out easily, as shown; if not, unscrew them.

RWR5. Take off the old beading and tap the old retaining tacks level with the wood.

RWR6. Slit the new beading so that it will follow the shape of the timber and tack it or staple it into place.

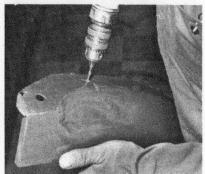

RWR7. Nowadays, new wings come with only one pre-drilled fitting hole at the lower front. Drill a series of 1/8 inch holes at the lower front. Drill a series of 1/8 inch holes around the flange following roughly the same spacing as the originals.

RWR8.   Use a good, long bright zinc plated wood screw with a large plain washer for the main front lower mounting.

RWR11.   . . . and insert the wood screw.

RWR14.   Tighten the jack, pushing the wing tight up into the wooden wheel arch, the large screw at the front holding the wing in place.

RWR9.   Offer up the new wing . . .

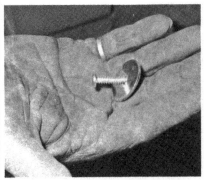

RWR12.   The rest of the screws will be 1 inch bright zinc plated self-tappers, with a large BZP flat washer, of course.

RWR15.   Next, drill a small pilot hole for the self-tapping screw that is to pass through the front hole (surely easier with the wheel off the car and an axle stand in place?) . . .

RWR10.   . . . drill a pilot hole . . .

RWR13.   Now place some sort of jack beneath the rear flange of the wing with a suitable soft pad between jack and wing.

RWR16.   . . . and insert the first screw. Work back, one hole at a time until the whole thing is tightly in place.

Saloons and Convertibles

RWR17.   Remove the old wing in a similar way to the Traveller wing, finishing off by unbolting the remnants of the flange.

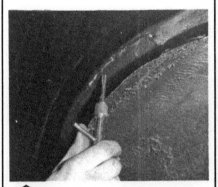

RWR18.   Tap out the mounting threads before offering up the wing. If you don't have a tap, saw ⅛ inch down the end of a spare bolt and run it through with some releasing fluid or paraffin as lubrication.

RWR19.   Offer up the wing and screw in the top bolt, washer and spring washer but don't tighten fully.

RWR20.   Fit all the bolts but, again, leave them quite loose.

RWR21. As with the Traveller rear wing, slit the beading so that it will follow the curve of the front lower portion of the wing. Cut a slot where it goes over the bolt.

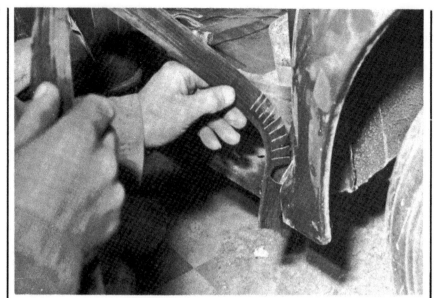

RWR22. Go around the wing, cutting more slots in line with each of the bolts . . .

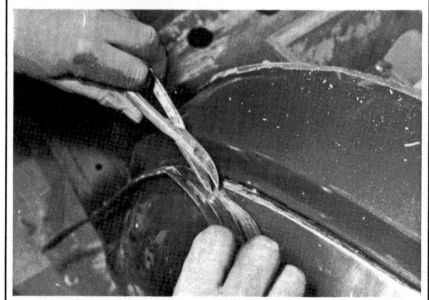

RWR23. . . . then tighten the wing, starting at the front and working back (use a length extension on a ratchet, as shown) pushing the beading carefully and accurately in position.

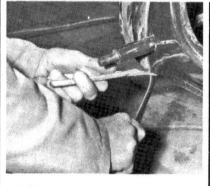

RWR24. Finally, at the rear, cut the beading to length.

Rear wheel arch patch/repair

If the rear wings of your Minor have corroded to the point where replacement is necessary, be prepared to have to repair the wheel arches, too. Most of the corrosion won't be evident until you take the wing off. See the preceding section for details of how to fit a new rear wing.

RWP1. Viewed from low down, this shot of the wheel arch shows how most of the rust was covered by the wing when it was fitted. Power sanding the paint from the area shows how much metal has to be cut out and this has been marked out.

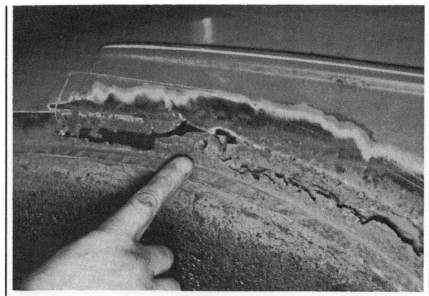

RWP2. Panel beater Mike Swinbourne has a curved template made out of aluminium for this part of the flange. You should spend time making an accurate one out of stiff card.

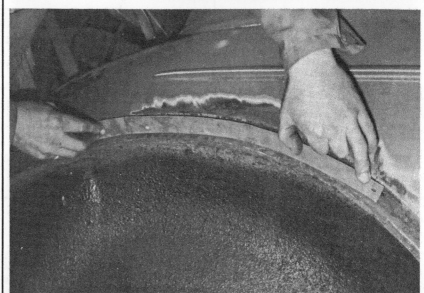

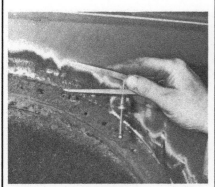

RWP3. Mike took a measurement with a pair of calipers representing the amount by which the repair was to go up the bodywork.

RWP4. He held his template down onto a piece of steel and scribed both lines at once, as shown.

RWP5. On the inside curve of the template, he made another pair of lines the width of the inner flange. (See RWP1.)

RWP6.   The excellent Sykes-Pickavant cutter was used to slice through the steel along the outer of the two first lines drawn.

RWP7.   Then Mike carried out the job that will be most difficult for beginners. He held the steel so that the first line he drew (RWP4) coincided with the edge of a steel anvil and started hitting over a fold. You should start at one end, work the fold over just a few degrees taking care to place it accurately and work right along the repair section. Then go back to the start and fold a bit further. Repeat the exercise again and again until you have the angle you want.

RWP8.   The excess steel had been useful as something to hold on to, but Mike next cut the surplus away with tin snips.

RWP9. Exactly the same procedure was used to take the small flange fold over in the opposite direction.

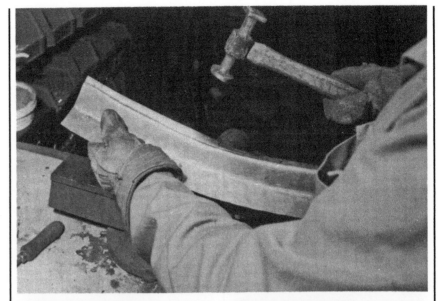

RWP10. Go to a lot of trouble to make both folds good and sharp so that the appearance and fit of the wing are not impaired.

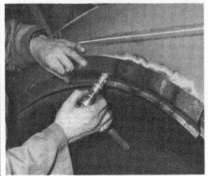

RWP11. Next, Mike pulled a crafty one! He drilled a carefully-placed hole in the repair and bolted it to the wing mounting nut, smack in the middle of the rusty area. Obviously, this gives a very positive reference point.

RWP12. Then the repair was clamped down . . .

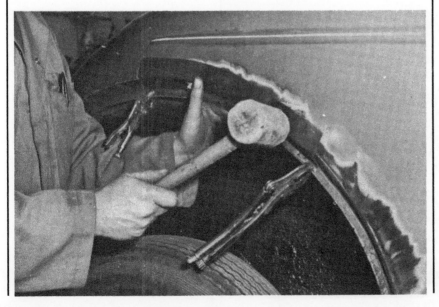

RWP13. . . . and the mallet used to improve the fit of the repair.

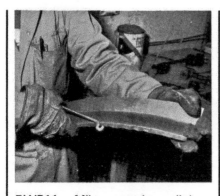

RWP14.   Mike wanted to pull the curve a bit tighter, so he crimped the small flange using the 'gate-latch' shown. The crimps were to be dressed out with the hammer and dolly when everything was welded in.

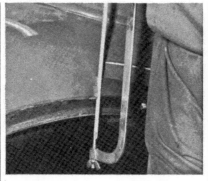

RWP16.   . . . except along the ends, where a hacksaw was used to cut the position at both ends of the repair which was still left in place.

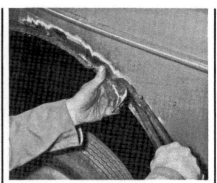

RWP18.   . . . so that the snips could cut along the scribed line.

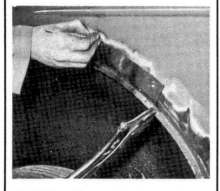

RWP15.   The repair was used as a template and scribed carefully around . . .

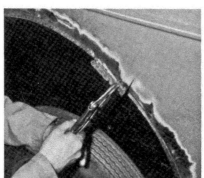

RWP17.   With template removed, a flap of the body panel was lifted up . . .

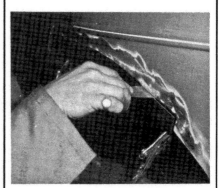

RWP19.   Mike then bolted and clamped the repair panel back onto the car and used a simple 'shoe horn' cut from a piece of flat, thin steel to jiggle the two pieces of steel level.

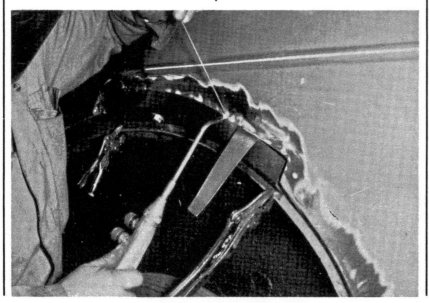

RWP20.   Then he tack-welded, 'jiggled' another part of the joint, and tack-welded again, until the whole butt joint was perfectly level.

RWP21. After welding the full length of the repair, Mike reached through to open boot to hold a dolly against the inside of the panel while tapping the outside of the panel true.

RWP22. If, during the course of tack welding, or before welding the bottom seam you have to push parts of the repair panel outwards, remember that access is easy from inside the car with trim removed.

⇨

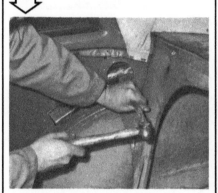

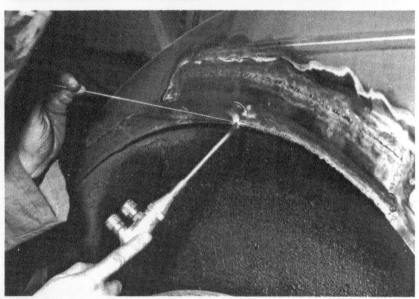

RWP23. The final weld is along the bottom of the small inner flange.

Author's Note: In two respects, Mike's choice of welding techniques are not so suitable for the non-expert. First, if the repair panel had been made ½ inch deeper and a 'set' or 'step' put on the enlarged portion with a tool that Sykes-Pickavant make for the job, then a lap-weld rather than a butt-weld could have been used which is far easier to carry out and is actually inherently stronger. Secondly, the non-expert could easily buckle the body panel when gas-welding it. MIG welding would be far less likely to induce distortion.

RWP24. The weld should next be 'linished' flat on the outside with a 36 grit disc . . .

RWP25. . . . and small blemishes removed with a smear of filler followed by rubbing down and a smear of stopper. (See 'Paint & Preparation section for more details.)

Two-door quarter-panel (rear sill) repair

TD1. This on-its-side Minor has had all its floorpan structures dealt with and all the filler has been ground out of the quarter-panel, exposing a great deal of rust.

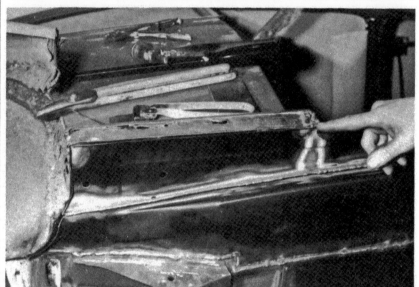

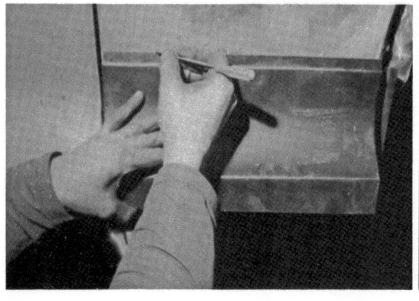

TD2. On this car, a full replacement quarter-panel is being fitted to the other side. The new panel is offered up and marked out . . .

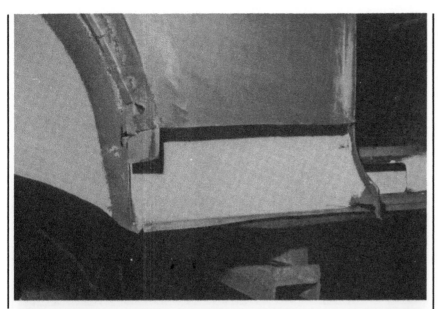

TD3. . . . and cut out, leaving sufficient metal for the overlap at the top of the repair panel. Note that the once-in-a-lifetime opportunity has been taken to paint hidden inner panels.

TD4. Back to the car shown in the first picture — a repair section for the base of the B-post had to be made up and welded in to the sill.

TD5. Since only the lower part of the quarter-panel had rotted, only that part was replaced.

TD6.   At the rear of the quarter-panel more repairs were needed, not forgetting to include a captive nut, held in place here with another nut and a bolt before welding the inner nut in place.

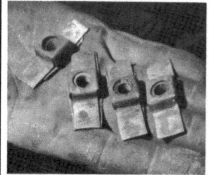

TD7.   If you can get hold of original-type captive nuts you may wish to use them — it all depends on how fanatical about originality you are.

TD8.   This is one of the few areas where a repair could show as a serious bodywork belmish. Linish off any raised welds to produce a surface which can be brought dead flat with a skim of polyester filler or, if you prefer, body solder.

Door repair and frame re-skinning

RSD1.   Most Minor doors split aroung the base of the quarter light and, if left unchecked, the split can go right the way through. Just welding the split gives only a temporary repair. To repair the area properly, remove the window frame as shown in the following section.

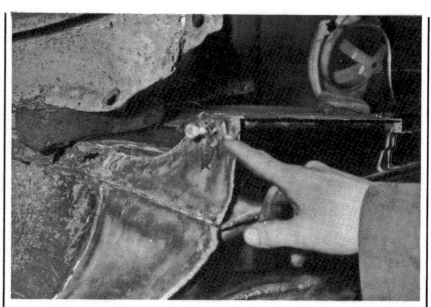

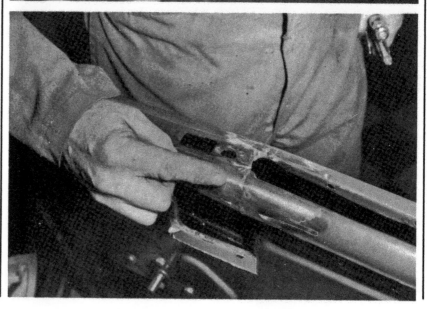

RSD2. Mike shows how to make a repair plate, shaping it to the curvature of the door frame top, first by hammering it around a suitable shape . . .

RSD3. . . . then increasing curvature by carefully squeezing the patch in the vice.

RSD4. The patch can be pulled to an exact fit by clamping and tack welding, finally welding right through the split to the repair patch beneath.

RSD5. Fitting a new door skin is a good job for a relative newcomer to panel beating to try. This door, however, had rotted along the bottom of the frame. Brian started by cutting away the base only of the door skin: it's important when repairing a frame that the correct door shape is maintained.

RSD6. Then corrosion along the door base was cut away . . .

109

RSD7. . . . and a patch clamped and welded against the inner panel. (A butt joint would be neater but a lap joint is easier for a beginner and a little stronger.)

RSD8. A new door bottom is available as a repair panel. Here it is being offered up . . .

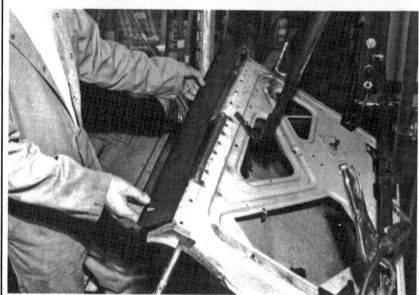

RSD9. . . . and then welded to the door frame and the door's internal support panels.

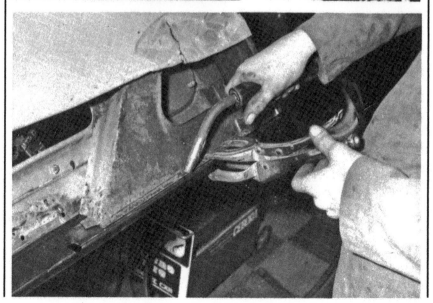

RSD10. To remove the old door skin, you grind away the edge of the fold and tap a thin bladed screwdriver into the fold to part any reluctant stretches. WEAR THICK INDUSTRIAL GLOVES because the edges produced will be razor sharp!

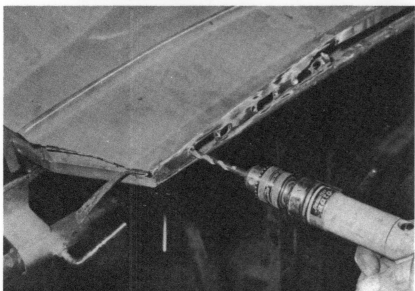

RSD11. The door skin overlaps the door frame at the top. Drill out the top half of the spot welds . . .

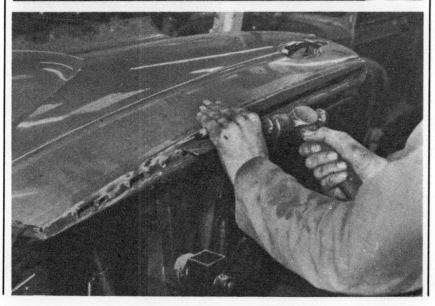

RSD12. . . . and part them with a thin-bladed bolster chisel.

RSD13.　Now the old skin can be lifted off, but take that warning about sharp edges very seriously!

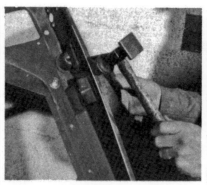

RSD15.　After this the flanges are dressed dead level with a hammer and dolly. (A simple set of Sykes Pickavant panel beating tools would be an excellent investment for this job and have the virtue that they are made to last a lifetime.)

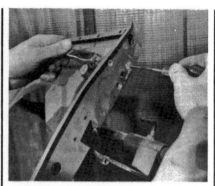

RSD17.　Dick also says that the latch/lock assembly should now be fitted so that the skin can be aligned with it.

RSD14.　A 36-grit flexible disc on the mini-grinder is used to clean all traces of rust from the door frame flanges.

RSD16.　The new door skin was fitted by panel beater, Dick. First he bent back this rainwater deflector which, he says, can sometimes foul the new skin and prevent it from fitting properly.

RSD18.　This is a MUST! Get hold of some 'Spot Weld Primer' from your local paint factor (they will supply non-trade customers in most cases) and spray the entire flange on the door frame and a similar area of the new door skin. It will help to protect the steel against rust and it won't burn off when spot-welded.

RSD19.　Next, Dick placed the skin on the frame . . .

RSD20. . . . easing it over the handle and locating it correctly for the lock.

RSD21. Just a little time should be spent moving the skin around to find the best possible position then clamping it in place.

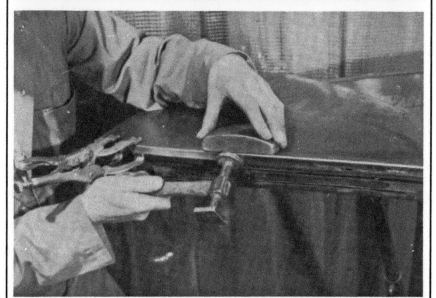

RSD22. With a flat dolly held against the outside of the skin, the flange was tapped over by Dick but NOT all in one go — that would have led to stretching and wrinkling.

RSD23. Several 'passes' were made, each easing the flange over a little further, great care being taken with the curved part of the door.

RSD24. This is the trickiest bit — hammering the flange flat without making marks on the door skin. The hammer must land flat; never hammer the outside of the door skin.

RSD25. New holes can be drilled in the overlap at the top of the skin and 'plug' welds carried out, in the holes themselves, with braze or MIG.

RSD26. At the rear of the door, this small seam should be welded down. Further welding should take place after the door has been fitted — see next section for details.

Fitting door gear and windows

This sequence shows how to fit-up a door after a door skin has been fitted. Removal of components, however, is very straightforward, being a reversal of assembly.

DG1. On the top face of the door latch mechanism is the key number; handy to know if you've lost the correct one.

DG3. . . . then held in place with three countersunk screws and special washers.

DG5. Next, the interior lock lever is fitted.

DG2. The latch is fitted by passing it through the opening shown . . .

DG4. Check the latch for correct free operation. If the door or catch needs adjustment, see the next section for details.

DG6. This pin, shown here with the latch assembly off the door, holds the lock lever in place.

DG7.   The 'remote control' assembly — simply the mechanism for operating the latch from inside the car — is fitted by weaving it through the appropriate holes in the door.

DG8.   It can be fitted upside down, so make a point of fitting it with the folded-over tabs in the position shown.

DG9.   Hook the free end over the pin on the end of the latch slide . . .

DG10.   . . . and secure it with a washer and light split-pin.

DG11.   Four screws hold the handle end in place.

DG12. This medieval looking contraption is the window winder gear. Again, there's an opening in the door casing for its insertion. Lubricate it thoroughly with grease.

DG13. It is held in place by the rectangle of four bolts, as shown.

DG14. Wind the lifting arm until it is approximately horizontal . . .

DG15. . . . insert the glass through the channel in the door top . . .

DG16. . . . and slip the glass channel over the wheel on the end of the lifting arm. Lubricate the channel with grease.

DG17. Next, the window frame can be slotted down through the same opening, not forgetting to place a new rubber gasket beneath the quarter-light panel.

DG18. Two studs are set into the bottom of the quarter-light panel but they are very prone to snapping when the frame is removed. Be prepared to drill them out or wind them out (of you're lucky) with a self-grip wrench or stud extractor and fit new bolts which can then have their heads sawn off. Make sure they're long enough!

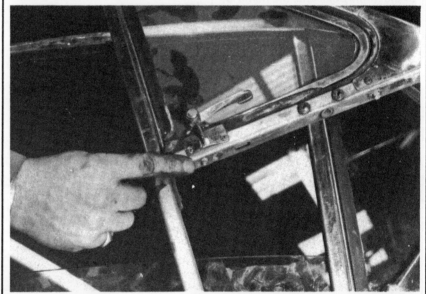

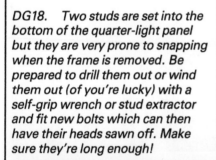

DG19. Nuts, flat washers and spring washers hold the frame down to the door.

DG20. This is not part of the door assembly, but a long socket spanner with an extension being used to insert the bolt and washers which hold in place the rear leg of the chromed frame.

DG21. A further, more accessible bolt holds the front leg of the frame . . .

DG22. . . . while this bracket, bolted through the door panel, is the bottom stop for the window glass.

DG23. You don't fully tighten any of the frame bolts until the frame is aligned with the panels that surround it, although on the Tourer, you don't have a roof alignment to worry about of course!

DG24. A little gentle 'persuasion' from a wooden mallet can work wonders in trueing the frame and bringing it back into 'square' but

wind down the window glass first, of course.

DG25. And don't forget of course, that the glass must run smoothly. (See 'Trim and Interior' section for information on fitting new channels and glass seals.)

DG26. The door stop bolts through the inner face of the door, a rubber, washer and (preferably) a lock-nut holding it in place.

DG27. At its simplest, the quarter-light is removed by undoing the two cross-head screws at the front of the frame.

DG28. The top of the hinge pulls out with the rubber . . .

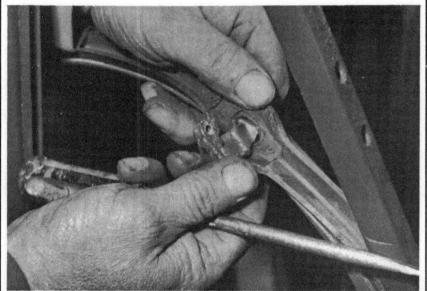

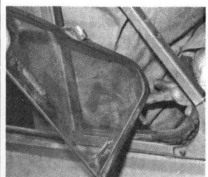

DG29. . . . allowing the quarter-light to be lifted off its bottom swivel.

DG30. The top hinge can be peeled out of the rubber, if necessary.

DG31. Refitting is a matter of easing the rubber back into place with a screwdriver, taking care not to scratch the paint, then re-inserting the two screws.

DG32. The lower half of the top hinge is held to the quarter-light frame with a pair of short cross-head screws.

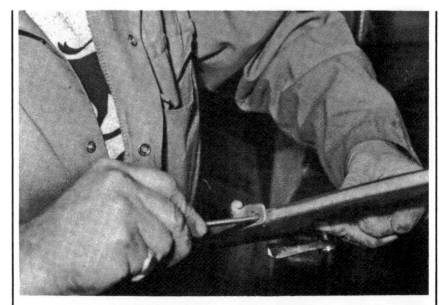

DG33. Meanwhile, back on the doorskin, the outer latch bezel is cleaned up before fitting, while it is easily accessible.

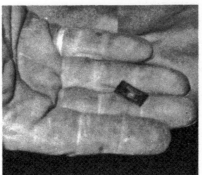

DG34. It is held on with a pair of spring clips like this . . .

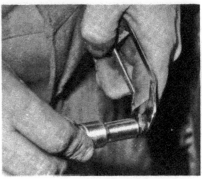

DG35. . . . which are best pushed on from inside the door frame with a socket, like this. (Bezel held off the door for illustration purposes.)

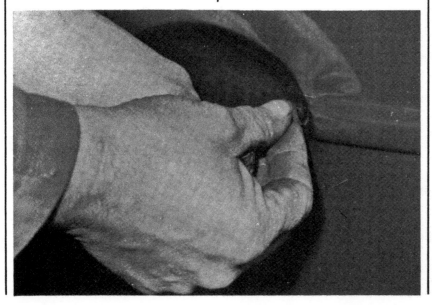

DG36. It's the little touches that count, so don't forget the tiny stop rubber that pushes into the hole in the door skin where the end of the outside handle would slap against the paint as it is released if there were no rubber fitted.

Fitting and aligning doors

FAD1. Firstly, it's no good trying to make the door fit perfectly if the hinges are worn out. Removing the old ones can be a battle — heat the screws with a gas flame (heat the captive plates if the door skin is off) and use an impact screwdriver to loosen the screws.

FAD2. Slackening the hinge bolts gives a little up-and-down and in-and-out adjustment but none forwards-and-backwards of course. Adjusting the front wing is the only way of manipulating the wing-to-door gap.

FAD3. The dovetail pin, which is crucial to door alignment, is fitted to the door, if not already there.

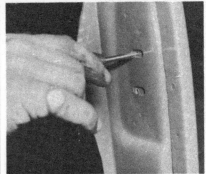

FAD4. After a rebuild, it may be necessary to tap out the threads in the captive plates in both door and door pillar

FAD5. The dovetail socket must also be fitted to the door pillar, of course.

FAD6. To a degree, you can line up the dovetail and socket by eye.

FAD7. More accurate alignment can be gained by placing masking tape over the socket, the dovetail pushing its way through either high or low and leaving its evidence in the masking tape.

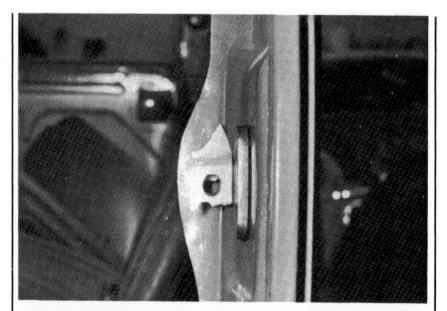

FAD8. Aligning the window frame is described in the previous section but a little 'kicking in' can be remedied by placing a wooden block between frame and body and pushing carefully. Ensure that the window glass is wound down!

FAD9. The top or bottom of the door frame can be pushed back a little by placing a small socket on one of the bottom nuts . . .

FAD10. . . . and closing the door against the socket. Remember that placing a socket within the bottom hinge will also lift the rear of the door.

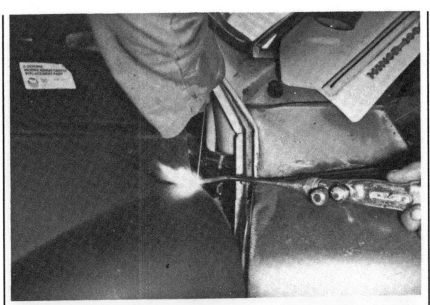

FAD11. With all the pushing, shoving and fitting out of the way, the skin can be locked into place by placing a tack weld on the inside of the flange at this point . . .

FAD12. . . . while the outer edge of the flange can be given three or four spot welds — a real belt 'n' braces job!

FAD13. The striker plate for the 4-door saloon's rear door looks totally different but its function is quite straightforward. It is released and re-tightened with similar countersunk head screws to those fitted to the front striker plate.

Making new guttering

NG1.   Strangely, Minor guttering cannot be bought but it can be made with surprising ease and fitting it is quite straightforward, too. Remove the old guttering by finding the spot welds holding guttering to roof panel, drill carefully through the guttering half of the weld only, insert a thin-bladed chisel to ease it away then clean up the roof flange, with the mini grinder.

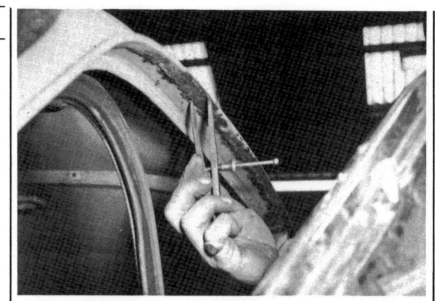

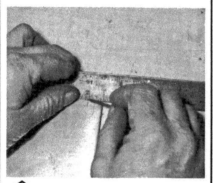

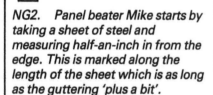

NG2.   Panel beater Mike starts by taking a sheet of steel and measuring half-an-inch in from the edge. This is marked along the length of the sheet which is as long as the guttering 'plus a bit'.

NG3.   The sheet is clamped onto a ¼ inch thick sheet of steel with a slightly radiused edge (a piece of angle iron would be perfect) and, held down with a dolly, hammered over using glancing blows from a 'slapper'. An ordinary hammer could be used, taking extreme care not to make marks on the steel.

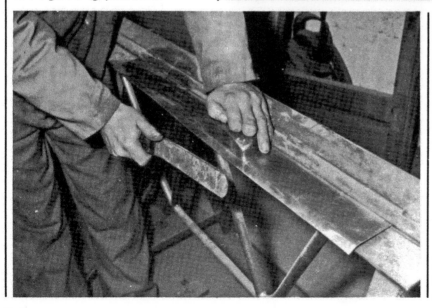

NG4.   The fold is taken over little by little, working from one end to the other . . .

NG5. . . . until it is brought tight round the steel.

NG6. Then the dolly is held beneath the fold and the 'slapper' used to tighten and make regular the fold all the way along.

NG7. Now the width of the guttering is taken from the old guttering (see NG1) and marked onto the half-completed new piece of gutter.

NG8. The Sykes-Pickavant sheet metal cutter is shown here being used by Mike to cut along the line made by the calipers.

NG9. The new guttering is held in place against the car . . .

NG10. . . . and gently, carefully bent to the curves of the roof panel using thumb and fingers only and avoiding a sharp, kink-inducing bend at any point.

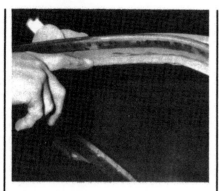

NG11. Here the finished gutter has been cut to length and spot welded in place.

NG12. It's important that no water is allowed in, so the tiny gap all the way along must be sealed with mastic forced in with a spatula.

Fitting front and rear bumpers

FRB1. Both front and rear bumpers (except Traveller) consist of a chromium plated blade over a painted shroud, shown here. The two should be separated for painting, cutting through the old bumper bolts if necessary.

FRB2. Behind the shroud is the bumper bar, with an over-rider bracket between bar and over-rider. These have to align in order that the bumper will go on. Slacken the over-rider bolt if necessary.
⇩

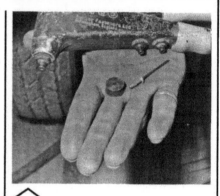

⇧

FRB3. Before offering up the front bumper assembly, ensure that each front wing has a pair of rubber buffers pop-riveted onto its front lower flange.

NG13. The excess can be wiped off with white spirit or paraffin.

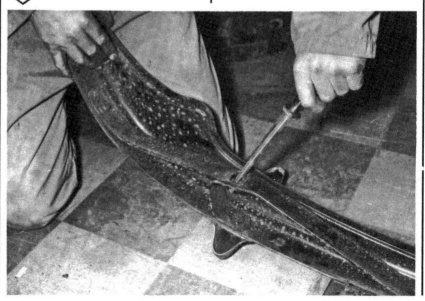

FRB4. It is best if two people offer up the front bumper because it is prone to scratching the front wings as it goes on.

FRB5. Behind the front bumper is a metal ferrule. This can be used to disguise the presence of flat washers used as shims to pack the bumper out so that it has the same position on both sides.

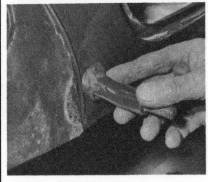

FRB7. The rear bumper stud protrudes through the body on all models. Seal the gap all around with caulking . . .

FRB9. There's no metal ferrule here, just a nut and flat and spring washers.

FRB6. Finally, tighten the bumper from underneath.

FRB8. . . . then fit the rubber ferrule in place.

FRB10. Run the nut along the stud thread, lubricating it well, before fitting the bumper.

FRB11. As with the front bumper, it's best if two people offer it up . . .

FRB12. . . . and, once again, tighten up from beneath.

FRB13. New chromework can make the world of difference to the appearance of your Minor. Here an old over-rider points up the contrast.

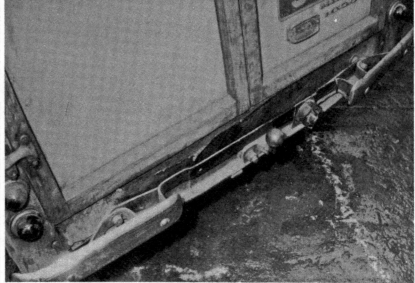

FRB14. Quite a number of Travellers have tow-balls fitted, which means that the number plate has to be moved. When the number plate is in the usual place, you start removing the rear bumper of a Traveller by disconnecting the bullet connectors and finish by re-connecting the wiring, sealing off the wiring's access to the body with an effective grommet and/or caulking.

Bonnet and boot lid removal

Removal of the bonnet and boot lid is essentially a similar process for each panel. Both are best undertaken by two pairs of hands. In the case of the boot lid, it will be necessary to disconnect the number plate wiring before disconnecting the hinges.

Prop the bonnet/boot lid open on its stay and place cloths around the bodywork if you wish to avoid scratching it. While an assistant holds the panel steady, take off the two nuts and washer sets from the same side as the stay and then from the other side and lift the bonnet/boot lid away. If the nuts are rusted on, apply releasing fluid and remove very carefully to avoid wrenching the fixed stud which is

part of the hinge. If it does shear and the hinge is re-usable, you will have to drill and tap the hinge to take a new bolt, the head of which can be sawn off once it is installed in the hinge. When replacing the bonnet or boot lid, remember to replace the gasket beneath each hinge to prevent the hinge from marking the paintwork. In both cases, the nuts should be tightened just enough to hold the panel in place but sufficiently free to enable you to adjust the fit of the panel to even up the gaps around it and fully tightened later.

Bonnet fitting

BF1. After a respray or a rebuild, fitting the bonnet is one of the important later steps. It's important because a good even gap and a level bonnet are crucial to the well-

finished appearance of your Minor. Here, the old bonnet hinge studs have screwed themselves out — a common occurrence — and are being replaced with bolts, spannered fairly tightly.

BF4. Don't forget to fit the rubber gaskets to the hinges before fitting the bonnet.

BF5. It takes two to offer up a Minor bonnet. Have all the washers and nuts to hand so that the nuts can be spun on by hand while the bonnet is held in place.

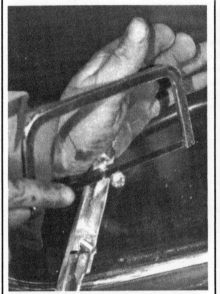

BF2. Then, of course, the heads have to be sawn off . . .

BF3. . . . and the thread ends cleaned up with a file.

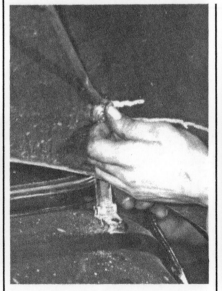

BF6. The top stud also supports the bonnet strut — don't forget the large washer that fits here.

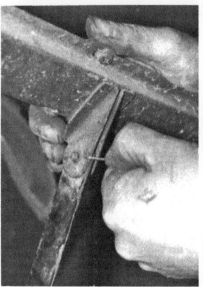

BF7. The bonnet stay is fitted to the bonnet with a clevis pin, which in turn is held in place by a split pin shown being inserted here.

BF8. Once the bonnet has been adjusted so that the gaps are correct, the bonnet catch must be adjusted.

BF9. The bonnet half of the catch is freed for adjustment at the front of the bonnet. . .

BF10. . . . while the grille-panel part of the mechanism is adjusted here.

BF11. Before attempting to true-up bonnet levels, fit the rubber seal across the bulkhead top.

BF13. But you won't achieve that aim without fitting the stop rubbers to the wing drain channels.

BF15. The large bonnet badge hooks on at the rear, bolts on at the front.

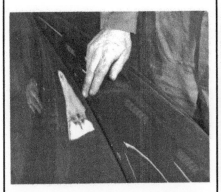

BF12. Of course, you should aim to get the bonnet sides nice and level with the wings.

BF14. Clean every piece of chrome with great care before re-fitting it because it's so much more get-at-able like this.

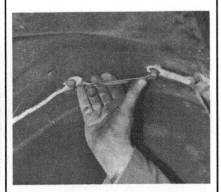

BF16. The front badge is also held on with threaded studs, this time two of them.

BF17. Having been sprayed separately, the two side finisher strips can be fitted . . .

BF18. . . . secured by a pair of spring clips, pushed onto prongs from the inside of the bonnet.

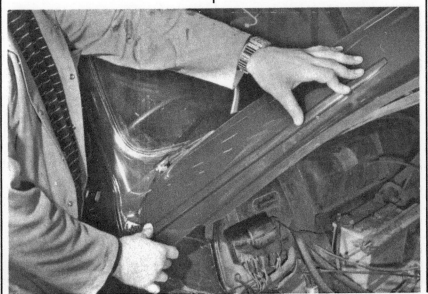

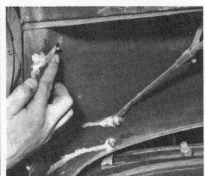

BF19.   The two 'Minor 1000' badges are also held on with two prongs apiece pushed through holes in the bonnet. These are fitted by pushing nylon fixings into the holes and then the badge prongs onto the fixings.

Windscreen and rear screen removal and refitting

Tool box

Thin-bladed screwdriver; broad-bladed screwdriver; sharp craft knife for cutting out the old rubber; finisher strip insertion tool.

Safety

Flex the glass as little as you possibly can to avoid breakage, the danger of which is self-evident. It is best to wear thick industrial-type gloves when handling the glass. If you are fitting a replacement for a previously broken windscreen note that tiny particles of glass will have fallen into the demister ducts. The particles MUST be removed and the heater unit must also be blown out otherwise particles of glass could be blown into the driver's or passenger's face with the obvious risk of damage to eyes.

One-piece screen removal and refitting

It pays to replace the windscreen or rear screen rubber every time unless the existing one is really supple and new. If you're scrapping the old rubber, the simplest way to remove the screen is to cut through the old rubber leaving the glass free to be just lifted away. If you must re-use the rubber, note that there will be a greater risk of breaking the glass as it is removed. In the latter case, start by taking off the finisher from the centre spreader strip and remover the spreader strip (front screen). Carefully push a screwdriver between glass and rubber and try easing the glass outwards a little (it has lust a LITTLE flexibility). Pull the rubber carefully away from both glass and body and work your way around the whole screen with an assistant pushing the whole time on the glass, especially at the early stage where the rubber has to be pulled free. Wear some sort of adequate hand and arm protection just in case your hand goes through the glass! Clean all traces of mastic from the metal frame and, if it is to be re-used, the rubber itself.

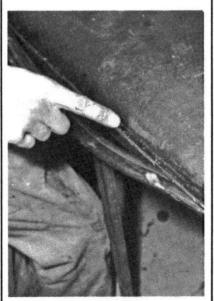

WF1.   Before attempting to refit the old screen, clean every trace of old mastic from the edges of the glass, the insides of the rubber . . .

WF2.   . . . and the screen surround. Be sure to paint any patches of surface rust and to repair anything worse.

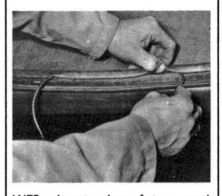

WF3.   Insert a piece of strong cord — nylon is ideal — into the lip of the rubber which fits over the screen surround.

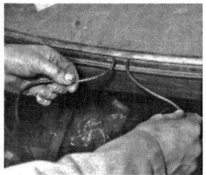

WF4.   Tuck it in carefully all the way around until the two ends meet in the middle of what will be the bottom of the screen.

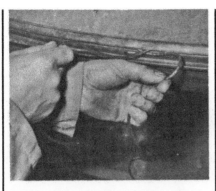

WF5. Then overlap them and continue to tuck the cord in for around 6 inches in each direction.

WF6. You'll now need an assistant. Lift the screen into position pushing it well into the aperture and centralizing it properly.

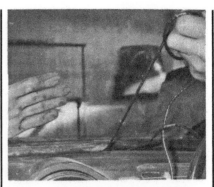

WF7. While one person pushes hard on the outside of the screen, one end of the cord is carefully pulled, easing the rubber over the aperture edge.

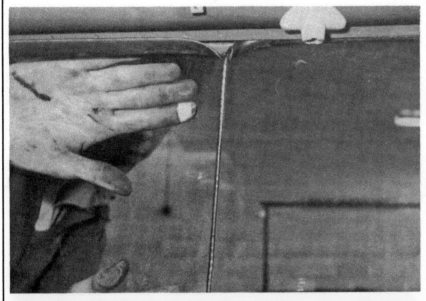

WF8. This is continued slowly and carefully all the way around taking special care that the cord does not pull out leaving the rubber the wrong side of the steel edge and taking care not to tear the rubber. An old rubber will almost certainly be too aged and brittle to fit.

WF9. Brian, one of The Morris Minor Centre's apprentices injects mastic between rubber and steel and between rubber and glass. It's best done now rather than before the rubber is fitted to avoid the incredible mess that squelching black mastic leaves behind.

WF10. For the next step, you'll need an inexpensive special tool, available from a Unipart dealer. The chrome spreader strip is inserted into the rubber, squeezing it tight. The tool is used to open the rubber and simultaneously push the chrome strip into the gap.

WF11. The plastic strip is cut to length with snips . . .

WF12. . . . and a screwdriver used to tease into place all the way around the last couple of inches of strip and any little turned-in lips of rubber. A chrome cover can be fitted over the filler strip joint.

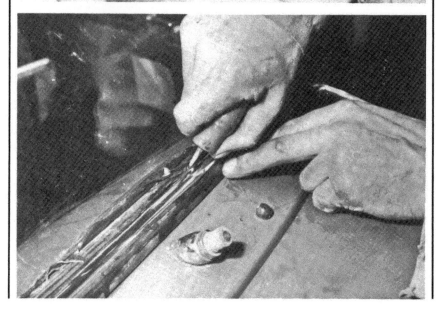

WF13. Finally comes the gooey job of cleaning off all the excess mastic, inside and out. A plastic filler spreader is the ideal tool for removing the worst, followed by paraffin or white spirit to remove the last smears.

Split-screen removal and refitting (to Car No. 26101 RHD, 10606 LHD)

Take out the fixing screws and the driving mirror bolt from the centre pillar and take off the exterior chrome strip.

Take off the small cover plates from the ends of the pillar and remove the pillar.

Unscrew and remove the metal mouldings from the inside of the windscreen. Press the glass towards the inside of the car starting at one corner and carefully easing it inwards with the rubber being carefully eased away from the metal edge of the windscreen housing with the aid of an assistant, and remove the glass.

For refitting, in general, follow the fuller instructions for refitting one-piece screens but don't bother to cross the string. Simply end it at the edge of the glass, where it abuts the central pillar, top and bottom. Position the interior metal surround before withdrawing the string and make sure that the rubber lip is pulled over the edge of the surround. Always start with the lower part of the surround and as soon as the lower part is fully in position replace two of the retaining screws, then do the same to the top part of the screen.

Use thin wooden packing pieces top and bottom to prevent the two pieces of glass moving close together and preventing the pillar from being fitted.

Refit all the metal surrounds but before doing so, straighten the rubbers.

Use strip-mastic sealer to seal each end of the channel between the screen glasses and then fill the entire gap with strip-mastic, overlapping the chrome finisher plate at each end.

When refitting the centre rubber sealing strip, ensure that the raised portion engages the channel between the screens. Make holes in the sealer for the finisher retaining bolts before replacing the finisher.

Refit the rubber seal outside the screen and place the chrome plated finisher over it. Have an assistant press it hard into place while the screws are tightened from inside the car. Then refit the two interior centre pillar cover plates.

Split-screen removal and refitting (from Car No. 26102 RHD and 10607 LHD)

(Some of the following instructions are abbreviated because of their similarity to those given above.)

Take out the interior fixing screws, driving mirror bolt and screen mouldings (held in place with self-tapping screws) and centre cover plate.

Remove the centre chrome pillar and cappings and prise the finisher strip from the rubber seal.

Push the glass inwards and away from the screen surround (see above).

Before attempting to refit the windscreen glasses, assemble them with the finishers and sealing rubber strips in the surrounding rubber channel. You will need to make up a 'dummy' centre pillar.

Fit the T-section interior weatherstrip, the outside weatherstrip (two are used if laminated glass is fitted) and fit the 'dummy' centre pillar.

Fit the inside finisher and replace the three or four (dependent upon model) slave nuts but do not fully tighten.

Refit the glass as shown for the earlier split-screen models. Inject a bead of non-setting windscreen mastic between the glass and rubber both inside and outside using a mastic applicator gun.

Remove the 'dummy' centre pillar and reassemble correctly with the correct centre pillar, tightening up fully as described for the earlier models.

Fit the external chrome moulding by running cord into the lip into which the moulding fits then offer up one end of the moulding whilst withdrawing the cord in similar fashion to that used when fitting windscreen glass, so that the rubber lip is pulled over that part of the moulding which is located in it.

Paint preparation

This section shows simply how to prepare the body panels of both

Saloons/Tourer and Traveller and how to paint them in cellulose lacquer paint. Contrary to popular myth, cellulose paint was not necessarily the type of paint in which Minors were originally painted, nor is it the best type of refinish paint available. It is, however, the best relatively safe type of paint for the home restorer to use.

What this section can't do is to show every variety of problem that can arise in car bodywork paint preparation and spraying. Haynes' *Car Bodywork Repair Manual* goes into every imaginable aspect of car bodywork repairs including all the paint types and how to apply them.

Tool Box

Spray gun/compressor: hired, borrowed or bought. Preferably high pressure, with a reservoir tank but excellent results can be achieved with even basic machines, given patience. Sanding block and various grades of wet and dry paper. Though not essential, a random orbit, D/A (Double Action) sander reduces the preparatory elbow work considerably.

Nowadays, there are many different types of automotive paints available including cellulose, synthetics and acrylics. More modern paints may be classed as having high gloss from the gun, whereas certainly with traditional cellulose enamel, some after spray compounding will be regarded as the norm in order to achieve the final desired result. Again, different paints require different setting conditions with some classed as air drying and others needing a low temperature bake. This obviously makes the latter unsuitable for the home restorer. A further paramount issue to the home restorer is that of safety. Fumes from modern two-pack iso-cyanate containing paints, as implied by the name, are deadly poisonous and should only be used in conjunction with full safety breathing systems usually well beyond the amateur as outlined below. Hence the only type of paint we can recommend for the DIYer to use is cellulose. Even with this paint a proper charcoal filter mask should be worn and other general safety adhered to.

Safety *Cellulose paint*

The spray is volatile and so are the fumes from the paint and thinners – keep away from all flames and sparks. Thinner dampened rags are also a fire hazard. The spray can cause you to lose consciousness if inhaled in a confined area. Always use a suitable filter mask (check with your paint supplier) and ventilate the work area. Simple cotton masks are simply not good enough (handkerchiefs over the face are worse than useless). Protect your hands with barrier cream or wear protective gloves when handling paint (ensure that any gloves are not themselves dissolved by the paint solvent). Keep well away from eyes.

"2-pack" paint

Spray from this type of paint is toxic to the degree that it can be lethal! (The hardened paint on the car is not dangerous, of course!) Only use with an air fed mask from a clean, isolated compressed air source (ie not from within the spray area) and never use this type of paint where the spray could affect others. It can also cause eye irritation and eye protection should also be worn. Protective gloves should be worn when mixing and handling paint. Those who suffer from asthma or any other respiratory illness should have nothing to do with this (or possibly with any other) type of paint spraying! There is also a fire risk with peroxide catalysts. In short, this type of paint can be seen to be totally unsuitable for DIY use and should be left entirely to the professional.

General

Don't eat, drink or smoke near the work area. Clean hands after the work is complete, but never use thinners to wash paint from the skin. Always wear an efficient particle mask when sanding down.

PP1. By now, most Minors have received so many coats of paint that one more could cause the whole lot to 'pickle' and wrinkle. Some Minors will have been painted with a type of oil-based paint that won't take cellulose paint without a very severe reaction (see 'Colour Schemes' appendix). In these cases, strip the paint down to bare metal using paint stripper. Always wear gloves and goggles – stripper is highly caustic.

PP2. Scrape the paint off after it softens, but still wear gloves. Note that surrounding panels are carefully masked off with non-absorbent plastic sheet when they are not also to be stripped.

PP3. You must always try to avoid digging the scraper into the metal because any scratches there may well show through the paint after a time but you should be especially careful when scraping the soft aluminium roof.

PP4. *Clean out the rain channel joint with a wire brush held in an electric drill. Wear goggles.*

PP5. *This is the tool that reduces by 90 per cent the time spent in all stages of sanding. It's a random orbit sander which oscillates as it rotates and doesn't cause the scratches that show through the paint like an ordinary rotary sander and it also causes few ripples. An air-operated tool is being used in this picture, which takes a rather large compressor to run it. Black & Decker, however, make a superb electrically operated random orbit sander which is ideal for the home restorer.*

OBTAIN AND THOROUGHLY READ THE MANUFACTURER'S DATA AND SAFETY SHEETS BEFORE USING BODY FILLER, THINNERS, PRIMER OR PAINT. ACT UPON THEM AS RECOMMENDED.

PP6. *You may have to use skims of filler to get a good level finish in certain areas of the body. For very small blemishes, try a stopper rather than filler.*

Note that if you apply filler to the aluminium roof, you must use an etch primer on bare aluminium otherwise filler (and paint for that matter) will flake off.

PP7. *Again, the random orbit sander comes in useful when sanding filler but as you can see, you must wear a mask of an efficient type.*

PP8. You can, of course, hand-sand but you'll obtain a more level finish if you wrap your abrasive paper around a flat block. Start with coarse paper, go through a medium grit and finish with a fine grit of paper, removing all the scratches from the previous grade before going on to the next.

PP9. Primer/filler is sprayed on in the same way as finish coat — see later pictures. Before sanding, then again before spraying the primer and, yet again, after flatting the primer but before spraying the finish coats, wipe all the bodywork with a proprietary brand of spirit wipe to remove contamination before it has the chance to ruin your paintwork.

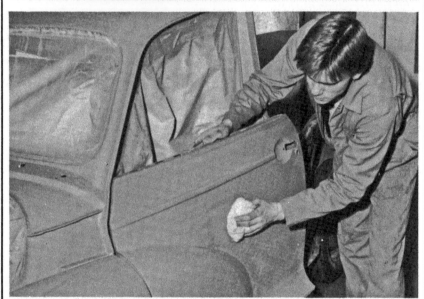

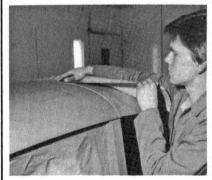

PP10. Spraying a Minor may be best carried out in broken-down sections. Here, a Traveller with woodwork removed is having its rear roof section masked off.

PP11. And here, the bare cab section is being sprayed. The seat is a spare which has only been placed temporarily in position for moving the car around — if you don't strip out the interior of your car, mask it off very thoroughly.

PP12. After giving the paint a day to harden off, masking paper can be stripped off the rear . . .

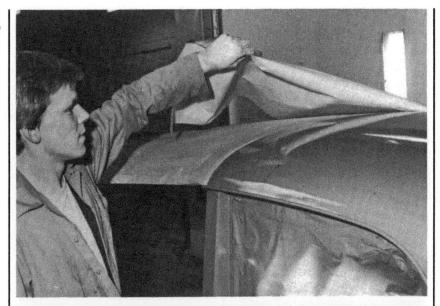

PP13. . . . more applied to the front, and the rear roof sprayed.

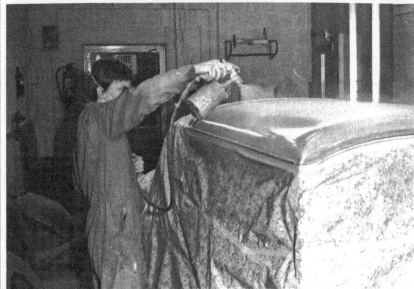

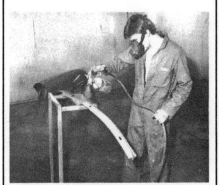

PP14. The best quality resprays are carried out like this: the front bumper apron has been stripped and is being sprayed here on a stand . . .

PP15. . . . while the bonnet and sill finishers receive the same treatment.

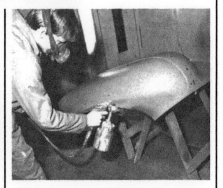

PP16. The bonnet should, ideally, receive the same off-the-car treatment. First, give all the edges a coat of paint, all the way round . . .

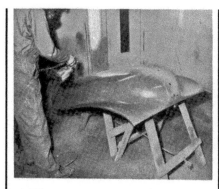

PP17. . . . then spray the bonnet in the usual strip-at-a-time spray pattern, starting on one side and working across.

PP18. Here, a set of Traveller aluminium panels have been stripped and primed and are ready for spraying. ▷

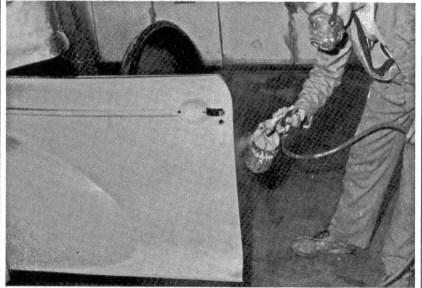

PP19. This is the start of a sequence showing a recommended sequence when spraying a Minor, following the procedure used by The Morris Minor Centre. First, all the edges should be given a coat of paint, as well as the 'fiddly bits' around the headlamp nacelles and anywhere where you would be tempted to pause with the spraygun in order to ensure coverage and so cause a run.

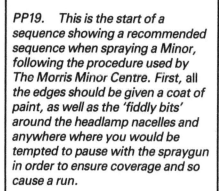

PP20. The insides of the wheel arches are other areas that should be given a preliminary coat. Don't wait for it to dry — it will be sufficiently dry by the time you come to give the car a decent coat of paint.

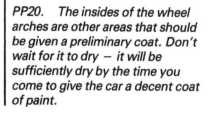

PP21.   Next, painter Adrian Chapman has painted one half of the bulkhead top and the windscreen pillar, and he is just starting on the roof, spraying in front-to-back strips. Had he been spraying a Saloon, he would no doubt have sprayed as shown in this sequence, then have sprayed the roof, stopping at the rear window, followed by the order shown here and finishing off by starting at the front of one door and working around the back of the car, a panel at a time, finishing with the other (front) door.

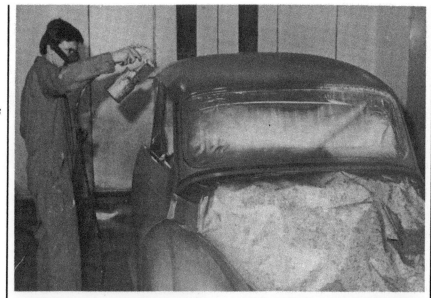

PP22.   He stopped at the middle of the roof, then quickly transferred to the other side continuing this time towards himself in front-to-back strips until the whole roof was painted . . .

PP23.   . . . and then spraying the rest of the bulkhead before going on to the door, front wing, grille panel and other front wing . . .

PP24.   . . . finishing off with the other door.

PP25.   Mastic and caulking are used in several places as a joint sealer. They can easily be cut to a good edge by using a plastic filler scraper but such edges are best cut after any dust-inducing work has been completed, to avoid getting bits in the 'new' edge of sealer, and also so that the mastic has had time to start going rubbery, which makes it easier to handle.

PP26. One of the great advantages in spraying with cellulose is that most blemishes — and some are inevitable in a home workshop, because of the amount of dust that is created — can be polished out. Cutting compound comes in various degrees of coarseness, rather like flatting paper. Even with four or five coats of paint in place, coarse compound will go right through fairly quickly so use a medium-smooth paste. Wipe a coat on with a rag, then buff it off.

PP27. You have to be extremely careful on edges because you can cut through in a few seconds. Hand cutting-back is recommended there. This is an air-operated tool which, again, uses far more air than any DIY compressor is likely to deliver. Once again, Black & Decker have come to the rescue with a super electrically-operated polishing mop.

PP28. Finish off with T-cut, (indeed, you can remove small blemishes by using only T-cut) and then hand polish to a final finish. Only ever cut-back or polish by hand with front-to-rear movements — anything else will show up as scratches.

PP29.   You can buy a stick-on pin stripe to your Minor but, since most Minor owners are traditionalists at heart, here's the way of adding a painted pin-stripe. You start off with a striping kit which is stuck on to the paint as shown.

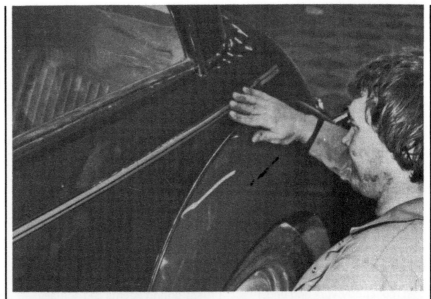

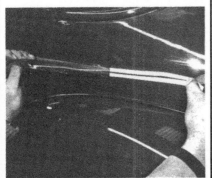

PP30.   After carefully sticking the tape down, peel off the top, clear layer of tape.

PP32.   Use a small paint brush to paint-in the stripe . . .

PP34.   . . . leaving an attractive stripe to set off a highly attractive little car. Certainly John Beasley, who painted this car, is proud of his handiwork.

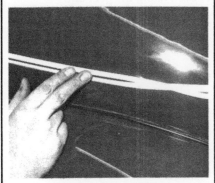

PP31.   Go over the tape left beneath, pressing it down firmly, in particular along its inner edges, so that it is stuck down tightly. Lift up and overlap the ends to give a tapered-off finish to the paint.

PP33.   . . . then as soon as the paint is touch-dry peel off the masking tape . . .

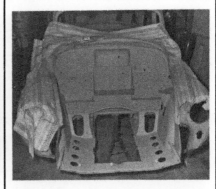

PP35.   If you aim to produce an as-new Minor, you will have to paint the engine bay. Stripping out the parts involves a lot of work but it's the only way to gain an acceptable finish in there.

Rustproofing

Anyone who spends a lot of time and a lot of money rebuilding a Minor, or anyone who owns a sound one, but who doesn't go that little bit further and rust proof it, really wants his or her priorities examining! You can't hope to stop a car from rusting; it's in the nature of all materials to degenerate and steel degenerates faster than a good many metals. You can, however, slow it down so that, with annual body maintenance and check-ups, your Minor will rust imperceptibly slowly – and here's how to do it.

First, you need to recognize that most bodywork and under-frame corrosion takes place from the inside out. So, while it's important to cover and protect outer surfaces, it's far more important to cover the inner ones! The only way to do so is to inject a spray of protective fluid into the enclosed section, sealing the inner surfaces from the moisture and air which are always around and, it is hoped, stopping any light rust dead in its tracks.

There are several schools of thought as to which type of rust-proofing fluid to use. Waxoyl, a wax-based product, is widely used but in this writer's view is best for new or only lightly rusted areas. Some studies have suggested that rustproofing agents can actually make matters worse if there is already corrosion present in the seams (where it tends to start), but one suggestion is that new oil or an oil-based product be injected into all such enclosed sections, this having the advantage that it will creep into all rusty areas over a period of time. It may well be best, for that reason, to treat a Minor with oil-based rust inhibitors twice in the first year after restoration and annually thereafter, bearing in mind that oil evaporates slowly. If this treatment seems a lot of trouble, then remember that body maintenance is far more cost effective than mechanical maintenance – and yet who in their right mind would quibble about the need to change engine oil?

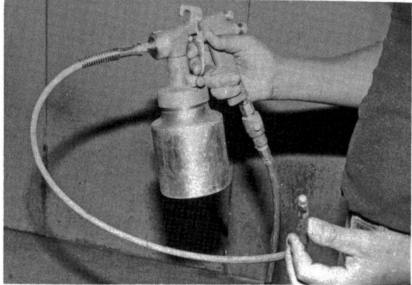

RP1. You can buy all sorts of cheap injector kits but they leave a great deal to be desired in terms of actual coverage – they dollop the stuff in streams rather than spraying it evenly. This DeVilbiss SGB-602 injector kit is a really professional tool, designed to give a coverage which meets manufacturer's latest specifications which is why it costs around the price of a set of tyres – but compare that to the cost of a rebuild, and you could even save a lot of the purchase price by sharing a gun between friends, rustproofing a couple of fellow-enthusiasts' cars or even hiring the gear out!

RP2. The SGB-602 uses a larger bore tube than the far cheaper Holts or Waxoyl DIY versions, so it is necessary to use a larger size of drill bit. This in turn means that you have to position the holes that much more carefully to avoid their looking obtrusive. Lay in a stock of blanking grommets before you start.

RP3. Here a different approach is being used to get some sort of barrier into a seam. WD40 is being injected and, although it is rather evaporative, it should leave some deposit; anything thicker would be unable to creep into there any way.

RP4. Another seam suitable for the WD40 is the one at the B-post. Look around your car and all such potential problem areas will be obvious. WD40 is also particularly good at creeping behind badges and the bonnet side-finisher strips.

RP5. Other parts of this car were protected with an aerosol rust inhibitor. Here, the seam between the front inner wing and the flitch panel is being sealed.

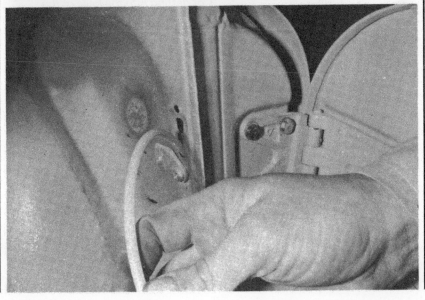

RP6. You'll be surprised at how many access points there are on the Minor without the need to drill holes. This one is by the door top hinge.

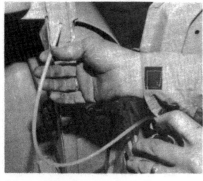

RP7. The windscreen pillar can be 'attacked' through this hole in the door pillar while the B-post can often be injected, on earlier cars, through the semaphore indicator aperture.

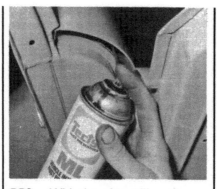

RP8. With the wing still on the car, you can get at some of the wing and hinge panel area this way but you may wish to drill a hole under the wing to gain better access.

RP9. An instance of where you will have to drill a hole in the inner sill . . .

RP10. . . . unless you remove the kick step. The DeVilbiss injector would undoubtedly give a heavier coating.

RP11. On the other hand, the aerosol injector does a splendid job of getting into the base of the complex door structure.

RP12. Unusually, the main cross-member is not a hollow box-section. It is important, however, to squirt a thin type of inhibitor into the seams around the cross-member and jacking point. Incidentally, the Minor Centre approach of seam welding these underbody seams would appear to give a useful degree of rustproofing.

RP13. The rear box-section beneath the rear seat will benefit greatly from the application of inhibitor, but the aerosol applicator is a very expensive way of covering a large area like this.

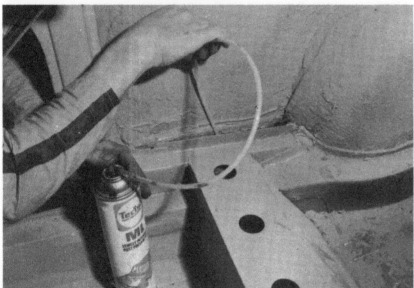

RP14. In the same area of a two-door car, the quarter-panel 'rear sill' area can be got at as shown.

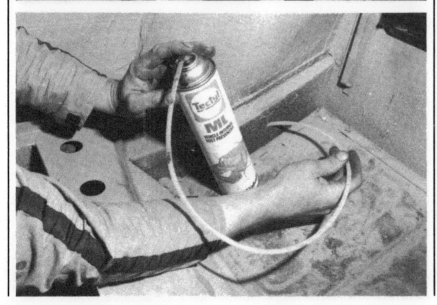

RP15. The long box-section that snakes its way from the middle of the car to the back can be easily reached from beneath the rear seat . . .

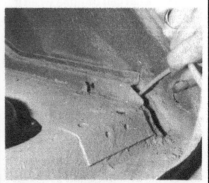

RP16. . . . and from the rear end of the box section.

RP17.   There are several small box sections, such as this one at the rear of the boot floor, but not all are as easy to reach as this one. Don't forget the cross-member beneath the front of the floor, the back of the bumpers and over-riders, the long box sections reaching from the cross-member right to the front of the car, plus the box-section extension which reaches up to the front bulkhead.

RP18.   You can, if you wish, inject a non-setting mastic into seams such as this around the rear inner wheel arch . . .

RP19.   . . . or you can use inhibitor fluid with the hope that it will 'creep' into the joint.

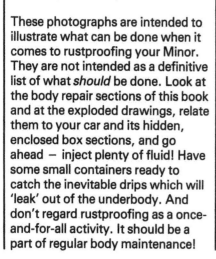

These photographs are intended to illustrate what can be done when it comes to rustproofing your Minor. They are not intended as a definitive list of what *should* be done. Look at the body repair sections of this book and at the exploded drawings, relate them to your car and its hidden, enclosed box sections, and go ahead — inject plenty of fluid! Have some small containers ready to catch the inevitable drips which will 'leak' out of the underbody. And don't regard rustproofing as a once-and-for-all activity. It should be a part of regular body maintenance!

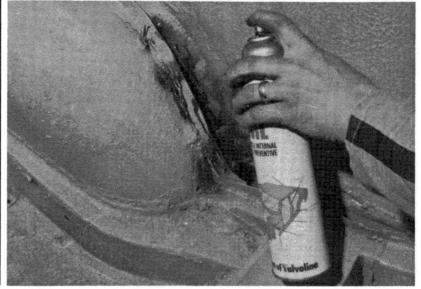

Ch 3 Bodywork, part IV: Traveller timber

When the woodwork on a Traveller has got to the point where rot has set in, it usually needs the 'works' to put it right — in other words, it's usually necessary to replace the lot! Unfortunately for the owner, a Traveller's timber is actually a structural part of the car and so it's theoretically possible for the annual MOT tester to fail the car on the grounds of unroadworthy half-timbering! In practice (and through the ignorance of most testers more than anything) this rarely happens. Anyway, when the rot sets in, there's only one thing for it and that's the replacement of the woodwork. There seems to be quite a few companies supplying Traveller woodwork but, sadly, some of their timber sections bear a stronger affinity to 'tree' than 'Traveller' — in other words, you have to do an awful lot of cutting and shaping to make them fit, and their shapes are extremely complex for the DIY-er to replicate.

Tool Box

Basic set of spanners and screwdrivers including impact screwdriver; mastic and caulking; wood chisels and mallets; fine and medium sand paper, varnish; wood preservative; aluminium paint; paint brushes; cross-pein cabinet maker's hammer; gimp pins (small nails); gimp pin holder; woodworker's plane; plastic filler spreader.

Safety

Follow the basic rule of using cutting tools summarized as, 'Always keep both your hands _behind_ the cutting edge!'

Figure 5. Here the wooden components of the Traveller rear end are shown broken down into individual items. In practice, however, you are only likely to want to buy complete assemblies. These are based on BMC's original specifications and should fit with the minimum of trimming. You could, of course, fit one side at a time, carrying out the work as you can afford it. (Courtesy The Morris Minor Centre)

It is anticipated that you can save 25-30 per cent of the cost of Traveller woodwork by fitting it yourself, but be warned that it's a rather ambitious, and certainly a time-consuming, project — not a job for someone with no DIY experience, perhaps, but one for the enthusiast with the time to proceed carefully, step-by-step and with the room required to get all around the car. The following sections show Barry Brewer, The Morris Minor Centre's resident 'chippy' working his way through timber repairs on a Traveller.

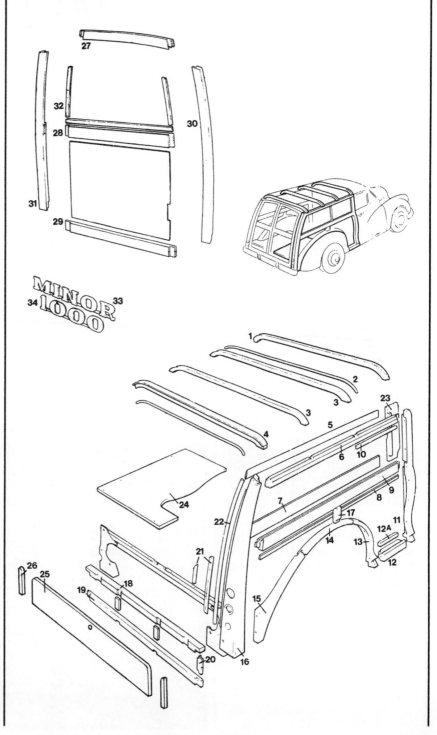

Woodwork dismantling

Step 1 Remove the rear lights and reflectors, the rear bumper assembly complete (see the section on 'Front and rear bumper removal'), the petrol filler pipe cover and the filler pipe itself, and blank off the petrol tank with masking tape.

Step 2 Take off the rear doors by removing the hinges from the rear posts, then take off the hinges from the doors. None are inter-changeable to another position, so label them all clearly.

Step 3 Remove the rear seat base complete with the rail to which its hinges are attached and also remove the trim-retaining strip along the edge of the floor.

TWD1. **Step 4** *Unscrew the seat belt top mounting, if fitted, and take out the four screws holding in place the front post capping. Temporarily replace the seat belt bolt and washers.*

TWD2. **Step 5** *Five screws hold the headlining tensioning rail at the rear of the cab roof. Take them out and carefully release each end of the headlining. Release the wires from the interior light and feed them back or cut them here to rejoin them later with 'bullet' connectors.*

TWD3. **Step 6** *Now the top rail must be freed from the cant rail (see Figure 5). A large, inaccessible screw passes through the roof rail from above (it was fitted in the factory before the aluminium roof), going through the tenon in the cant rail and into the front post. Prise it out of the redundant side-rail, cut or break it off and later cut it off level. It is fitted in a totally different way when reassembling.*

TWD4. **Step 7** *Remove the waist rail cappings and the sliding window catches.*

TWD5. **Step 8** Take out the screw at the top of each wheel arch and remove the trim from the wheel arches. The screws which go through the wheel arch flange and into the wheel arch timber can be unscrewed (including those beneath the rear floor) or prised away if necessary.

TWD6. **Step 9** Next, the windows and then the front upright window channels are removed.

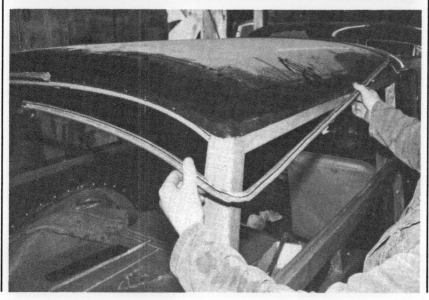

TWD7. **Step 10** There are two lots of nails holding the roof to the timber framework: one goes through the roof panel only and the other goes through both the drip moulding and the roof panel. Barry Brewer recommends driving an old wood chisel between the woodwork and roof to shear off the nails. Before the roof is pulled free, Barry recommends marking both the roof and the rear top rail to aid accurate re-alignment later. Before attempting to chisel through the roof-to-timber nails, the drip moulding should be opened up as in Figure 6. It would be so much more difficult to attempt to open up the moulding off the car and there would be a very strong risk of distorting it.

Drip moulding to be opened
out to expose head
of nail

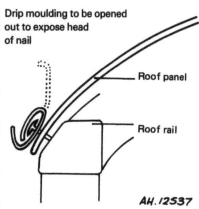

Roof panel

Roof rail

AH. 12537

Figure 6.   A cross-section through the drip-moulding, showing how it can be opened up for removal and reuse.

Step 11   If metal finishing panels are fitted to the side frames, just ahead of the rear wheels and beneath the woodwork, these should be unscrewed next. (See next Section for details.)

TWD8. **Step 12**   *After unscrewing the corner top support brackets . . .*

TWD9. **Step 13**   *. . . undoing the bolts through the front posts, behind where the glass 'runners' were fitted . . .*

TWD10. **Step 14**   *. . . and unbolting the rear post bottom bolts (if they need it).*

Step 15   . . . the rear wings must be removed – see Rear Wing Removal and Refitting section for full details.

Step 16 Then it will be possible to lift one complete sideframe away and lower it a few inches, still attached to the roof rails.

TWD11. **Step 17**   *This enables you to get a 'stubby' screwdriver into the roof gap so that the screws angled downwards can be removed.*

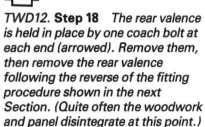

TWD12. **Step 18**   *The rear valence is held in place by one coach bolt at each end (arrowed). Remove them, then remove the rear valence following the reverse of the fitting procedure shown in the next Section. (Quite often the woodwork and panel disintegrate at this point.)*

Step 19   Finally, remove any remaining traces of rotten wood, mastic, and any screws or nails which are still attached. Be prepared to have to carry out welding repairs to steel that has been in contact with wood. Remove the aluminium side panels, any metal fittings, rubber bump stops. Any reusable fillets should be removed, sanded and revarnished ready for reuse.

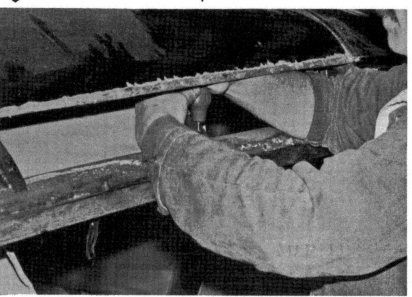

Fitting new woodwork

TWF1A. You'll see from the 'Paint & Prep' section that the ideal time to respray a Traveller is with all the woodwork removed. You'll also see that the rear roof section can be left attached to the rear of the cab (unless — pretty unlikely — the cab flange has corroded badly) and it will be self-supporting, although it wouldn't exactly support a barn dance, of course! This picture shows just how showroom-new a Traveller can look with all-new timber. You are best advised to paint the aluminium panels first then fit them to the woodwork whilst it is off the car, applying plenty of mastic in the joints. Clamp the sill rail fillet (Figure 5, 12A) in place and then screw it into position.

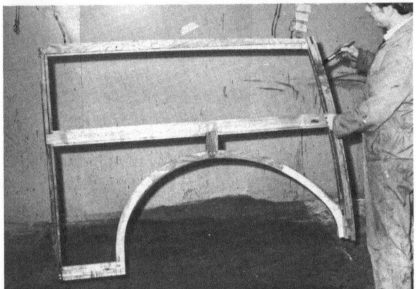

TWF1B. **Step 1** New individual timber side pieces can be bought separately, but there's no point in making extra work for yourself. It's best to buy sides as complete units. After carefully sanding the timber and varnishing it with at least two initial coats of yacht varnish (sanding between coats) you can offer the timber up to the car, preferably with the help of a friend. The author recommends sealing the end grain of front and rear posts with several coats of well-stirred aluminium paint, at least at the bottom of each post. Take care not to break off any of the end grain as the sides are moved around and fitted.

Step 2 Bolt the front posts securely to the rear of the cab, aligning them accurately because there will be no need to remove them again. Make sure that two continuous lines of mastic or caulking are run down the B-post before fitting up.

TWF2. **Step 3** If you are fitting a new top rail, now is the time to slot its joints into position.

TWF3. **Step 4** Fit the rear valence woodwork by bolting it down with four bolts to the rear floor extension. Then insert the bolts at the base of each rear corner post but do not fully tighten them. Leave a small gap between the valence woodwork and the corner post.

TWF4. **Step 5** The rear doors are used as templates around which the woodwork must be accurately aligned.

TWF5. Offer them loosely up into place, then pack them at the bottom with thin plywood until top and bottom gaps are even.

TWF6. **Step 6** Now push the whole assembly to one side or the other — and spend some time 'fiddling around' with door packing until you have a good even gap — or at least the best compromise you can manage — all around the rear doors.

TWF7 This is the sort of situation you sometimes get, but by sharing out the excess door gap so that it is evenly spread top and bottom and then by taking out some of the 'bow' by careful planning, the gap can be made acceptable.

TWF8. **Step 7** When you are satisfied that the rear corner posts are spot-on, screw the corner brackets to the top and corner rails and posts, drilling ⅛ inch pilot holes to guide the screws.

TWF9. **Step 8** Tighten up the coach bolts at the rear post bases so that the position of the framework is now locked into place. Now check the measurement across the inside of the bottom of the wooden wheel arch just to ensure that you haven't induced any distortion. The

measurement should be 45 inches but not over, although 44¾ inches is acceptable.

TWF10. **Step 9** If you haven't already done so, tighten up the four bolts holding the rear valence timber in place . . .

TWF11. . . . slip the new rear valence, suitably painted inside and out, over the bumper mountings . . .

TWF12. . . . and tap in the two coachbolts from the rear.

TWF13. The valence is actually nailed down through its flange.

TWF14.   Don't forget to seal the joint. Barry recommends something called 'Seal 'N' Caulk' but anything similar will do. Don't trim it back yet – you'll see why later!

TWF16.   The top rails will now be screwed down from below. Drill a pilot hole right through the cant rail and into the top rail and drill a clearance hole in the cant rail.

TWF18. **Step 11**   Use 1 inch wire nails to hold the roof down to the timbers. Nail through the countersunk holes in the roof – the others are for the drip moulding. Old-timer's tip: *dip the nails in varnish before hammering them in. It should help to prevent the steel causing discoloration in the ash.*

TWF15. **Step 10**   Starting in the centre, working forwards and back, ease the top rails into position.

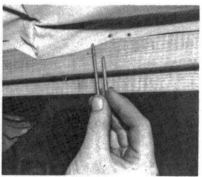

TWF17.   Then screw a counter-sunk head bright zinc plated woodscrew up into the top rail to hold it in position.

TWF19. **Step 12**   Then, using the same type of nails, pin down the drip moulding using a cross-pein hammer with great care so that the aluminium moulding is not damaged.

TWF20.   The nails can be seated properly using a cold chisel as shown here.

TWF21. **Step 13** Hammering down the fold in the moulding is an extremely difficult exercise to carry out. Barry used a home-made tool (which he uses to prise up the flap) as a flat drift to even out the hammer blows. You could use a small block of wood.

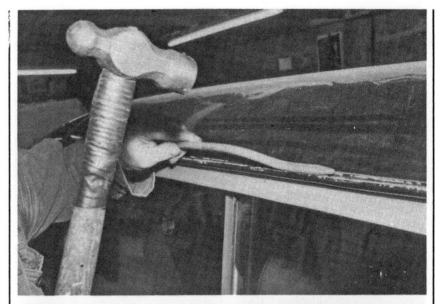

TWF22. Around the corners, the hammer must be used carefully to restore accurately the line of the moulding as the fold goes down. Barry reckons, by the way, that to fit a brand new moulding, rather than refitting the old one, would be beyond the expertise of the home restorer.

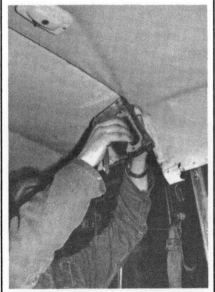

TWF23. **Step 14** After rewiring the courtesy light, start to refit the headlining. Staple or tack it down to the front rail working from the middle outwards . . .

TWF24. This is the so-called tensioning rail — the piece of wood that shows over the headlining. It's shown here with pilot holes being drilled to screw it into place. It has the effect of pushing the headlining right into the corner, so pulling it nice and taut.

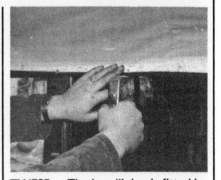

TWF25. The headlining is fitted in the same way at the rear and is also stapled or tacked onto the cant rail.

TWF26. Bits of the headlining come down over the B-post. They should be held down with carpet tape or something similar.

Step 15 The next stage is a logical progression which involves fitting the channels in the right order, sealing them against the elements and fitting the sliding window.

TWF27. New glass channels are bought as a complete kit, as shown.

TWF28. The top outer channel is best pinned in place. Here a grip pin punch is being used, which enables the pin to reach into the channel. You can use original-type screws but there's a good chance of distorting the channel.

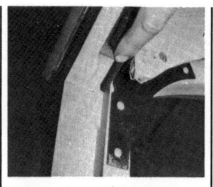

TWF29. Next, fit the top inner channels in the same way but note that they are cut slightly longer than the outers.

TWF30. You can cut the channel with a sharp pair of pincers as shown but perhaps a hacksaw would be less likely to distort the channel.

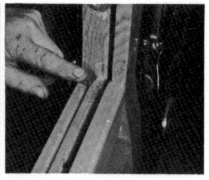

TWF31. Seal the top of the waist rail to B-post mortice and tenon joint to stop water running into it, but don't seal it at the bottom, so that any water that might accumulate can run out again. Seal the hole at the end of the rail, too, or you will wonder why the carpets get soaked!

TWF32. Cut the bottom-outer channel to length (the one with chrome finishers), then hold the channel onto the bottom of the outer glass, fit the glass into the top outer channel and slot glass and bottom channel into place. A helper is almost vital here! Push the glass to the front and pin the rear of the channel; push it the other way and pin the back. You can't get at the middle 5 inches or so. Pin at an angle so that the channel is pushed tightly into the corner of the rebate, leaving it level and tidy-looking.

TWF33. Fit the lower-inners in the same way but pin right into the bottom corner which is the only place where there is sufficient timber in the waist rail for the pins to hold.

TWF34. Cut the uprights carefully to length . . .

TWF35. . . . and pin them at the sharp angle shown, through the bottom corner of the channel so that they are held as tight into the rebate as possible.

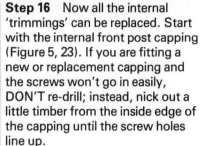

Step 16 Now all the internal 'trimmings' can be replaced. Start with the internal front post capping (Figure 5, 23). If you are fitting a new or replacement capping and the screws won't go in easily, DON'T re-drill; instead, nick out a little timber from the inside edge of the capping until the screw holes line up.

TWF36. Offer up the new waistrail capping for size and trim if necessary, but only trim from the back because the cut-outs for brackets are fixed and ready routed-out. Do the same with the cant rail capping.

TWF37. Screw the metal finisher to the back of the capping after first drilling shallow pilot holes. (Use the old ones as a guide).

TWF38. Thumb a strip of sealer into the waist rail-to-channel joint to prevent any water ingress and run a second line of sealer along the bottom and ends of the waist rail to form a second line of defence and so that the waist rail capping will not tilt when screwed down.

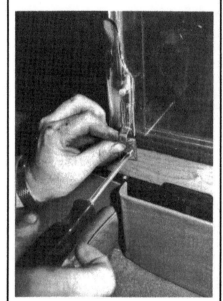

TWF39. Screw the window catches to the waist rail. Fit the cant rail fillet (Figure 5, 10) not forgetting to fit the rubber bump stop on the end.

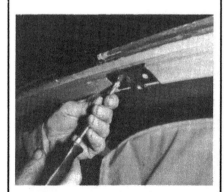

TWF40. Fit the door closing plate/s to the rear of the car.

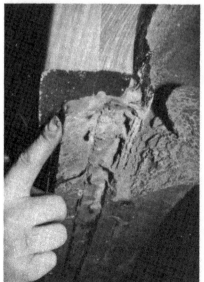

TWF41. Back inside the car, screw back into position the fixing screws holding the trim and replace the seat and trim.

TWF42. **Step 17** Seal every joint with caulking to stop water getting in and rotting the timber again. This is the bottom of the rear corner post.

You can cut back the mastic or caulking with a plastic filler spreader, but don't do so until the dusty jobs are completed because bits inevitably stick to the caulking. If this happens to the cut-back edge, you won't be able to get the unsightly bits out.

TWF43. A capping plate fits on the bottom of the sill rail. Both the top of the plate and the bottom of the rail should be painted well before fitting. It is a good idea to coat the plate very liberally with Waxoyl or something similar, so that no water can get between the two.

Timber fitting tips

● Woodscrews will go in very much more easily if you: drill a pilot hole; use a screwdriver with a good, square end; dip the screw in grease (or, in some cases varnish — see text) before screwing in.

● Keep *all* old timber and channels as constant reference points when fitting the new.

● Consider renewing the headlining because, compared with the cost of the whole job, it is an inexpensive item and has to be virtually re-fitted in any case.

● Treat every inch of timber with a colourless preservative such as Cuprinol before doing anything at all with it. Paint several coats all over, but take note of the safety precautions on the tin and particularly avoid splashing preservative or varnish into the eyes.

The final step, that of fitting the rear wings has not been covered in this section — see 'Rear wing renewal' — nor has the fitting of electrical components which is a common sense reversal of removal, nor fitting the rear bumper which is also shown elsewhere in this book.

Rear door repair

The section on Traveller Woodwork Dismantling offers some advice on dismantling the twin rear doors but here it's gone into in some depth. Just as with the main wood sections, keep every part of the old timber until the new work is completed so that you have an adequate reference point. Remember that none of the hinges are interchangeable regarding their position so label them clearly when they are removed. As with the body sections, treat the doors with a clear preservative and varnish before fitting — see previous section for details. There is nothing to stop you reusing old doors or to fit new doors to existing timber, of course.

Dismantling

Step 1 Undo the screw holding the door handle to the inside of the mechanism.

TRD1. Take out the screws holding the outside of the handle to the timber. Theoretically, the handle and square shaft should pull out but they're often rusted solid. You may have to drill out and replace the handle and lock, or you may want to try the application of heat, if the door is to be renewed. Remove glass first and have an adequate means to hand of putting out a small wood fire!

TRD2. **Step 2** *Dismantle the lock, rods and brackets following the reverse of the order shown in the section dealing with reassembly. Note their positions very carefully.*

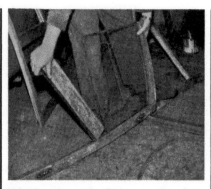

TRD4. **Step 4** *Take out the glass by dismantling the woodwork — you'll probably find it half way there!*

Rebuilding

TRD6. **Step 1** *Place the varnished door upon a piece of carpet to protect its surface, apply mastic to the rebates, put the glass in place and press each edge carefully down into the mastic. Take care not to apply too much pressure in one place so cracking the glass.*

TRD3. **Step 3** *Unscrew and remove the aluminium panels ready for flatting and repainting.*

TRD5. *Scrape stuck-on mastic off the glass and clean the glass with thinners.*

TRD7. *Try the fillet strips just to check that they do go in, then tap them into place. They will tell you whether the glass has gone down far enough or not.*

TRD8. *When the fit is right, drill pilot holes through the pre-drilled holes in the fillets . . .*

TRD9. . . . and screw down the fillets.

TRD11. From the inner shoulder of the rebate at the top of the door, measure 3 inches downwards and put a pencil mark. (Make sure you are measuring the hinge-side of the door.)

N.B. When drilling the holes for the hinge bolts, it is essential that you apply the following points. Drill ⅛ inch pilot holes from the inside (where you have marked out) to the outside of the door, then the ¼ inch bolt hole, from outside-to-inside so that any breakthrough caused by the drill does not look unsightly. Also do NOT simply hold the drill in a vertical position and drill; hold it at a right angle to the curve of the door (or more exactly, to the arc of the curve at the point where the hinge fits).

TRD10. **Step 2** The fit of the aluminium is straightforward. Once again, screw down.

TRD12. Make a cross over the centre of that part of the timber shown in the photograph then use the (correct) hinge to mark the position of the other hole.

TRD14. Fit the bolts through the door timber and fit the hinges with spring washers.

Step 3 So far, so easy — but the business of fitting the hinges to the doors comes next and it must be carried out with meticulous care or there will be a risk of destroying your very expensive ash door. Each of the following measurements is as supplied by Barry Brewster at the Morris Minor Centre, but check every one of them against your old door as a confirmation that they apply to *your* car.

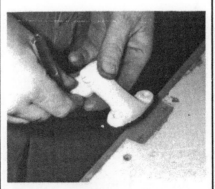

TRD13. The position of the lower hinge is determined by the cut-out in the aluminium panel.

TRD15. **Step 4** You can now fit the lock, rods and brackets. Use the old timbers to establish the correct positions.

TRD16.   Start by drilling pilot holes and fitting the lower of the two top brackets.

TRD18.   . . . slide the top rod into the top two brackets . . .

TRD20.   Screw the bottom bracket down . . .

TRD17.   Then fit the very top bracket . . .

TRD19.   . . . and slip the top one of the two lower brackets onto the rod.

TRD21.   Slide the only loose bracket up to its correct position and screw it down.

TRD22.   Accurately locate the lock assembly, drill pilot holes and screw it down.

TRD23.   If reusing the old lock, check that it works before refitting.

TRD24.   Ensure that the lock/handle shaft does not foul the hole in the timber (it may have to be opened out) then screw it back into place.

TRD26.   If you have to carry out any planing, do it equally on the centre edges of each door, but don't take off too much. Revarnish later.

TRD29.   . . . followed by a ¼ inch drill, that being the actual size of the hinge bolts.

TRD27.   Use the drill to mark the positions of the bolts . . .

TRD30.   Insert the bolts from the rear, bolt the hinges on . . .

Re-fitting

TRD25.   **Step 1**   With hinges fitted to the doors, pack the doors to obtain the best fit (or the best compromise) as described in the previous section.

TRD28.   . . . then remove the doors again, drill right through the wood and, at the bottom, the steel brackets behind, with a ⅛ inch drill . . .

TRD31.   . . . and use a 'junior' hacksaw to cut the bolts down to length. Finish off with a file.

TRD32. If the doors bind a little against the rear posts, take off a whisker with a rasp. See how to fit the rubber seals (which are virtually a 'service' replacement even with sound timber) in the section on trim.

TRD33. As with the main timber sections, leave cleaning off the surplus mastic from glass and aluminium panels until everything else is complete to avoid getting 'foreign bodies' in the cleanly-cut edges of mastic.

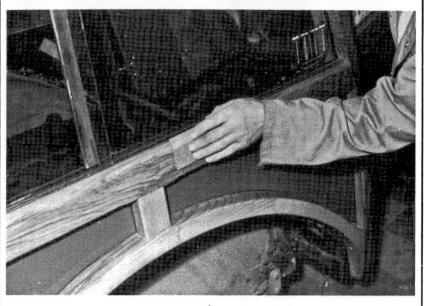

Revarnishing Traveller Timber

Occasionally, sound timber will become discoloured on the surface and the varnish will peel without the structure of the timber deteriorating. When that happens, the timber must be stripped and revarnished before the rot sets in.

RTT1. Old varnish should be removed with a woodworker's cabinet scraper followed by coarse then fine sandpaper, all of it used only in the direction of the grain. If you try sanding across the grain, you will leave scores that can be the very devil to get out again. If there are black stains on the wood that won't sand out, visit your nearest chandler (boat supplies merchant) where there will undoubtedly be a range of bleaches and other products for the very job. You may consider using yacht varnish to protect your timber. Some swear by it, others claim that polyurethane varnish is best. After wiping the wood down with a rag dampened in white spirit, paint on a thinned coat of varnish (50% varnish/50% white spirit) then follow with a full coat of varnish when the first is dry. When that is dry, rub down with the grain using fine grade sand paper, wipe down with white spirit again and repeat the process until you feel you have sufficient depth and coverage — at the very least, there should not be any dull, dry looking patches when the varnish is dry.

4 Interior and Trim

Tool box

Sharp scissors; chalk for marking carpets; basic spanners and screwdrivers.

Safety

Impact adhesive fumes can be dangerous in a confined area, and they and the adhesive are highly flammable.

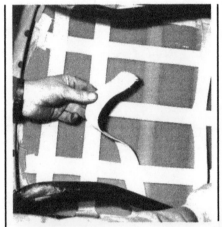

Front seat removal

FSR.   There can be nothing less 'high tech' than the simple, sensible way a Minor front seat is held in place. It's secured by a couple of steel straps which pass over the frame tubing and which are each held in place by by two bolts and washers. There are actually two positions provided for these brackets. If you want to move the seat back, take out the bolts, find the alternative threads just a little way back, clean out the threads and refit the seat. Easy! But do remember to seal the original threaded holes with mastic.

Front seat repair

SR1.   Sooner or later all Minor owners come to know the undignified feeling of driving with their rear-end virtually on the floor, hands and feet stretching for the controls like some under-age joy rider. This − a piece of broken webbing − is almost invariably the cause.

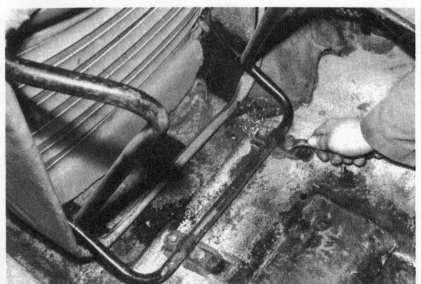

SR2. Along with broken webbing usually goes damaged seat covers. Start taking the old ones off by pushing off the clips holding the cover in position at the rear — underside of the frame.

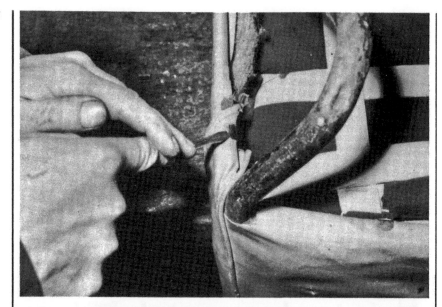

SR3. You will then be able to see that the front and back of the backrest cover were folded and clipped together onto the seat frame.

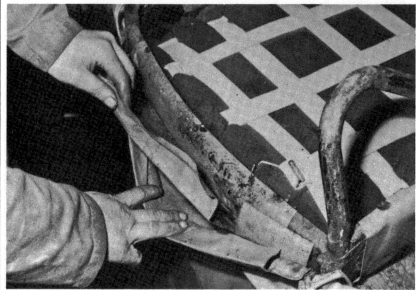

SR4. Unwrap them, then just pull the backrest cover up and off like an armless T-shirt.

SR5. Go back to the seat base and push off the clips holding the base cover in place. (Don't lose these clips!)

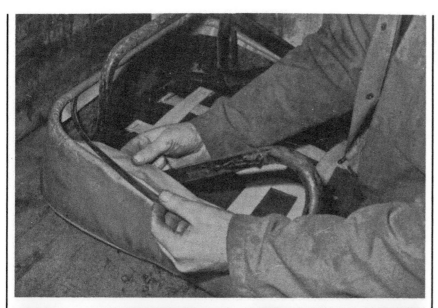

SR6.   The seat cover is held around the front of the frame with a rubber strip pushed into the fold of the frame.

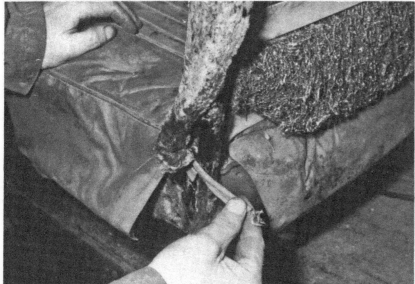

SR7.   There's also a small strip attached to the frame tube, designed to pull the seat cover back nice and tight. You could tie it or glue it when refitting.

SR8.   Quite often, the seat foam has been cut by the webbing. If the cutting action has been severe, it can go right through necessitating renewal of the foam.

SR9.   Now's the time to fit new webbing if necessary. The way it fits is self-explanatory when you examine it. Refit the foam and pull on new covers in the reverse order shown in the previous pictures.

SR10.   New foam, wadding, covers and webbing — in fact every part of the seat — is available as a replacement item including single-colour and duo-tone styles of cover.

SR11.   Later seats are held by clips all around the base instead of the rubber strip shown in SR6 . . .

SR12.   . . . while the very latest seats had a one-piece rubber membrane as shown here, and many were recliners, making them very much more comfortable.

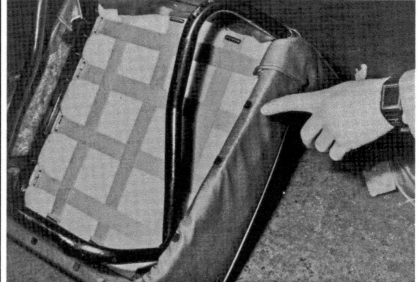

Removal and refitting door trim

DT1. Start by unscrewing the very obvious screws holding the door handle and window winder in place, and remove the handles.

DT2. Similarly, take off the door pulls.

DT3. Then, very carefully, ease the trim boards forwards at one corner so that the clip springs out . . .

DT4. . . . working down the door a clip at a time. But be especially careful at the bottom that the clip doesn't pull out of a soggy trim panel instead of the door!

⬇

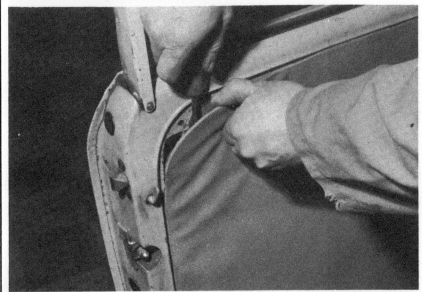

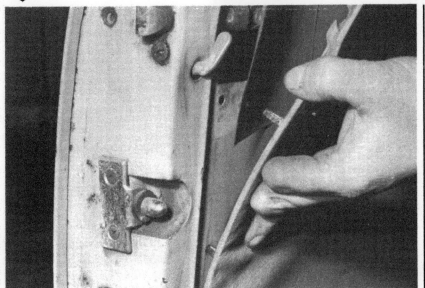

DT5. Replacement is the easiest thing in the world: just bang the panel back into place with the flat of your hand, so that each clip springs back into its appointed hole.

Making new trim panels

This is the story of an old trim panel taken from the car and used as a model to make a replica. And that's the way you have to do it! The vast majority of Minor trim wasn't made or fitted by modern machine-intensive methods, so take the old trim apart with care, see how it's made up and make a new version of it using original covering.

NTP1. Here's the old quarter-panel from the side of the rear window. The cover has been carefully stripped to be used as a model and the card is to be reused.

NTP2. After marking out the new cloth to suit the card, (referring to the old cloth as well) . . .

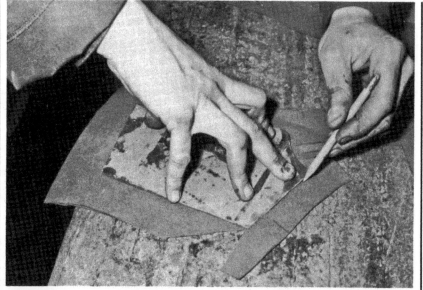

NTP3. . . . the new cloth is cut carefully to shape and glued to the card.

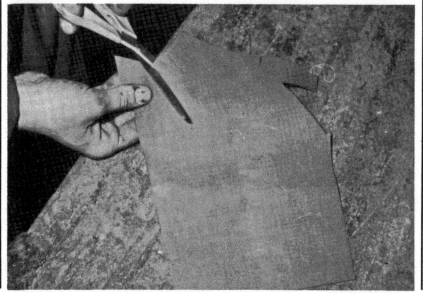

NTP4. Then it's a simple matter of gluing, clipping, screwing, or folding the 'new' panel back in place as it was originally.

Fitting new carpets

FNC1.   New carpets are installed with the front seats out of the way. Start by gluing down smoothly the side-member pieces.

FNC2.   Fit the rear seat panel, make any necessary cut-out for the seat belt mounting, and use the back of your scissors to push the carpet neatly into the corner.

FNC3.   Place the gearbox tunnel piece in place after removing the gearstick gaiter. Refit the gaiter and trim, feeling through the carpet with a bradawl or nail to find the original screw holes.

FNC4.   Today's carpets don't perfectly replicate the old, so put a tuck into the carpet behind the handbrake to take account of the changing tunnel shape.

FNC5.   Original-type soundproofing 'underfelts' are next fitted into place . . .   ⇨

FNC6.   . . . not forgetting the area beneath the rear seat.

FNC7.   This carpet needed a shade trimming to make it fit properly up against the parcel shelf.

FNC8. *It was also necessary to cut pedal apertures and to fit the carpet around the dipswitch. A straight cut was made up to the end of the carpet in line with the middle of the switch . . .*

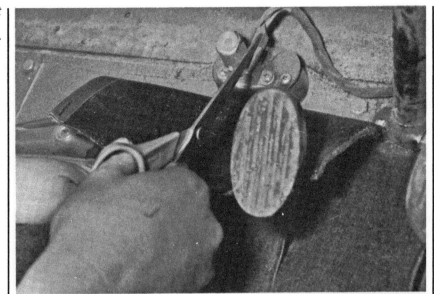

FNC9. *. . . then the shape of the dipswitch was cut out of the slit one half at a time.*

When buying carpets — beware! There is so much cheap-and-nasty, ill-fitting rubbish about that it is worth paying a little more and buying the best, original-quality carpets.

Headlining removal and fitting

HL1. *It is often considered that removal and fitting or the Morris Minor headlining is just a little too tricky an operation for the DIY-er to tackle. Plastic headlining is simple to wipe clean, however, and cloth headlining can be cleaned with a proprietary brand of cloth upholstery cleaner but do take care not to soak and shrink the cloth.*

For those feeling adventurous, here is the procedure for removal and fitting of the rexine headlining

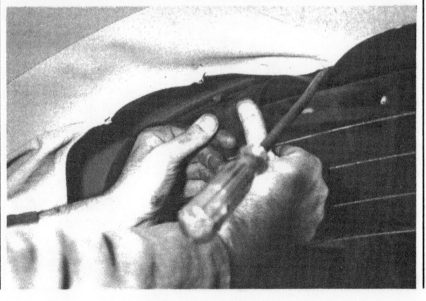

fitted to later models (replacement of cloth headlining really is a job for a coach trimmer).

Take out the self-tapping screw holding the tensioning cable beneath the dash reinforcement panel on each side of the car. Tie a piece of wire to the end of the cable, so that it can be reinserted through the front pillars when it is replaced.

The headlining is retained in the channel section above the windscreen by two concealed spring clips. Free them from the reinforcement front plywood fillet with a flat bladed screwdriver, taking great care.

Two more self-tapping screws are found holding the rear of the tensioning cable to the real pillar flange behind the rear quarter liners. Unscrew and again attach a length of wire to the cable.

On four-door models, remove the centre pillar trim pads. Where trafficators are fitted, a side tensioning screw is fitted to the top fixing screw; later models have a separate screw. The rear screws are fitted to the rear quarter inner reinforcement panel.

Slacken the self-tapping screw which secures the side tensioning cable which passes through each roof rear reinforcement and gusset plate.

Take out the top lining from the rear parcel shelf. The cable runs down each side of the rear window and there are two more screws to be removed. On most models, the headlining is fixed to clips welded to the body and can be removed after folding the rear window rubber back as shown in the picture.

On early models, the rear screen has to be removed by pushing the glass and rubber inwards until it is free. Then the bottom edge of the headlining can be freed from the fibre strip to which is it held with tacks.

Remove the headlining from the rear of the car. IMPORTANT! Make sure that the wires which you fixed to the cables are removed from the ends of the cables before taking them right away, leaving the wires running through the front and rear pillars. When refitting, which is the reverse of the process given here, re-attach the cables and use the wires to draw them through the pillars.

Fitting new door seals

NDS1.   Fit door seal clips to the opening flange as shown.

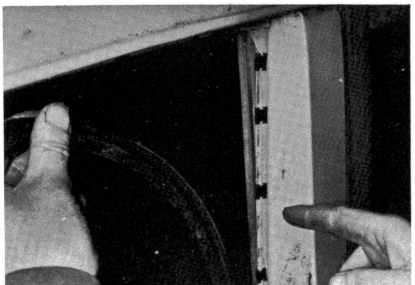

NDS2.   Open the door seal lip just a shade with a screwdriver, or it can buckle instead of going each side of the flange.

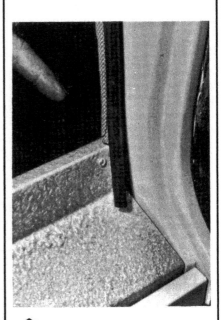

NDS3.   At the bottom of the rear of the door opening, cut the seal so that although the clip-on part stops at the base of the flange, the rubber seal continues down to the angled part of the kick plate.

Fitting door window seals

DWS1.   The upright channels slot into the window surround channels and are pushed down from above with the window lowered, the top being eased in with a screwdriver.

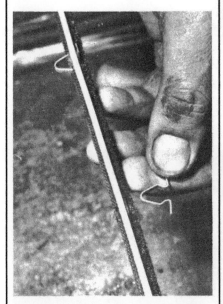

DWS2.   The door window seals are held with small spring clips that pass through ready made holes in the seals and clip into holes in the door.

DWS3.   The seals are trimmed to length . . .

DWS4.   . . . then with window glass fully lowered, the seal is eased, with the clips half in place, into the door opening. You can gain extra clearance by removing the door glass bottom stop and winding down a little further — an essential when fitting the strips to four-door rear doors. ⇩

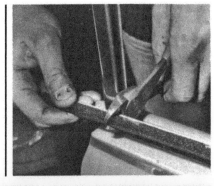

See the section on stripping and reassembling a door for details of how to fit the steel surround and how to replace a quarter-light rubber.

Traveller side panels

TSP1.   Over the top of the side panel is a stiff crescent-shaped strip, held in place with a line of self-tapping screws. ⇩

TSP2. *The top of the panel is eased out of/back into a rebate at the bottom of the waist rail.*

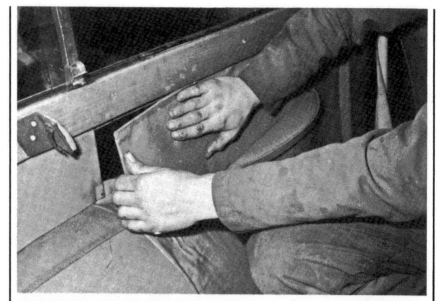

TSP3. *Invariably the edges of these panels come loose. Glue them back down with a contact adhesive such as Dunlop Thixofix.*

Traveller rear door seals

RDS1. *These are simply strips of quadrant-shaped rubber stuck into the rebates. Cut them exactly to length . . .*

RDS2. . . . then apply with a brush a type of contact adhesive that allows you a little shuffling time (movement) such as Thixofix to both the rubber and the rebate. Clean off any excess with petrol, then stick the rubber into place.

Traveller side-window pulls

SWP1. The side window pulls are held on by rubber strips and friction, so they shouldn't pull off.

SWP2. If one does pull off, clean out the insides of the pull, add a wipe of adhesive then, taking precautions against the risk of shattering glass (goggles, gloves), tap the pull back into place or even resort to the use of a woodworker's sash cramp used with extreme care. ⇨

Traveller load bay boards

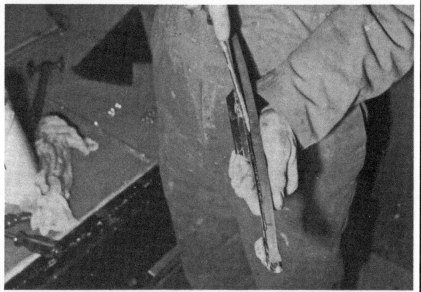

LB1. First, take out the rear seat backrest by undoing the countersunk-head machine screws (not woodscrews) in the hinges.

LB2. Take off the aluminium strips and the floor covering by removing the self-tapping screws.

LB3. The boards beneath are also held in place with self-tappers . . .

LB4. . . . and they, simply, lift straight out.

Fitting a Minor Tourer Hood

Tool box

Box of ¾ in. cut steel tacks. Light hammer. Screwdriver. Heavy-duty staple gun. Heat source such as fan blower heater.

Safety

Watch out for the sharp ends of old tacks when removing the old hood. Don't use the fan blower heater other than as recommended by the manufacturer.

Chris Newman specializes in fitting Tourer hoods at The Morris Minor Centre and he showed me how it was done. He recommends fitting a new frame as well as a new hood because most have worn their pivots to the point where they won't hold up satisfactorily. If you've got the time and patience, you could of course save money at home by reconditioning the frame yourself, drilling out the rivets and replacing them with larger ones to take out the slack. Hood removal is perfectly straightforward and simply involves pulling out the tacks that hold it in place using a pair of carpenter's pincers. The following sequence of how it all goes together also allows you to see just as clearly how it comes apart.

TH1. If, after stripping off the old hood, you find that the rear rail has rotted beyond redemption, you may have to replace it. You can buy new ash timbers, (almost) correctly shaped to fit the rear quarter panel — you may have to carry out a little final shaping yourself — and the correct type of covering material which has to be cut (carefully remove the old material and use it as a template) and glued into place.

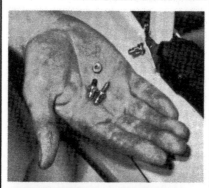

TH2. Clips to hold the hood to the base of the rear window come in two types: self-tapping and thread-and-nut. Chris used the latter type then filled the gap at the base of the screen frame carefully with mastic to prevent the ingress of water.

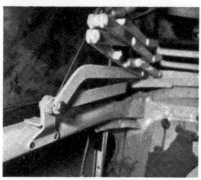

TH3. Next the frame was fitted in place: These are the wear-prone rivets mentioned earlier.

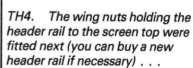

TH4. The wing nuts holding the header rail to the screen top were fitted next (you can buy a new header rail if necessary) . . .

TH5. . . . and the frame fitted in place by first lifting it high into the air to straighten all the joints . . .

TH6. . . . before being fitted to the windscreen top.

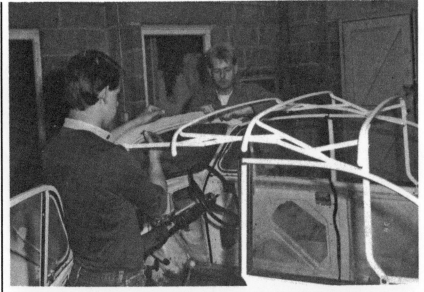

TH7. It's essential that the frame lies parallel to the door tops and that there's symmetrical clearance with no fouling. A little judicious bending and pushing may be called for.

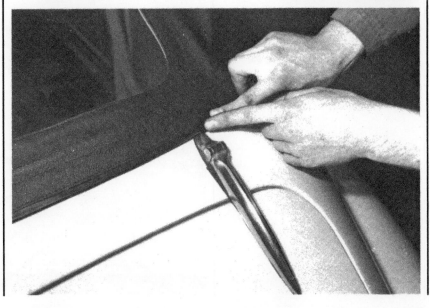

TH8. Make sure that the tensioner rail on the hood frame is in the folded down position and is not tensioning the hood. The hood can now be placed over the frame and correctly lined up at the back. The weather flap on the back should just overlap the top of the boot lid hinges, as shown.

TH9.   Inside, the hood must be eased over the rear side window frame so that it fits properly there.

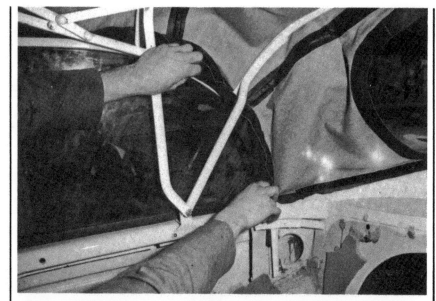

TH10.   Clip the hood onto the two fittings shown in TH2.

TH11.   Then, starting from the middle and working outwards, staple the hood to the rear rail. Use the staple gun upside down, as shown in this shot.

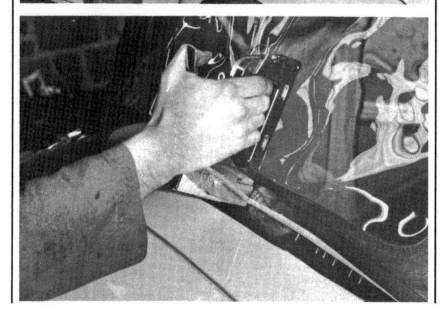

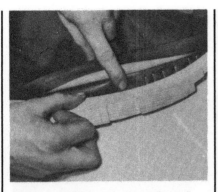

TH12. This is a spare section of rear rail, held against the fitted one to show a recess on the apex of each curve: Don't try to staple here. (You can feel its position through the hood fabric.)

TH14. Place the fan blower heater in the car — and wait! You will probably have to leave the heater in place for around half-an-hour before the hood warms up sufficiently to become stretchable, which is the aim of the exercise.

TH16. . . . and give the hood a very strong, even pull forwards, stapling it in place with just a few staples once again.

TH13. You can now transfer your attentions to the front of the car. Pull the hood forwards and temporarily tack it to the header rail with just a couple of staples in the centre of the rail.

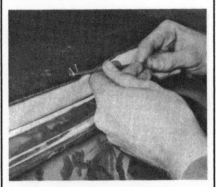

TH15. Lever out the staples with a screwdriver . . .

TH17. You should be taking great care that the hood is coming forwards fairly evenly, although being fabric, you can't assume that the seams will be precisely even. The aim will be to get the cross seams lining up with the frame rails beneath.

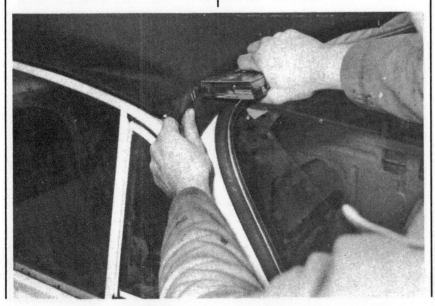

TH18. The process of tack and tension, tack and tension must continue until you are satisfied with the fit of the hood. But don't overdo it or you might conceivably damage the material or, and this is a greater risk, you may find that, in use, the hood will come off like a relieved rubber band and then be somewhat difficult to get back on again, especially on a cool day.

TH19. The hood should be held with closely spaced staples, as shown and then the front corner properly formed by tucking and tacking . . .

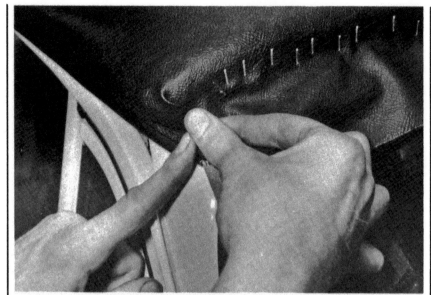

TH20. . . . tapping the staples all the way along the rail to ensure that they are fully home.

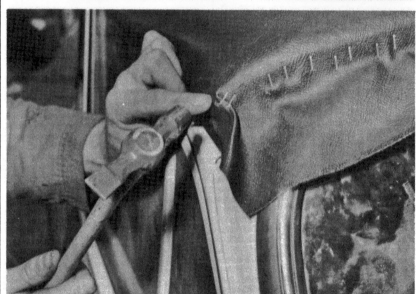

TH21. Use scissors to trim off the surplus material just a shade up from the bottom edge of the header rail.

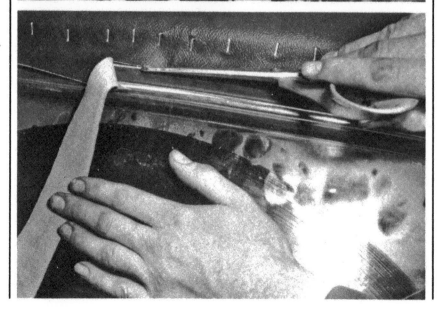

TH22. Offer up the new front weather strip and check it for symmetry of fit. You may want to measure and mark the centre point of both header rail and weather strip.

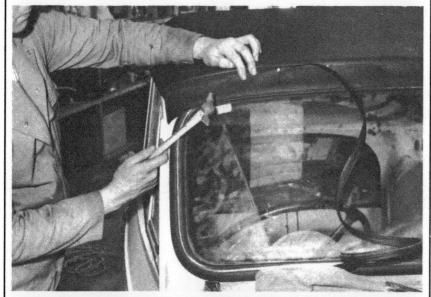

TH23. After tacking it in place with the cut tacks, quite near to its top edge, you can then fit the finisher strip which is designed to cover both top edge of the weather strip and the tacks holding it in place. Once again, ensure that it is centralized before fitting.

TH24. The tacks holding the finisher strip in place have to be driven out of sight as shown.

TH25. The finisher strips themselves have end finishers which are simply held in place with the tacks provided.

TH26.   You may want to carry out a 'belts & braces' job, in which case you should add tacks to the rear hood attachment, about every three inches. Of course, you may have wanted to be totally 'original' and to have used tacks throughout. But do note that, at the time of writing, absolutely original-type hoods were not available; these are a close approximation although they do look different in the way that the front weather strip is fitted into place.

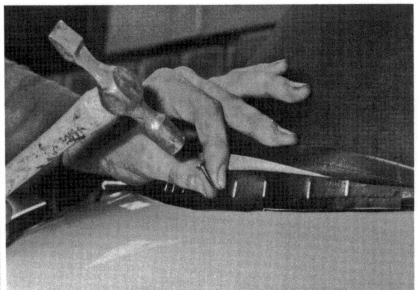

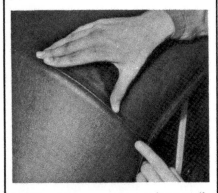

TH27.   Here you can see how well the hood seam lines up with the frame beneath. If you have fitted a new frame, there's one more step you will have to take. Lift the hood tensioner rail from inside the car . . .

TH28.   . . . then, just at the point shown, drill a ⅛ in. hole through the centre of the rail on each side.

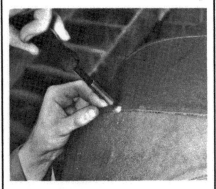

TH29.   Screw in a ½ in. × No. 8 domed, chrome-plated screw with cup washer to hold the hood to the frame when is it folded down.

TH30.   The finished job will not only look rather smart, it will also make the car far more fun to own by abolishing those leaks, gales and sounds of flapping canvas!

5 Mechanical Components

Engine removal

The engine can be removed either by itself or in conjunction with the gearbox. In practice it is not recommended that both components are removed together other than in exceptional circumstances because either the radiator and radiator surround have to be removed or engine and box can be removed with the car over a pit or raised very high, the engine and box tilted very sharply indeed and also lifted very high. Moreover, the gearbox mountings have to be removed from the cross-member, which is a difficult job to carry out in situ.

Tool box

Full range of socket, ring and open-ended spanners; pliers; range of screwdrivers; large lever; engine hoist; self-grip wrench.

Safety

Never work or stand beneath an engine held up on a hoist; the sturdiest of models can give way and ropes can break. If possible, make a mechanical fixing to the engine rather than using ropes. When working on the engine, either ensure that it cannot slip from the bench on which it is placed or, better still, work on the floor. Take care when moving around the very heavy weight of an engine and its major components.

ER1. *Fortunately for the owner, there is plenty of space in which to work, the Minor engine bay being most capacious. On early models such as this, remove the air cleaner and the battery as a first step. Also, drain the water out of the block and radiator using the taps provided. Drain the engine oil from the sump.*

ER2.   Pull out the split pin, remove the Clevis pin from the bonnet stay and, with the aid of an assistant, remove the bonnet (see 'Bonnet removal and refitting' for details). Alternatively prop it fully open or even tie it with a piece of light rope to the boot lid handle.

ER3.   Disconnect the heater hose and heater cable (later models only) or, alternatively, leave both connected and remove the heater tap.

ER4.   Disconnect the top and bottom hoses, remove the bolts holding each side of the radiator in place and lift out the radiator taking care not to damage it on the fan blades.

ER5.   Leave all the carburettor connections on the carb, unbolt it and place it out of the way. Take off the distributor cap, mark the leads and remove them from plugs and coil.

ER6.   Slacken the two exhaust clamp bolts (you'll probably need to grip the bolt head with a spanner, too) and let the exhaust pipe drop out of the way.

ER7.   Unbolt the engine tie-rod from the bulkhead and from the cylinder block and remove it.

ER8.   Take the wires off the coil. Tag them for identification but, since they are often incorrectly fitted, note that the white wire should go to the side marked 'SW' and the white and black wire to the side marked 'CB'. Remove them also from the starter motor.

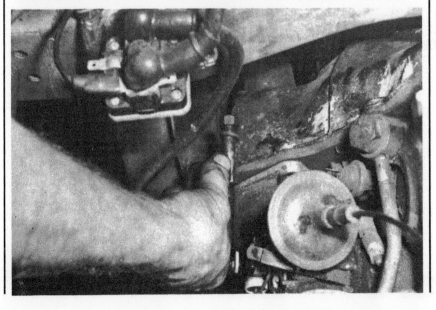

ER9.   Remove the large nuts and bolts holding the starter motor in place . . .

ER10. . . . and pull the starter motor out. You can now take out the ring of bolts around the bellhousing reached from inside the engine bay and from beneath the car.

ER11. This is the Minor Centre's own way of removing the engine: from the dynamo side, remove the engine mounting bottom nut and washers.

ER12. Do the same to the other side but also remove the top nuts and washers.

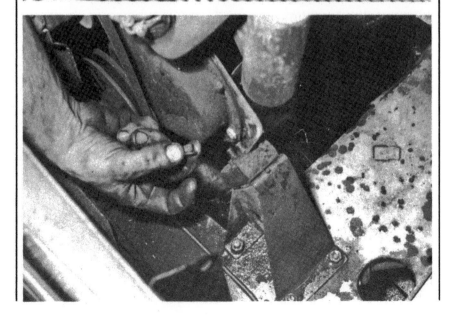

ER13. Use your hoist to take the engine weight. Place a jack below the front end of the gearbox so that the weight is just taken.

ER14. Prise up, twist and remove the exhaust-side engine mount . . .

Authors note: What looks simple in ER14, I have found sometimes to be very tricky. It is then much easier to cut your losses and remove the four bolts that hold the engine mounting tower to the chassis/floorplan. You can then, if you wish, leave both engine mountings attached to the engine.

ER15. . . . and the other side will come free allowing you to lift the engine up a touch, pull it forwards off the gearbox splines and lift it away, taking care not to place any pressure on the clutch or gearbox splines.

Clutch renewal

You can refit the new clutch by removing either the gearbox or the engine but, while either option was equally open whilst the Minor was new, the probable presence of

CR1.   Refit the clutch with the aid of an aligning tool. Here, an old spline (first motion shaft) is being used from a scrap gearbox but accessory shops sell a tool that does a similar job. Obviously, if the gearbox is out you can use that. Make certain that the longer part of the driven plate spline faces away from the engine.

corroded screws and captive nuts means that you are likely to encounter fewer problems if you stick to removing the engine for clutch renewal.

Remove the six bolts holding the pressure plate to the flywheel. Examine the face of the pressure plate for cracks or scoring, which will require its renewal. If the clutch has been 'juddering' badly it could mean that oil has got onto the clutch or that there are broken springs in the pressure plate.

CR2.   It is advisable to have fairly clean hands and to wipe any traces of oil off the flywheel and clutch pressure plate. Tighten the cover bolts finger-tight, then spanner them up, screwing each in by a turn at a time. Then withdraw the aligning tool.

CR3.   The clutch release bearing lives inside the gearbox bellhousing. Even if the old one is not particularly worn, it is false economy not to renew it at this stage. It is held in place by a pair of spring clips.

You will finally need to slacken the clutch adjustment locknuts, remove temporarily the clutch return spring and adjust the clutch to give ¾ inch of free movement at the pedal.

Engine stripdown

See 'Engine Removal' section for tools and safety references

The cylinder head

ESC1.   You can strip the engine down on a bench but perhaps the simplest and safest place for the home restorer to work is on the floor, the engine placed on a large opened-out cardboard box. Have plenty of containers handy for storing bolts and brackets from each of the main components. Whenever possible, store studs or nuts, along with their washers, by placing them on the component from which they came.

ESC2.   Undo the two internally threaded studs holding the rocker cover down . . .

ESC3.   . . . and lift it off, giving it a tap with a hammer handle if necessary.

ESC4.   You can, if you wish, remove the sparking plugs to avoid their being broken but you may decide to leave them in place to prevent rubbish from being stuck in the head threads.

ESC5.   Undo the three nuts holding the thermostat housing but be prepared for a struggle to remove it! In some cases, you may have to accept a breakage.

ESC6.   Slacken the head nuts working from the centre outwards and remove the rocker retaining nuts, too.

ESC7.   Don't forget to note the position of the locating plate which prevents the rocker shaft locating screw from coming unscrewed.

ESC8.   When unscrewing the head and rocker shaft nuts, don't be surprised if the whole stud comes out. Remove the nut separately.

ESC9. Remove the rocker assembly complete, as shown. Pull the brackets against the springs to expose the rocker shaft. Check it for wear and so determine whether it needs replacement.

ESC10. Pull out the pushrods. Shake them vigorously first to leave the tappets properly located in the block (See ESB15 for details).

ESC11. Don't try to remove the head without removing the bypass hose between the front of the head and water pump. If the engine is in situ cut the hose and remove it later. You should always renew it anyway.

ESC12. Lift off the head. If (when?) it sticks, tap it upwards with a soft-faced mallet beneath the thermostat housing at the front and a casting boss at the back. Don't prise the head upwards.

ESC13. Unbolt and remove the manifold.

ESC14. Start stripping the valves out by first removing the valve retainer circlip.

ESC15. Mark the heads of the valves with a centre punch so that they can be identified and refitted from where they came.

ESC16. Tap each spring cap to free it then compress the spring with a proprietary brand of compressor. Lift out the retainers, release the compressor and the springs and valves can be released.

    With the valves held in or near the closed position, attempt to rock the valve in the valve guide. If there is anything more than the slightest movement you will have to renew the valves and guides. Look especially carefully at the exhaust valves and valve seats. Slight pitting can be ground out but it is far from unusual to have to fit new exhaust valves and to have the seats professionally recut or valve seat inserts fitted.

The cylinder block assembly

Cylinder head removal and stripdown were described in the previous section. The internal components of the block are shown in Figure 7.

ESB1. Start by removing the fan and water pump pulley. Store the bolts by screwing them back into the water pump.

ESB2. Unbolt and remove the water pump, tapping rather than levering it free.

Figure 7. A typical A-series engine.

1 Cover – rocker gear
2 Cylinder block
3 Block – head
4 Crankshaft
5 Sump
6 Water pump body
7 Cover – cylinder block front
8 Flywheel
9 Starter ring
10 Fan blade
11 Fan belt
12 Oil filler cap
13 Elbow – water outlet
14 Thermostat
15 Piston assembly
16 Connecting rod
17 Exhaust valve
18 Exhaust valve guide
19 Inlet valve
20 Inlet valve guide
21 Outer valve spring
22 Inner valve spring
23 Shroud for valve guide
24 Valve packing ring
25 Valve spring cup
26 Valve cotter
27 Valve cotter circlip
28 Camshaft
29 Camshaft bearing liners
30 Tappet
31 Pushrod
32 Tappet adjusting screw
33 Locknut
34 Rocker (bushed)
35 Valve rocker shaft (plugged)
36 Rocker shaft plug (screwed)
37 Rocker shaft plug (plain)
38 Rocker shaft bracket (tapped)
39 Rocker shaft bracket (plain)
40 Rocker bush
41 Rocker spacing spring
42 Rocker shaft bracket plate
43 Cover joint gasket
44 Rocker shaft locating screw
45 Spring washer

46 Washer
47 Split pin
48 Nut
49 Cup washer
50 Distance piece
51 Cover bush
52 Rocker bracket long stud
53 Nut
54 Spring washer
55 Elbow joint gasket
56 Water outlet elbow stud
57 By-pass adaptor
58 Rocker bracket stud (short)
59 Cylinder head nut
60 Washer
61 Cover nut
62 Spring washer
63 Cover plate
64 Cover plate joint gasket
65 Cover plate stud
66 Cylinder head gasket
67 Cylinder head stud (short)
68 Cylinder head stud (long)
69 Exhaust manifold stud (medium)
70 Cylinder head stud (long)
71 Exhaust manifold stud (short)
72 Small washer
73 Large clamping washer
74 Exhaust manifold stud (long)
75 Core plug
76 Dynamo pulley
77 Dynamo fan
78 Bearing distance piece
79 Bearing
80 Outer retainer for felt
81 Felt
82 Inner retainer for felt
83 Retainer circlip
84 Bearing grease retainer
85 Bearing
86 Water pump gasket
87 Distance piece
88 Seal
89 Seal rubber
90 Pulley key
91 Spring locating cup

92 Spring
93 Spindle with vane
94 Water pump body stud (short)
95 Water pump body stud (long)
96 Oil gallery plug
97 Spindle nut
98 Spindle washer
99 Screw to pulley
100 Spring washer
101 Cover gasket
102 Front bearer plate
103 Bearer plate joint gasket
104 Plain washer
105 Spring washer
106 Front bearer plate screw
107 Cover felt
108 Rubber front mounting block
109 Block attachment bolt
110 Camshaft sprocket (upper)
111 Sprocket nut
112 Camshaft drive chain
113 Tensioner rings
114 Locking plate
115 Plate to crankcase screw
116 Shakeproof washer
117 Gearbox bearer plate
118 Joint gasket to plate
119 Cover joint washer
120 Rear cover
121 Cover screw
122 Screw to block
123 Spring washer
124 Dowel (top) to block
125 Drain tap (water)
126 Tap washer
127 Oil priming plug
128 Copper washer
129 Block front side cover (with elbow)
130 Side cover gasket
131 Screw to block
132 Fibre washer
133 Fume vent pipe (with clip)
134 Clip screw
135 Spring washer
136 Stud (blanking plate)

137 Nut
138 Washer
139 Pulley retaining bolt
140 Lockwasher
141 Crankshaft pulley
142 Oil thrower
143 Crankshaft sprocket
144 Packing washer
145 Crankshaft key
146 Upper thrust washers
147 Lower thrust washers
148 Main bearing
149 Main bearing cap dowel
150 Lockwasher
151 Bearing cap bolt
152 Shakeproof washer
153 Bearing cap screw
154 Lockwasher for bolts
155 Cap bolt
156 Bearing cap screw
157 Shakeproof washer
158 Big end bearing
159 Dowel
160 First motion shaft bush
161 Flywheel to crankshaft screw
162 Lockwasher
163 Sump right-hand gasket
164 Sump left-hand gasket
165 Main bearing cap seal
166 Sump drain plug
167 Drain plug washer
168 Screw
169 Washer
170 Ignition control pipe
171 Pipe clip
172 Pipe nut (distributor end)
173 Pipe nut (carburettor end)
174 Pipe olive
175 Oil gallery plug
176 Oil pressure relief-valve passage plug
177 Stud nuts
178 Big end cap
179 Block rear side cover

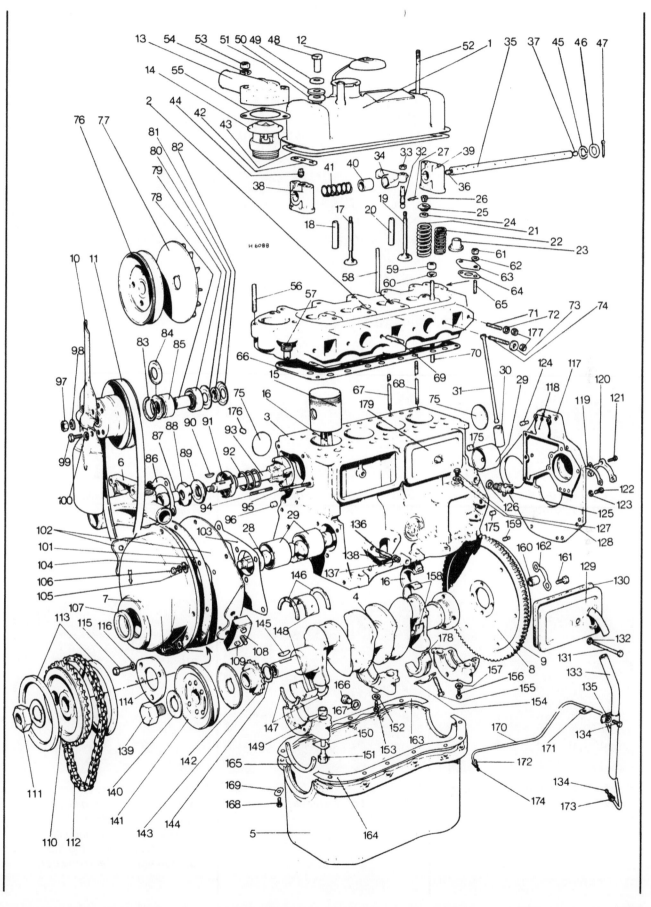

H 6088

ESB3. You may be able to remove studs by locking a pair of nuts onto a stud and unscrewing the bottom nut. If this doesn't work, you may have to beg, borrow or buy a stud extractor, use a self-grip wrench in conjunction with the above method or leave it to the reconditioner.

ESB4. Take out the two bolts holding the distributor to the block . . .

ESB6. Take out the distributor housing screw . . .

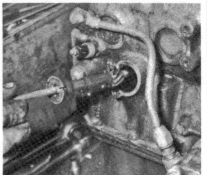

ESB8. Insert a 5/16 UNF bolt into the distributor drive (a tappet cover bolt is ideal) and lift and turn the shaft slightly clockwise as it comes out.

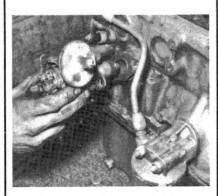

ESB5. . . . and lift the distributor away.

ESB7. . . . and the housing itself will pull out of the block.

ESB9. Take off the external main oilway pipe; hang on to all the copper washers (when reassembling, fit one end very loosely before connecting the other end, then tighten each one up).

ESB10. Take out the domed nut holding the oil pressure release valve spring in place.

ESB13. Pull it off the studs, being prepared for the inevitable mess, and remove the studs.

ESB16. The almost inevitable 'stickers' can be pulled out with pliers, as shown.

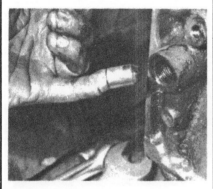

ESB11. Use a little finger to 'thimble' the release valve itself out of the block.

ESB14. Take off the tappet chest covers, hanging on to the gaskets.

ESB17. At the rear of the engine, knock back the two pairs of tab washers and remove the bolts and flywheel.

ESB12. Unbolt the oil filter housing and tap it loose.

ESB15. As with the release valve, so the tappets can be removed.

ESB18. Take out the bolts holding the backplate in place and remove it.

ESB19. Take out the three oil pump bolts then, to enable you to get a grip on the oil pump in order to remove it, insert the bolts a little way and grip them as shown.

ESB20. Turn the block onto its top face and, from the sump flange, remove and store the retaining screws and special washers.

ESB21. Sumps are sometimes (wrongly) 'glued' down with gasket cement. Tap with a wooden or soft-faced mallet to free it.

ESB22. Disconnect the oil pick-up and coarse filter bracket and disconnect the pipe from the block.

ESB23. The crank nut will be extremely tight. Don't use a ratchet here because you could break it. Lock the crank with a piece of wood and, if you're working on a bench, take care not to lever the block off the bench!

ESB24.   Tap the crank pulley off along its keyway and carefully retain the crescent-moon-shaped woodruff key if it comes out of the crank nose.

ESB25.   Remove the ring of bolts holding the timing chain cover in place. If you have to lever it, do so only at the top because if any distortion should take place there leaks are unlikely to occur as a result. If yours is the type of cover with a felt seal try getting hold of a later one, second-hand if necessary, with the superior front oil seal in it.

ESB26.   Whichever type of oil thrower is fitted, note carefully which way round it goes. The type on left has the concave side to the block; the one on the right is convex side to the block.

ESB27. Knock back the tab washer on the camshaft, take out the bolt . . .

ESB29. Remove the camshaft retaining plate.

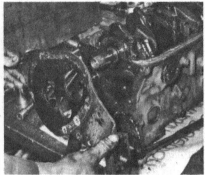

ESB31. Take off the front plate.

ESB28. . . . and slide both timing gears and the chain off. Start them moving by levering both simultaneously with a pair of screwdrivers.

ESB30. Knock back the tab washers on the front main bearing bolts and remove these along with the other front plate bolts.

ESB32. The camshaft can be wriggled forwards, taking care not to damage the white metal bearing with the cam lobes as they bump their way past.

ESB33. Inspect the tips of the cam lobes for wear, in which case a new or reprofiled cam will be needed.

ESB34.   The drive pin (if this type of drive is fitted) in the end of the cam can't come out whilst the cam is in situ but check that it hasn't slipped out whilst the cam was being withdrawn.

ESB36.   Loosen a pair of big end bolts . . .

ESB38.   . . . pull the bolts part out then pinch and pull to take the cap free of the oil's surface tension on the crank. Inspect the face of the bearings — any red showing through the leaden grey colour indicates quite heavy wear as does scoring on the crank.

ESB35.   Mark each conrod and cap with centre-punch marks so that they don't get confused and so that the caps don't get reversed.

ESB37.   . . . tap them to free the conrod . . .

ESB39.   With all conrods free, the pistons can be driven up and out. They may, however, need a good thump to clear the wear ridge in the top of the bore.

ESB40.   Here's a couple of typical problems: a broken piston ring and a piston with 'blow-by' marks on it from the hot gases inefficiently escaping downwards.

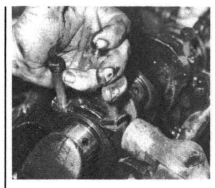

ESB41.   Slacken the main bearing bolts and remove them in a similar way to the big ends with the extra help of a tap from the hammer.

ESB42.   Lift out the crank. Note that conrods and big-ends have been reassembled after removal as a double guarantee against confusion. It's best to have both crank and bores checked by an expert with micrometers and/or a clock dial gauge to see whether machining is needed or not.

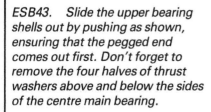

ESB43.   Slide the upper bearing shells out by pushing as shown, ensuring that the pegged end comes out first. Don't forget to remove the four halves of thrust washers above and below the sides of the centre main bearing.

ESB44.   Finally, remove all remaining plugs or taps so that when the block is scoured out at the reconditioners, all the accumulated 'gunge' in oil and waterways is completely removed.

ESB45. Whilst having block and crank machined and purchasing all necessary new parts and gaskets before reassembling, it would be wise to dismantle the oil pump and check for scoring, renewing it if in any doubt. Fill the pump with oil before refitting it to the engine and, just to be sure, prime it after fitting through the plug shown in ESB44. Fill with oil. Examine the timing chain for wear — look for grooving on the rollers and check the sprockets for slightly concave shaped teeth, instead of perfectly straight-sided teeth, in which case they will require renewal. If there is any hint of wear, especially if the engine has covered 60,000 miles or more, it is sensible to renew the timing chain in any case.

At the very least, renew the rubber tensioner rings (where fitted) which are recessed into the outsides of the camshaft gearwheel.

Before refitting the rocker shaft, remove the plugs from its ends and clean it out — remember that it acts as the oil passage for the valve gear — and clean out its oil holes, too. If the shaft shows any wear ridges, renew the shaft.

Check the rocker bushes for wear by gripping the rockers one by one and attempting to rock each sideways. If they are very loose, the rocker bushes will need renewal (but do not mix forged and the newer-type pressed steel rockers — keep to the same type). Check the ends of the rockers for any cracking or pitting and if wear is apparent, replace the rocker.

When reassembling the engine, ensure that all oilways are clear, including those through the crank journals, and thoroughly lubricate all bearing surfaces as reassembly is carried out. Always use new spring washers, and new gaskets. A torque wrench is essential.

Reassembly is not necessarily the reverse of dismantling and, unless you are fully familiar with the engine, reassembly is best carried out with the aid of Haynes Minor 1000 Owners Workshop Manual,

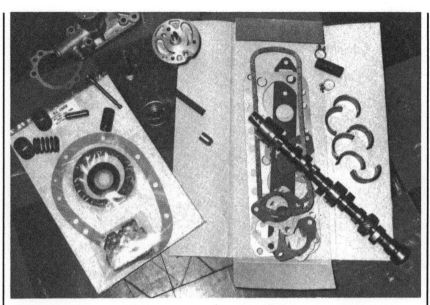

where piston ring positions, timing gear alignment, order of assembly, and so on, are all given in detail.

Gearbox removal

If you need to change the clutch, leave the gearbox in place and remove the engine (see the appropriate section), unless the gearbox has recently been removed, and any fitting problems overcome, in which case it is probably easier to remove the gearbox than the

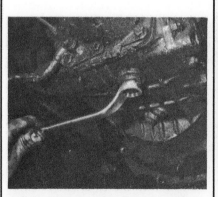

GR1. Remove the drain plug and drain the gearbox oil. Also, remove the speedometer drive (use pliers or a self-grip wrench used loosely if the nut is very stiff).

engine. See 'Engine removal' section for tools and safety references.

GR2. Put the gearbox in 'neutral', remove the gearstick gaiter and take out the three bolts holding the gearstick retaining plate in place. Lift out the gearstick. Disconnect

the battery and remove the heater tap from the engine. Take out the two nuts and bolts holding the starter motor in place and withdraw the starter motor, leaving it connected, if possible, and lying in the engine bay.

GR3.   Take off the clutch linkage, as follows: Take off the return spring and disconnect the pedal arm by taking out the split pin and cotter pin. Take out the two bolts and washers holding the shaft to the chassis. Take off the packing plate, bracket and bush and pull the shaft away, taking note of the spring. Also release the engine steady cable (after chassis number 264013) connected from the rear cross-member to a bracket on the gearbox. Unscrew the cable from the gearbox by means of the flats on the cable end fitting.

Figure 8.   The clutch release shaft. (Courtesy The Morris Minor Centre)

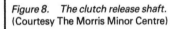

GR4.   The front of the propshaft pulls off the splines on the rear of the gearbox . . .

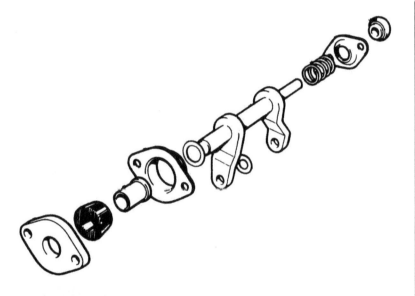

GR5.   . . . but before it can do so, the four propshaft-to-differential bolts must be removed. Mark both flanges so that they are reassembled in the same place. Removal of these bolts is not required if the engine has been removed.

GR6.   The cross-member is held on each side by two brass screws that hold the floorpan down from inside the car. (Take care not to damage wires or fuel pipe which pass through this area, when the gearbox cross-member is being removed or refitted.)

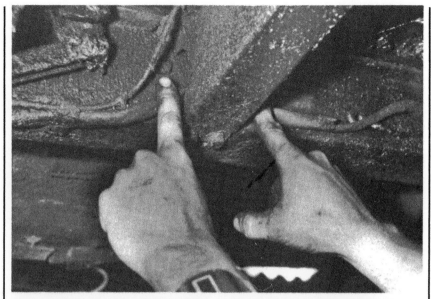

GR7.   These are the two screw positions. You may consider replacing them later with bright zinc plated hexagon-head bolts. Use an impact screwdriver or even drill them out if absolutely necessary.

GR8.   Two more bolts on each side screw up into captive nuts in the chassis rail. (Remember to refit the earthing strap when refitting.)

GR9.   The captive nuts into which they are screwed frequently break off inside the chassis rail, rotating uselessly when unscrewed. Grind the bolt heads off if necessary but do not completely remove them without supporting the gearbox in some way.

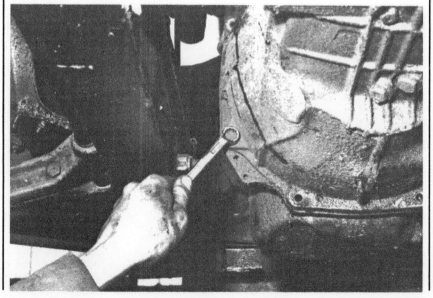

GR10.   Undo the ring of bolts around the bellhousing — this is so much easier with the engine and 'box lowered at the rear. (Make sure that the cooling fan blades are placed horizontally so that they cannot pierce the radiator; removal of the heater tap removes the risk of breakage and allows the engine to tilt further.

GR11. Allow the cross-member to drop, easing it down and away from the pipes and wires, take the weight of the gearbox and turn it clockwise so that the bellhousing clears the steering rack and slide it away from the engine.

GR12. To renew the mountings, unbolt them from the gearbox here . . .

GR13. . . . and from the cross-member here. Cross-members have often been butchered in the past and may need repair or, in some cases, replacement. Captive nuts in the 'chassis' rails are best replaced by a pair of bolts passing through and welded to a strip of metal. The bolts are then placed downwards through the box-section and the cross-member pushed up onto them from beneath. The master-cylinder has to be removed first on the driver's side of the car to gain access to the old captive nuts and for fitting of the bolt/plate assembly. Once in place the master cylinder will prevent the new bolts being pushed out; on the passenger side, however, the strap should be made extra-long and folded at its ends, giving a squared-off U-shape. The two vertical pieces should be almost the height of the inside of the box section so that they prevent the bolts and strap being pushed upwards as the cross-member is fitted.

Suspension, steering and brakes – general

Before starting any job concerned with repair of the suspension, steering or brakes read the following notes on tools and safety, and refer to the information on safety in Appendix 1.

Tool box

The only special tool necessary for these sections will be a good quality hub puller for front and rear hubs, although both can be removed with a little ingenuity. Otherwise: a good set of spanners; a trolley jack; a pair of axle stands.

Safety

Only carry out work on brakes if you are competent to do so; if in doubt ask a trained mechanic to check your work. NEVER work on a car supported by a jack; always support the car on axle stands with wheels chocked when working on suspension or brakes.

Brake dust contains asbestos and can be lethal! NEVER blow it away, but use a damp cloth for wiping it off components (dispose of the cloth in a sealed plastic bag). Follow the instruction in the text but try the brakes carefully when first using the car after the work is finished – wet brake shoes will not stop the car.

Beware the latent energy in a spring and always release the tension in the spring safely and slowly.

Front suspension overhaul and steering rack removal

See section on 'Front floor and cross-member repair' for details of how to remove and replace a torsion bar.

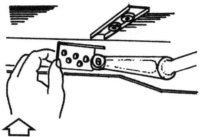

Figure 9.   Torsion bar adjustment. Behind this plate is a slot in the chassis. Choose which hole to bolt the torsion bar lever through in order to adjust the torsion bar and 'trim' the front suspension so that both sides are the same height. To set the car upwards, choose a lower hole than was previously used (and choose a higher hole to set the car lower, of course). Each successive hole raises (or lowers) the car by approximately ¼ inch. Tapping the lever forwards and off its splines then replacing it one spline 'out' raises or lowers the car by approximately 1 ½ inch.

FSS1.   The bump stop often breaks off its mounting plate in which case a new one should be bolted on in its place.

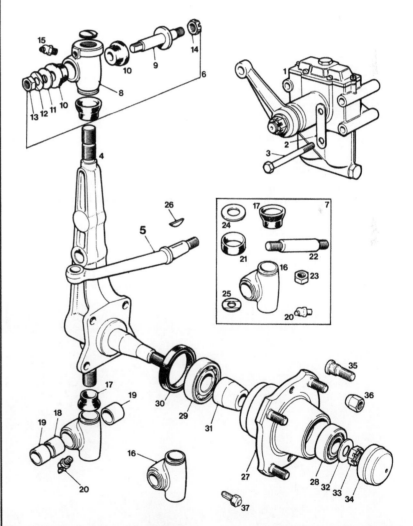

Figure 10.   Front suspension components. Remember when examining and repairing a top or bottom trunnion (6 and 17-20) that it is not necessary to remove the whole kingpin, and that if the kingpin is to be removed, the brake backplate complete with shoes and hydraulics should be removed as a piece, which avoids having to break into the hydraulic system. (Courtesy of The Morris Minor Centre.)

FSS2. Remove the front hub by first tapping off the dust cover.

FSS3. Pull out the split pin through the castellated nut . . .

FSS4. . . . and remove the nut. You can then lever off the hub using a pair of stout levers using the brake shoes or wheel cylinders as fulcrum points. If the inner bearing stays on the stub, it may be necessary to use a puller to remove it.

Before refitting the hub the inner bearing, oil seal and bearing spacer must be fitted correctly into the hub. If they are not in their correct positions, the oil seal can fail to seat, allowing grease to reach the brake shoes.

Note that cars after chassis number 228267 were fitted with angular contact bearings which have to be installed the correct way round. The thrust side of each bearing — that with the part number stamped on it — MUST face towards the solid bearing spacer. Earlier bearings are not of the thrust type. They should be fitted to the hub with the chamfered side of the bearing spacer towards the small outer bearing then the large bearing pressed into position. Pack both types with grease before reassembly.

Before refitting the hub, fit a new oil seal with the metal face of the oil seal away from the bearing. The castellated nut should be tightened to between 55 and 65 lb/ft (later type) and the holes aligned before fitting a new split pin.

FSS5. Test for wear in the top and bottom trunnions by jacking a road wheel a very short distance off the ground beneath the suspension arm. Take care that the car cannot slip off the jack and cause injury. Lever the top and bottom trunnions vigorously, attempting to lift the top arm away from the swivel pin.

FSS6. The top pin (or 'pivot' — Figure 10, 9) can wear badly, as shown, giving a lot of free play. You will need to fit a new pin and bushes and possibly a complete trunnion kit.

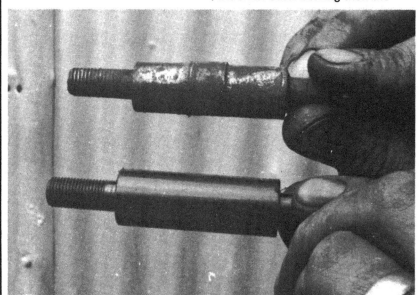

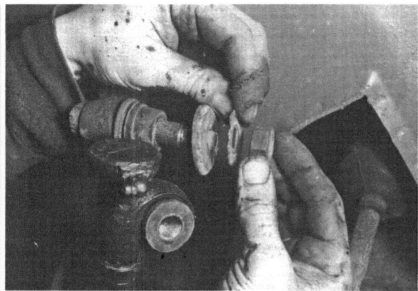

FSS7. Jack up the front suspension just sufficiently to take the pressure off the top pivot pin. (Place an axle stand beneath the chassis rail — this is essential! Take care to locate the jack so that it cannot slip.) Knock back the tab washer and unbolt the top pivot, removing the shocker arm and the bushes.

FSS8. You may be lucky enough to get away with replacing just the bushes if the top pin is not worn.

FSS9. Quite often, the trunnion is worn where it threads onto the swivel pin which means that a new trunnion and a new pin will be required to prevent the possibility of disastrous suspension collapse. Check the bottom pin and bottom trunnion, too.

FSS10. The top pin passes through the trunnion and through a clearance in the thread in the top trunnion, as shown. Very early Minors did not have screwed pivots but here special machining may be necessary to recondition them, or it may be necessary to convert to later components. The Morris Minor Centre will advise on individual cases.

FSS11. *Another source of suspension 'clonks' on the Minor can be worn bushes in the torsion bar eye-bolt which passes through the chassis leg.*

Dismantling the lower suspension arm is described under 'Front Chassis Leg Repair'. It should be dismantled after disconnecting the top suspension arm and then lowering and removing the jack. The steering arm (Figure 10) will have to be removed from the swivel pin if that is to be replaced.

Note for Riley 1.5/Wolseley 1500

The supply of swivel pins for these cars is drying up. You will see in Figure 10 that two bosses were cast into the swivel pin, the bottom one being machined out for Minors, the top one for Wolseleys and Rileys. Early swivel pins were machined in both places but these are no longer available. Owners of Riley 1.5s and Wolseley 1500s should check with their suppliers to see if the correct swivel pin is still available and if not, they can get over the problem by having new Minor swivel pins machined out in the top boss by a competent engineering firm. Specialist Riley/Wolseley suppliers may be able to have this operation carried out for you.

Notes on reassembly

● It is most important that, when the shock absorber arm is refitted to the top swivel, there is a little play otherwise the suspension will be locked solid. The gap should be measured with a feeler gauge and

should be .002 inch. (0.5mm). Give it a tap with a hammer to ensure that it is properly seated as far as it will go and that you are taking a 'real' reading.

● The swivel pins and links fitted to the left-hand side of the car have left-hand threads. Those on the other side have right-hand threads.

● So that the top pin does not foul the swivel pin (see FSS10) when the steering is turned assemble as follows. Fit the top pin to the trunnion which is itself fitted to the swivel pin. Screw the trunnion down as far as it will go. (It should give three revolutions between the top pin fouling at the top and fouling at the bottom) then screw the trunnion back 1 ½ turns to give

maximum clearance in each direction. The bottom swivel should also be centralised *before* the brake back-plate is replaced and before the swivel pin is fitted to the suspension arm.

FSS12. *Obviously this trunnion is not attached to the swivel pin but it illustrates that there are sealing rings to be located beneath the cover seals which must be fitted before the two halves of the bottom suspension arm are reassembled.*

Steering rack removal

FSS13. First disconnect the track rod end from the steering arm. Take off the retaining nut then strike the tapered eye on the steering arm vigorously to free the pin. You can try using two hammers, hitting both sides of the eye simultaneously and/or using an accessory tool to apply pressure to the track rod end. If you wish to reuse the track rod end again, take care not to damage the rubber. If it is removed or renewed, have the 'track' correctly set at a garage with specialist equipment.

FSS14. The steering rack passes above the gearbox and is bolted through two aluminium split brackets . . .

FSS15. . . . the bolt heads of which can be found beneath the carpets at the very front of the floor, ahead of the gearbox tunnel (removed from this car).

Rear suspension overhaul and axle removal

RSA1. Here the rear spring U-bolt and mountings have been loosely assembled showing how the buffer is held into place.

RSA2. To detach the axle from the springs undo the U-bolt nuts. Because they're so exposed, they can rust immovably in which case chisel through the side — the thinnest part of the nut — with a sharp cold chisel.

Figure 11. These are the components of the rear suspension as depicted in the Minor Centre Catalogue.

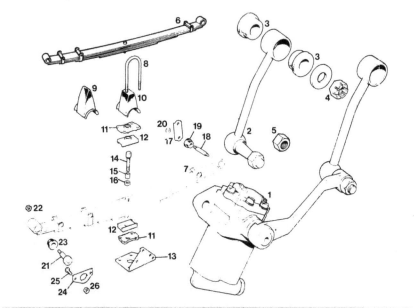

RSA3. If you're taking off the spring but leaving the axle in place, you'll have to hold both the body and the axle up on axle stands.

RSA4. If removing the axle by itself or the axle and springs together, hold the body up at the front shackles and wheel out the axle or axle/springs on a trolley jack. ⇨

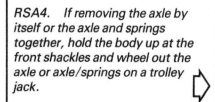

RSA5. See 'Bodywork' chapter for details of how to dismantle and reassemble both front and rear shackle pins.

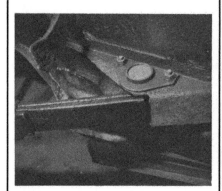

RSA6. Van and Pick-up rear spring mountings are attached to the rear chassis via special brackets as shown here.

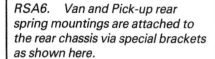

Rear axle hub, half-shaft and differential removal

Figure 12.   These are the components of the rear axle, Austin-type. See 'Production changes' for change point. (Courtesy Morris Minor Centre)

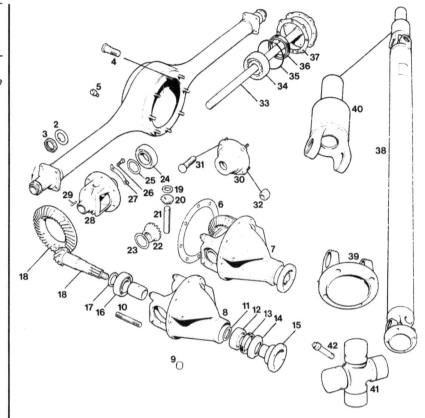

Figure 13.   The early-type Nuffield back axle is rather different to the Austin-type but parts can be obtained by special order from The Morris Minor Centre. (Courtesy Morris Minor Centre)

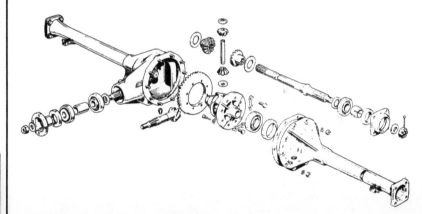

RAH1.   Whether you're aiming to remove the diff, change the half-shaft or change the oil seals, you will need to start here! Take out the cross-head screws holding the brake drum. (You may need an impact screwdriver.) Slacken the brake adjuster then tap off the drum with a soft-faced hammer.

RAH2.   Unscrew the single screw holding the half-shaft to the hub (this is an impact screwdriver!) . . .

RAH3.   . . . and tap the half-shaft flange to free it, if necessary.

RAH4.   Next the half-shaft can be withdrawn. If the differential is being removed, the half-shaft only needs to be pulled a little way out. It's worth remembering, if the axle is to remain in the car, to park the car sufficiently far away from the garage wall to enable you to remove the half-shaft if that's what you intend to do. Otherwise there could be much annoyance, frustration and gnashing of teeth!

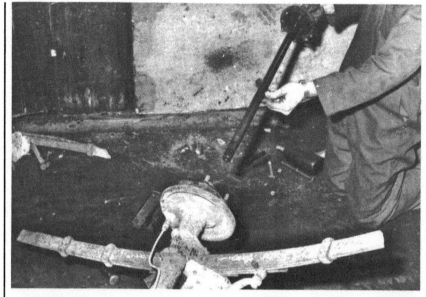

RAH5.   Don't hit the flange too hard with the hammer because it can easily become distorted which leads to an oil leak into the brake drum.

RAH6.   After draining the differential oil, take off the ring of nuts holding the differential carrier in place and lift off the spring washers, too, because that makes removal much easier.

RAH7.   Push the brake pipe out of the way (there's no need to disconnect the brake line of course) and lift the diff out. If you're on your back beneath the car remember that it's very heavy — keep your face and body from beneath it and take care not to trap fingers.

RAH8.   To remove the hub, knock back the tab washer (Figure 12, 2) and remove the retaining nut. Use a puller to pull the hub off the axle casing.

RAH9. If the bearings have gone then, obviously renew them — but the most likely fault is an oil seal failure. The bearing can be awkward to tap out from the hub: you can easily remove lots of rubber but the steel shell is trickier. Use a thin-bladed screwdriver as a drift and keep it really close to the shoulder inside the hub.

RAH10. Examine the face on the axle casing where the oil seal has been running. If it's worn or pitted, note that even the new oil seal will leak. Look carefully at the hub and you will see that it is not necessary to tap the oil seal tightly against the shoulder in the hub. This allows the seal to run on a fresh piece of the axle casing and keeps it sealing. (It also makes it easier to replace next time!)

Shock absorbers

The Minor is, like all cars — perhaps more than most — shock absorber critical. If the shockers become weak, handling and roadholding will worsen dramatically.

D1. The front absorbers are fitted to the bulkhead by four long bolts held by tab washers and screwed into captive nuts (except in the case of Wolseley 1500/Riley 1.5 which have free nuts on their inner ends and therefore require two pairs of hands to remove and retighten them). The section on front suspension shows how to remove the shock absorber arm from the suspension top pin. Because the shocker linkage is an integral part of the suspension system, check for play very carefully, replacing the shocker if necessary.

D2.   The rear shocker bolts to the spring/axle plate and can sometimes be difficult to detach because of corroded threads.

If the shock absorbers require topping-up, the area around the plug should be thoroughly cleaned before removal. Unfortunately, the rear shockers must be removed simply in order to top them up.

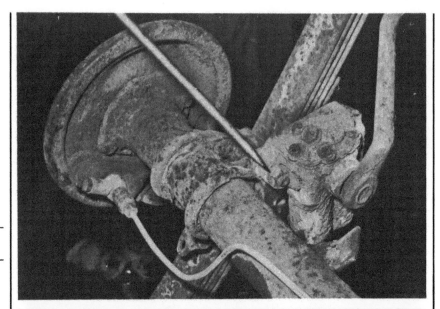

Braking system

For full information on overhauling the braking system on your Morris Minor see the Haynes *Morris Minor 1000 Owners Workshop Manual*. However, there follows some general information of relevance to the home restorer/repairer.

BS1.   Only ever use the best components when repairing the brakes of your Minor. It is considered acceptable to use new rubbers when a wheel or master cylinder leak is found provided that the cylinder inner bore is perfectly smooth (check with a qualified mechanic to be sure). For safety's sake, however, and for the sake of convenience in the case of the hard-to-get-at master cylinder, this writer recommends the use of new components.

BS2.   Brake linings can only be checked after slackening the adjusters and removing the drums. BRAKE DUST CAN BE LETHALLY DANGEROUS! Do this job out of doors if possible. DON'T blow dust out of the backplate or drum — spray on soapy water with a hand sprayer, make sure that the asbestos impregnated dust is soaked and WIPE it away. (The author strongly recommends the wearing of a respirator and gloves.) Dispose of dust and contamination in a sealed plastic bag. Some asbestos-free linings are now becoming available — obtain them if you can.

BS3. You can see here the layout of the rear brake shoes and the correct positioning of the springs at the rear of the shoes.

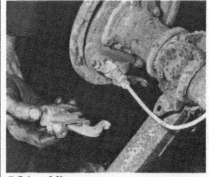

BS4. Minors are very prone to rear wheel cylinder failure. If you replace all the wheel and master cylinders, consider using silicone brake fluid which does not absorb water from the air and does not, therefore, induce corrosion inside the hydraulic cylinders.

BS5. When corroded it may be possible to move the brake operating shoe, but the piston inside may be seized. Sometimes both seize solid.

BS6. Remove the rear wheel cylinder by taking out the split pin and clevis pin and removing the end of the handbrake cable from the handbrake operating lever on the wheel cylinder. Slacken and remove the brake pipe from the union on the wheel cylinder.

BS7. Unbolt the union, taking care not to lose the copper washers shown. When reassembling, ensure that the bleed nipple points upwards. (The brake pipe will not, as in this shot, be connected.)

BS8. Take out the wheel cylinder, wriggling it free after first removing the dust cover. Refitting is the reverse of removal but remember to add special brake grease to the backplate so that the wheel cylinder can slide freely. Remember to bleed the brakes properly on reassembly.

BS9. Flexible hoses should be changed if there is any evidence whatsoever of cracking when they are bent sharply in the hand. They are held at one end to a plate on the body or axle. Remove the steel (or copper) brake pipe, grip the hose with a spanner and undo the nut holding it in place with another spanner.

Figure 14. This shows the layout of the whole braking system. The brake pipes most likely to corrode are the one that enters the rear of the master cylinder especially inside the box section where it cannot be seen, and the one across the top of the front cross-member where it is, again, a little difficult to see easily. This writer strongly recommends the use of Kunifer brake pipes for use with the Minor because of these concealed brake lines.

Another maintenance problem is the brake pedal bush, spacer and shaft. Sometimes wear can develop to the point where operation of the brake causes the clutch pedal to be depressed. The only solution is to strip the shaft and replace the bushes and, if necessary, the shaft.

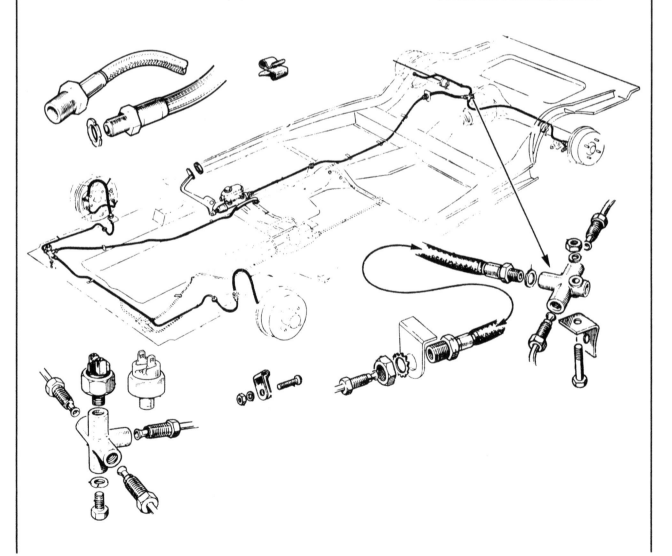

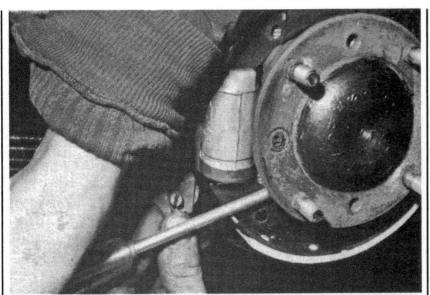

BS10. When replacing the rear brake shoes, fit the springs to the shoes as previously shown. Fit one spring, place the shoes behind the half-shaft flange but not fully in place, and fit the other spring. Carefully lever the shoes into place, one end at a time but without dislodging the springs. Last of all, lever the bottom front end of the shoe away and fit the adjuster into place.

BS11. Some Minors had extra springs designed to stop sideways movement of the brake shoes and possibly to stop some brake noise. In the view of the Minor Centre, they often stretch, they seem to achieve little and they can safely be left off. (They are also a 'pain' to remove and refit!)

BS12. Master cylinder removal — the best left until last! Start by removing the eight screws holding the cover in place. (If only one seizes, you are in luck if it comes free far enough for you to swivel the plate out of the way!) Theoretically, you should remove the torsion bar in order to remove the retaining bolts which pass right through the 'chassis' leg and the master cylinder. This is a horrible job so, instead, carefully lever the torsion bar out of the way while the bolts are tapped out then refit them from the other side when reassembling. Disconnect both brake pipes from the union at the back of the master cylinder and lift it out.

Brake Lines

Tool Box

Open ended spanners; Brake pipe forming tools if making your own pipework.

Safety

If you make your own brake pipes, make absolutely certain that all flares are properly formed so that a good seal is achieved inside the brake pipe union. Always renew brake pipe nuts with those of the correct type. Make certain that you, or whoever makes the replacement pipe, make a 'single' or 'double' flare, to match the one of the pipe being replaced. Use Kunifer rather than steel tubing because it will not corrode. Copper stands a theoretical risk of snapping after work-hardening from the vibration found in certain locations.

Always use the old brake pipe as a pattern for making the new one. Even if it breaks as you remove it, it will still be invaluable for this purpose. Don't bother straightening it to measure the new length of pipe; instead lay the old pipe against the new one a section at a time, rolling the new pipe against the old at the bends.

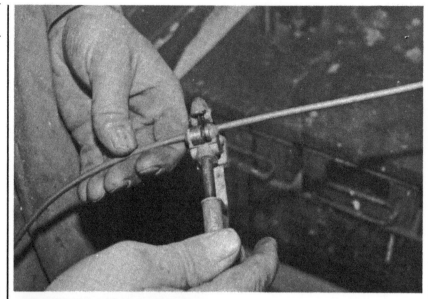

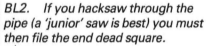

BL1.   If you have access to a proper pipe cutting tool, use it, because the quality of the cut will be much higher. You tighten the cutter until it touches the pipe, turn the cutter a couple of times round the pipe, tighten half a turn, rotate the cutter round the pipe again, and so on until the pipe is cut through.

BL2.   If you hacksaw through the pipe (a 'junior' saw is best) you must then file the end dead square.

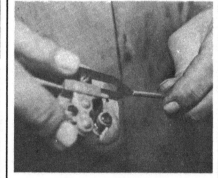

BL3.   Whether you use a cutter or a saw, use a deburring tool to clear any burr from the inside of the pipe. Then blow through thoroughly to get rid of any swarf or filings.

BL4.   Place the wing nut (A) of the flaring tool over the pipe, push the end of the pipe into the throat of the tool and fit the collets (B) each side of the pipe with the pipe sticking out of the collets by a small fraction.

BL5.　Next, use the dolly (C) to push the collets back into the throat of the tool and the pipe end dead level with the front of the collets.

BL6.　The dolly is pushed into the receiver on the end of the screw thread which acts like a press, pushing against the collets and pipe. The collets are held tight into the throat of the tool by the wing nut (left) which screws onto a thread on the back of the collets and draws them back into the taper of the throat.

BL7.　With the pipe tightly gripped, the dolly is changed for a flaring tool which is forced into the end of the pipe by the screw thread and handle in the foreground.

BL8.　When a double flare is required, a single flare is first formed and then the 'Number One' flaring tool changed for a 'Number Two' which is again forced into the end of the pipe making a double flare.

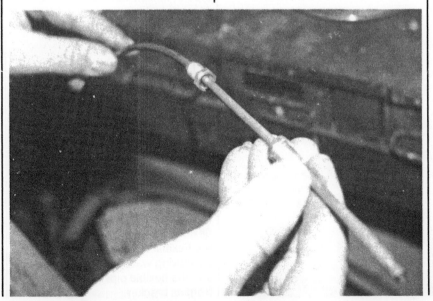

BL9.　Before the other end of the pipe is flared, both nuts must be slipped onto the pipe (facing the correct ways of course).

BL10. To illustrate the point – both of them, in fact – from left to right is a double flaring tool; a double flared pipe with 'female' nut (for fitting to the 'male' ends of the flexible brake pipe); a single flared pipe with 'male' nut for fitting to wheel cylinders, brake light switches and other fittings with an internal thread.

BL11. After making the pipe as a long straight piece, use the old pipe as a guide to bending the new piece of pipe to fit the car. Don't bend the pipe too accurately.

You will probably have to make final adjustments when fitting up. Make absolutely certain that new pipes cannot chaffe on wheels when they are on full lock, or on the full limits of suspension travel, and that they cannot rub on any other moving parts or cause an electrical short-circuit, and that any long runs, such as under the car's body or along the rear subframe, are properly supported. Pipes have to meet their unions squarely or you will have difficulty getting the nut to screw in or on. If you have great difficulty, take the union off or loosen it, fit the pipe nuts up and then refit or retighten the union.

If you intend renewing a complete set of brake lines, you may well be better off going to a firm like 'Handy' who make, for specific cars, complete brake pipe sets all of the correct length and with flares and nuts already fitted.

Flexible brake hoses

FBP1. In time, flexible brake hoses can perish and become weakened. Check them by bending them back: if any cracks or any other form of deterioration then shows, renew the hose before it gets to the stage where it can burst when the brakes are applied hard, which is always the time when you need them most, of course!

You may wish to go over to a rather more expensive but tougher type of flexible hose such as the 'Aeroquip' hose covered in braided metal. Removal and refitting of all types is as follows.

First, unscrew the brake master cylinder cap and screw it back down tight with a piece of plastic sheet beneath it. This seals it and greatly reduces the amount of fluid lost and thus the amount of brake bleeding required.

Now release the union joining the rigid brake pipe to the end of the flexible hose with a spanner to lock the flexible hose. The retaining nut and spring washer can be removed and the flexible pipe pulled away from its bracket.

It is now a simple matter to unscrew the brake wheel cylinder end of the flexible pipe in the usual anti-clockwise direction.

Bleeding the brake hydraulic system

After the fitting of any brake lines or brake components, it is essential to bleed all air out of the brake hydraulic systems otherwise air bubbles trapped in the pipe will compress instead of pressure being available to work the brakes. The main symptom is pedal 'sponginess' (softness when the brake pedal is pushed), compared with the firm 'pedal' which is obtained from air-free brake lines.

When bleeding the brakes, remember to top the reservoir with fresh fluid every 6-8 strokes of the pedal. Do not reuse even fresh fluid as it comes out of the braking system, because it will almost certainly be aerated by tiny bubbles, which is exactly what you are trying to get rid of, and do not use brake fluid that has been standing uncovered to the air because brake fluid is hygroscopic, which means that it absorbs water vapour from the atmosphere. Once water is absorbed, the high pressures/temperatures inside brake pipes make it form a vapour lock which has the same effect as air in the brake lines or can even render the brakes totally ineffective in severe cases.

Brake bleeding involves slackening off a bleed screw on each of the wheel cylinders in turn and pumping fluid through the system until all the air is expelled. When bleeding brakes, it is strongly recommended that you use one of the many so-called 'one-man' brake bleeding kits. These incorporate a one-way valve so that, as the foot is removed from the brake pedal in the following process, air is not drawn back into the system. However, the system is not infallible because it is often possible for air to be drawn

through the bleed tube where it push-fits onto the bleed screw, but such systems are invariably superior to the more long-winded system involving a clean jam-jar, a length of clear plastic tubing that is a tight fit over the bleed screw, and a ring spanner.

Brake bleeding without a 'one-man' kit

Clean the area around the bleed screw. Push the clear plastic tube over the bleed screw after first locating the ring spanner on the screw with enough clearance to first untighten and then retighten it.

Pour an inch or so of brake fluid into a clean jam jar and hold the free end of the plastic tube beneath the level of the fluid in the jar. (Check that the master cylinder is topped up.)

Have an assistant inside the car with a foot on the brake pedal. You position yourself near to the wheel cylinder and release the bleed screw by half a turn or slightly more. Say the word 'Down' to your assistant, who should push the pedal right down to the floor steadily, but not too slowly, taking perhaps a couple of seconds. He/she should then reiterate the word 'Down' to indicate that the stroke is complete. You then retighten the bleed screw to prevent air re-entering the system, and tell your assistant to let the pedal 'Up'. He/she says 'Up' to tell you that it is now up! As the pedal is pushed down, you may see nothing at first as air is pushed out of the system, or you may see bubbles rising through the fluid in the jar. Continue bleeding at each bleed screw until no more air is pushed out, which can take anything from half-a-dozen pumps, depending on the length of the brake line, whether a servo is fitted and whether any bubbles of air are trapped in the pipe. Try asking your assistant to give four steady pushes to every two hard, rapid pushes. If your assistant notices any pressure at the pedal you may not have slackened the bleed screw sufficiently. The master cylinder

level must be kept up through this whole process.

Brake bleeding with a 'one-man' kit

It becomes possible with such kits to bleed brakes without an assistant (although the author would always go back later and re-bleed for a couple of strokes with the aid of an assistant, to make certain that no air was creeping back in). Even with an assistant, bleeding becomes much quicker because the bleed screw does not have to be tightened/untightened between each stroke.

Brake bleeding general notes and sequence

During bleeding top up the master cylinder every 6-8 strokes. THIS IS VITAL because if you do not and the fluid level falls too low, you will draw air into the system and have to begin bleeding the whole system again from scratch. DON'T SPILL FLUID ON THE PAINTWORK OF YOUR CAR because it can act like paint stripper and remove or at least damage your paintwork. Wrap a rag around the neck of the master cylinder to catch any fluid spillage (it makes a mess of the engine bay too) and use a flash lamp to check the fluid level. If you have renewed something at one of the extremities of the brake system, such as a wheel cylinder or flexible pipe, you should easily get away with bleeding only the section of brakes which you have worked on. If you exchange the master cylinder or a major section of pipework you will have to bleed the whole system as follows:
1. Bleed the l.h. front brake.
2. Bleed the r.h. front brake.
3. Bleed the l.h. back brake.
4. Bleed the r.h. back brake.
5. Go all the way round the whole system once more to remove any air bubbles that may have been pushed from one part of the system to another. If the pedal still feels spongy, repeat the process until a) no more air bubbles can be seen to come out and b) the pedal ceases to feel spongy.

6 Electrical Components

The following 'Tool Box' and 'Safety' notes apply generally to auto-electrical work and are relevant to every section of this chapter.

Tool box

B.A. spanners sometimes needed for earlier cars. Engineers and long-nosed pliers. Soldering iron and pre-fluxed solder. Selection of new electrical connectors. Insulation tape.

Safety

ALWAYS disconnect the battery before working on any electrical system. An electrical short circuit can destroy parts of the wiring system in a second or cause a car-wrecking fire.

The vast majority of car breakdowns occur because of electrical faults, so it pays to give regular attention to your car's wiring and electrical components. This section gives an overview of some of the most important areas in the maintenance or rebuilding of a car's electrical system.

Wiring and wiring loom-general

The wires used in the Minor are colour coded, so rewiring a Minor is fairly straightforward provided that a correctly colour-coded loom is used. Each lighting component already has a coded tag of wire coming from it so all you have to do is link it to the relevant part of the loom with a connector.

The seven basic colours are:
Brown – battery and dynamo/alternator circuits.
White – ignition
Blue – headlamps
Red – side and tail lamps
Green – auxiliary (accessories, etc) circuits protected by fuse terminal 4, and only live with ignition 'on'.
Purple – other auxiliaries not wired through the ignition switch. Protected by fuse terminal 2.
Black – earth wires

With care, an older cloth-covered loom can be cleaned to make it appear fresh and new. CAREFULLY remove the loom, noting the location of the clips which hold it in place and, to speed up refitting, fold a piece of double masking tape, but leaving an inch at the end single and sticky. Wrap this around the end of each wire as it is disconnected and write its location on the masking tape. Wire brush the clips and repaint them with a hammered metal finish paint. Coil the wiring loom and place it into a shallow pan with warm soapy water. SQUEEZE BUT DO NOT SCRUB the loom until it is as clean as it will get before it begins to unravel, then hang it in the garage until completely dry. PVC covered wires can be cleaned to almost new lusture by spraying a rag and the wires with aerosol carburettor cleaner, and wiping the sludge and grease from the wires.

As a rule, the wires themselves do not fail. The connectors may lose contact with the wires but the wires themselves rarely break. Any splicing or correction to the loom should be made outside the wrapping. There should be no connections within the loom itself. If changes are made in the loom, solder Lucas bullet connectors to the wires and use the black female connectors of the type used with the rest of the system. NOTE: Prior to removing the loom from the car, remove ALL the black female connectors as they impede the free

movement of the loom through the bulkhead, boot etc. Prior to refitting the loom in the car, clean each bullet connector with fine emery paper to ensure a good connection.

The interior light switches in the door pillars become bent and corroded so that they do not work. Remove them from the pillar and from the purple/white wire. Wire brush them so that they will make good contact with the pillar and with themselves. Straighten bent plungers with pliers.

WL1. If you decide to fit a new loom, start by laying it out alongside the car to work out its general layout in comparison with the existing loom. The new loom comes in two parts: the front section goes back through the bulkhead to the back of the car and includes the front light wires which cross the car beneath the radiator area; the electrical control wires, which cross the car between bulkhead and dash; and the electrical component wires which run down the front of the bulkhead. Use a new special type of screw-on grommet at the bulkhead, not just a rubber electrical grommet. The rear lighting section is a separate section of loom.

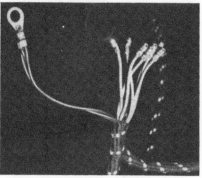

WL2. Making all the right connections is easy by referring to the wiring diagram and the wiring colours shown there and comparing them with the colours on the loom.

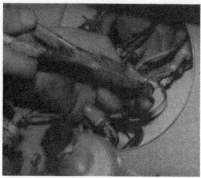

WL3. When removing the old loom, snip the wires a couple of inches from where they join the component so that you have an instant cross-referencing colour code to hand.

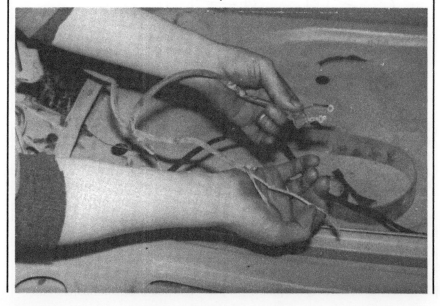

WL4. You may simply wish to repair the existing loom, in which case many terminals will probably need to be renewed. Sometimes they are corroded and hanging on by a thread of dangerous bare wire.

WL5. You really need three hands to solder bullet connectors onto the ends of wires: one to hold the wire, one the iron and one for the solder itself! Cleanliness is the key to obtaining a good soldered joint. Remember the solder will tend to be drawn towards the heat and try not to heat for so long that the wire's insulation melts. When fitting new spade-type connectors, do remember to push on the plastic insulator before soldering the spade in place!

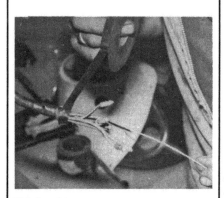

WL6. You can tape up any additions, or replacement sections, with plastic insulation tape wrapped around the wire in a spiral, each wind covering about half of the one that went before.

Distributor overhaul

Figure 15. The component parts of the Lucas distributor.

1	Distributor cap	12	Contact breaker points
2	Brush and spring	13	Driving dog
3	Rotor arm		
4	Condenser	14	Bush
5	Terminal and lead	15	Clamp plate
6	Moving baseplate	16	Cap retaining clips
7	Fixed baseplate	17	Shaft and action plate
8	Cam screw	18	Bob weights
9	Cam	19	Vacuum unit
10	Advance spring	20	O-ring oil seal
11	Earth lead	21	Thrust washer
		22	Taper pin

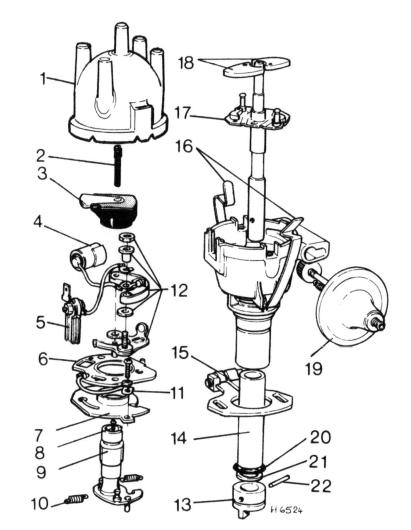

Many parts of the distributor can wear and malfunction. In particular, the following points should be checked (for component identification see Figure 15).
1) The vacuum advance unit perforates and no longer functions (check by releasing the pipe from the carb, suck it and look and listen for distributor base plate movement).
2) The plates holding the points wear, allowing the points to contact the distributor cam at an angle and causing the vacuum unit to work jerkily.
3) The mechanical advance screw seizes.
4) The cam develops sideplay on the distributor shaft.
5) The distributor shaft wears where it fits the body bush, which also wears.
6) The points and condenser fail.

DO1. Wire insulation inside the distributor is inclined to disintegrate and cause a car-stopping short. Replace the wire with a new piece.

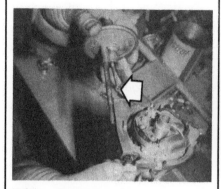

DO2. To remove the vacuum advance on the distributor, lever off the clip that holds the advance/retard finger nut (held in right hand here) in place, disconnect the spring from the baseplate (arrowed) and unscrew the nut completely before withdrawing the advance mechanism. Don't loose the spring from behind the knurled nut.

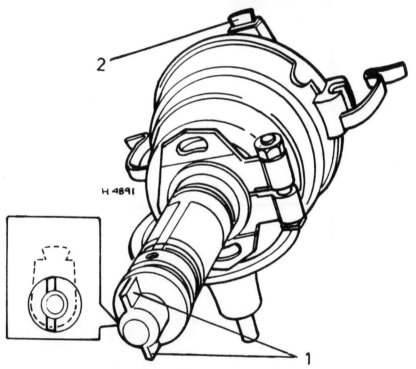

H.4891

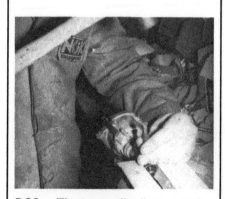

DO3. The Lucas distributor shaft assembly is held in place by a pin (Figure 15, item 20) which must be driven out with a pin punch, after which the distributor components can be pulled apart. Note: when reassembling the distributor, make certain that the drive dog is offset relative to the position of the rotor arm as shown in Figure 16 or the ignition spark will occur 180° out, i.e. the wrong plug will fire.

Figure 16.   Correct relative positions of drive dog and rotor arm.

1   Offset drive dog   2   Rotor arm
    tongues

DO4. When refitting the distributor, make sure the clamp plate is not distorted; if it is it can damage the distributor mounting flange, like this.

Horn – general

The Minor horn operation with steering wheel horn push operates in a similar fashion to the following:

H2. The horn button (removed here) pushes down on the contact to which the wire (shown sticking out of the top of the column in the previous photo) is fitted. This action creates a complete circuit which sounds the horn. If you're not sure whether the horn or switch is faulty, put a test lamp in place of the horn and see if it lights up when the horn is 'sounded' (ignition on).

BAT2. When a car stands, its battery can quickly go flat which is irritating and shortens a battery's life. The Exide 12V Charger Battery Saver Plus provides a constant trickle charge from the sun – free and continuous!

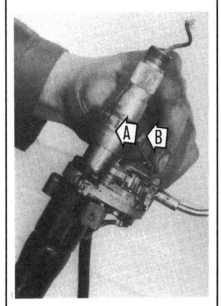

H1. So that the horn works from the centre of the steering column (earlier cars) without getting its wiring in a twist, it operates from a slip ring (A) and a contact (B) which bears on the slip ring. The contact is connected to a feed wire; the slip ring is connected o the piece of wire shown here sticking out of the top of the column. Make sure that the contact spring has sufficient life in it to hold the contact in place and that neither contact nor slip ring are dirty and thus preventing the flow of current.

On charge!

BAT1. These are quite different from conventional batteries. The plates are coiled and the acid is sealed-in gel. As a result, an Optima battery is smaller, more powerful and can be recharged in an hour without damaging it. It can be mounted at any angle – even upside down! Well, you never know . . .

Appendices
1 Workshop Procedures

Professional motor mechanics are trained in safe working procedures, whereas the onus is on you, the home mechanic, to find them out for yourself and act upon them. However enthusiastic you may be about getting on with the job in hand, do take the time to ensure that your safety is not put at risk. A moment's lack of attention can result in an accident, as can failure to observe certain elementary precautions.

There will always be new ways of having accidents, and the following points do not pretend to be a comprehensive list of all dangers; they are intended rather to make you aware of the risks and to encourage a safety-conscious approach to all work you carry out on your vehicle.

Be sure to consult the suppliers of any materials and equipment you may use, and to obtain and read carefully operating and health and safety instructions that they may supply.

Essential DOs and DON'Ts

DON'T rely on a single jack when working underneath the vehicle. Always use reliable additional means of support, such as axle stands, securely placed under a part of the vehicle that you know will not give way.

DON'T attempt to loosen or tighten high-torque nuts (e.g. wheel hub nuts) while the vehicle is on a jack; it may be pulled off.

DON'T start the engine without first ascertaining that the transmission is in neutral (or 'Park' where applicable) and the parking brake applied.

DON'T suddenly remove the filler cap from a hot cooling system – cover it with a cloth and release the pressure gradually first, or you may get scalded by escaping coolant.

DON'T attempt to drain oil, automatic transmission fluid, or coolant until you are sure it has cooled sufficiently to avoid scalding you.

DON'T grasp any part of the engine, exhaust or catalytic converter without first ascertaining that it is sufficiently cool to avoid burning you.

DON'T allow brake fluid or antifreeze to contact vehicle paintwork.

DON'T syphon toxic liquids such as fuel, brake fluid or antifreeze by mouth, or allow them to remain on your skin.

DON'T inhale dust – it may be injurious to health (see Asbestos below).

DON'T allow any spilt oil or grease to remain on the floor – wipe it up straight away, before someone slips on it.

DON'T use ill-fitting spanners or other tools which may slip and cause injury.

DON'T attempt to lift a heavy component which may be beyond your capability – get assistance.

DON'T rush to finish a job, or take unverified short cuts.

DON'T allow children or animals in or around an unattended vehicle.

DON'T park vehicles with catalytic converters over combustible materials such as dry grass, oily rags, etc., if the engine has recently been run. As catalytic converters reach extremely high temperatures, any such materials in close proximity may ignite.

DON'T run vehicles equipped with catalytic converters without the exhaust system heat shields fitted.

DO wear eye protection when using power tools such as an electric drill, sander, bench grinder, etc., and when working under the vehicle.

DO use a barrier cream on your hands prior to undertaking dirty jobs – it will protect your skin from infection as well as making the dirt easier to remove afterwards; but make sure your hands aren't left slippery. Note that long term contact with used engine oil can be a health hazard.

DO keep loose clothing (cuffs, tie, etc.) and long hair well out of the way of moving mechanical parts.

DO remove rings, wrist watch, etc., before working on the vehicle – especially the electrical system.

DO ensure that any lifting tackle used has a safe working load rating adequate for the job, and is used precisely as recommended by the manufacturer.

DO keep your work area tidy – it is only too easy to fall over articles left lying around.

DO get someone to check periodically that all is well, when working alone on the vehicle.

DO carry out work in a logical sequence and check that everything is correctly assembled and tightened afterwards.

DO remember that your vehicle's safety affects that of yourself and others. If in doubt on any point, get specialist advice.

IF, in spite of following these precautions, you are unfortunate enough to injure yourself, seek medical attention as soon as possible.

Fire

Remember at all times that petrol (gasoline) is highly flammable. Never smoke, or have any kind of naked flame around, when working on the vehicle. But the risk does not end there – a spark caused by an electrical short-circuit, by two metal surfaces contacting each other, by a central heating boiler in the garage 'firing up', or even by static electricity built up in your body under certain conditions, can ignite petrol vapour,

which in a confined space is highly explosive.

Always disconnect the battery earth (ground) terminal before working on any part of the fuel system, and never risk spilling fuel on to a hot engine or exhaust.

It is recommended that a fire extinguisher of a type suitable for fuel and electrical fires is kept handy in the garage or workplace at all times. Never try to extinguish a fuel or electrical fire with water.

Fumes

Certain fumes are highly toxic and can quickly cause unconsciousness and even death if inhaled to any extent. Petrol (gasoline) vapour comes into this category, as do the vapours from certain solvents such as trichloroethylene and those from many adhesives. Any draining or pouring of such volatile fluids should be done in a well-ventilated area.

When using cleaning fluids and solvents, read the instructions carefully. Never use any materials from unmarked containers – they may give off poisonous vapours.

Never run the engine of a motor vehicle in an enclosed space such as a garage. Exhaust fumes contain carbon monoxide which is extremely poisonous. If you need to run the engine, always do so in the open air or at least have the rear of the vehicle outside the workplace.

If you are fortunate enough to have the use of an inspection pit, never drain or pour petrol, and never run the engine, while the vehicle is standing over it; the fumes, being heavier than air, will concentrate in the pit with possibly lethal results.

The battery

Never cause a spark, or allow a naked light, near the vehicle battery. It will normally be giving off a certain amount of hydrogen gas, which is highly explosive.

Always disconnect the battery earth (ground) terminal before working on the fuel or electrical systems.

If possible, loosen the filler plugs or cover when charging the battery from an external source. Do not charge at an excessive rate or the battery may burst.

Take care when topping up and when carrying the battery. The acid electrolyte, even when diluted, is very corrosive and should not be allowed to contact the eyes or skin.

If you ever need to prepare electrolyte yourself, always add the acid slowly to the water, and never the other way round. Protect against splashes by wearing rubber gloves and goggles.

Mains electricity

When using an electric power tool, inspection light, etc., which works from the mains, always ensure that the appliance is correctly connected to its plug and that, where necessary, it is properly earthed (grounded). Do not use such appliances in damp conditions and, again, beware of creating a spark or applying excessive heat in the vicinity of fuel or fuel vapour.

Also, before using any mains powered electrical equipment, take one more simple precaution – use an RCD (Residual Current Device) circuit breaker. Then, if there is a short, the RCD circuit breaker minimises the risk of electrocution by instantly cutting the power supply. Buy from any electrical store or DIY centre. RCDs fit simply into your electrical socket before plugging in your electrical equipment.

Ignition HT voltage

A severe electric shock can result from touching certain parts of the ignition system, such as the HT leads, when the engine is running or being cranked, particularly if components are damp or the insulation is defective. Where an electronic ignition system is fitted, the HT voltage is much higher and could prove fatal. Consult your handbook or main dealer if in any doubt. Risk of injury while working on running engines, e.g. adjusting the timing, can arise if the operator touches a high voltage lead and pulls his hand away on to a projection or revolving part.

Welding and bodywork repairs

It is so useful to be able to weld

when carrying out restoration work, and yet there is a good deal that could go dangerously wrong for the uninformed – in fact more than could be covered here. **For safety's sake** you are strongly recommended to seek tuition, in whatever branch of welding you wish to use, from your local evening institute or adult education classes. In addition, all of the information and instructional material produced by the suppliers of materials and equipment you will be using must be studied carefully. You may have to ask your stockist for some of this printed material if it is not made available at the time of purchase.

In addition, it is strongly recommended that *The Car Bodywork Repair Manual,* published by Haynes, is purchased and studied before carrying out any welding or bodywork repairs. Consisting of 292 pages, around 1,000 illustrations and written by Lindsay Porter, the author of this book, *The Car Bodywork Repair Manual* picks the brains of specialists from a variety of fields, and covers arc, MIG and 'gas' welding, panel beating and accident repair, rust repair and treatment, paint spraying, glass-fibre work, filler, lead loading, interiors and much more besides. Alongside a number of projects, the book describes in detail how to carry out each of the techniques involved in car bodywork repair with safety notes where necessary. As such, it is the ideal complement to this book.

Compressed gas cylinders

There are serious hazards associated with the storage and handling of gas cylinders and fittings, and standard precautions should be strictly observed in dealing with them. Ensure that cylinders are stored in safe conditions, properly maintained and always handled with special care and make constant efforts to eliminate the possibilities of leakage, fire and explosion.

The cylinder gases that are commonly used are oxygen, acetylene and liquid petroleum gas (LPG). Safety requirements for all three gases are: Cylinders must be stored in a fire resistant, dry and

well-ventilated space, away from any source of heat or ignition and protected from ice, snow or direct sunlight. Valves of cylinders in store must always be kept uppermost and closed, even when the cylinder is empty. Cylinders should be handled with care and only by personnel who are reliable, adequately informed and fully aware of all associated hazards. Damaged or leaking cylinders should be immediately taken outside into the open air, and the supplier and fire authorities should be notified immediately. No one should approach a gas cylinder store with a naked light or cigarette. Care should be taken to avoid striking or dropping cylinders, or knocking them together. Cylinders should never be used as rollers. One cylinder should never be filled from another. Every care must be taken to avoid accidental damage to cylinder valves. Valves must be operated without haste, never fully opened hard back against the back stop (so that other users know the valve is open) and never wrenched shut but turned just securely enough to stop the gas. Before removing or loosening any outlet connections, caps or plugs, a check should be made that the valves are closed. When changing cylinders, close all valves and appliance taps, and extinguish naked flames, including pilot jets, before disconnecting them. When reconnecting ensure that all connections and washers are clean and in good condition and do not overtighten them. Immediately a cylinder becomes empty, close its valve.

Safety requirements for acetylene: Cylinders must always be stored and used in the upright position. If a cylinder becomes heated accidentally or becomes hot because of excessive backfiring, immediately shut the valve, detach the regulator, take the cylinder out of doors well away from the building, immerse it in or continuously spray it with water, open the valve and allow the gas to escape until the cylinder is empty. If necessary, notify the emergency fire service without delay.

Safety requirements for oxygen are: No oil or grease should be used on valves or fittings. Cylinders with convex bases should be used in a stand or held securely to a wall.

Safety requirements for LPG are: The store must be kept free of combustible material, corrosive

material and cylinders of oxygen.

Cylinders should only ever be carried upright, securely strapped down, preferably in an open vehicle or with windows open. Carry the suppliers safety data with you. In the event of an accident, notify the Police and Fire Services and hand the safety data to them.

Dangerous liquids and gases

Because of flammable gas given off by batteries when on charge, care should be taken to avoid sparking by switching off the power supply before charger leads are connected or disconnected. Battery terminals should be shielded, since a battery contains energy and a spark can be caused by any conductor which touches its terminals or exposed connecting straps.

When internal combustion engines are operated inside buildings the exhaust fumes must be properly discharged to the open air. Petroleum spirit or mixture must be contained in metal cans which should be kept in a store. In any area where battery charging or the testing of fuel injection systems is carried out there must be good ventilation, and no sources of ignition. Inspection pits often present serious hazards. They should be of adequate length to allow safe access and exit while a car is in position. If there is an inspection pit, petrol may enter it. Since petrol vapour is heavier than air it will remain there and be a hazard if there is any source of ignition. All sources of ignition must therefore be excluded.

Lifting equipment

Special care should be taken when any type of lifting equipment is used. Lifting jacks are for raising vehicles; they should never be used as supports while work is in progress. Jacks must be replaced by adequate rigid supports before any work is begun on the vehicle. Risk of injury while working on running engines, e.g. adjusting the timing, can arise if the operator touches a high voltage lead and pulls his hand away on to a projection or revolving part. On some vehicles the voltage used in the ignition system is so high as to cause injury or death by electrocution.

Consult your handbook or main dealer if in any doubt.

Work with plastics

Work with plastic materials brings additional hazards into workshops. Many of the materials used (polymers, resins, adhesives and materials acting as catalysts and accelerators) readily produce very dangerous situations in the form of poisonous fumes, skin irritants, risk of fire and explosions. Do not allow resin or 2-pack adhesive hardener, or that supplied with filler or 2-pack stopper to come into contact with skin or eyes. Read carefully the safety notes supplied on the tin, tube or packaging.

Jacks and axle stands

Special care should be taken when any type of lifting equipment is used. Any jack is made for lifting the car, not for supporting it. NEVER even consider working under your car using only a jack to support the weight of it. Jacks are only for raising vehicles, and must be replaced by adequate supports before any work is begun on the vehicle; axle stands are available from many discount stores, and all auto parts stores. These stands are absolutely essential if you plan to work under your car. Simple triangular stands (fixed or adjustable) will suit almost all of your working situations. Drive-on ramps are very limiting because of their design and size.

When jacking the car from the front, leave the gearbox in neutral and the brake off until you have placed the axle stands under the frame. Make sure that the car is on level ground first! Then put the car into gear and/or engage the handbrake and lower the jack. Obviously DO NOT put the car in gear if you plan to turn over the engine! Leaving the brake on, or leaving the car in gear while jacking the front of the car will necessarily cause the jack to tip (unless a good quality trolley jack with wheels is being used). This is unavoidable when jacking the car on one side, and the use of the handbrake in this case is recommended.

If the car is older and if it shows signs of weakening at the jack tubes while using the factory jack, it is best

to purchase a good scissors jack or hydraulic jack – preferably trolley-type (depending on your budget).

Workshop safety – summary

1 Always have a fire extinguisher at arm's length whenever welding or when working on the fuel system – under the car, or under the bonnet.
2 NEVER use a naked flame near the petrol tank.
3 Keep your inspection lamp FAR AWAY from any source of dripping petrol (gasoline); for example, while removing the fuel pump.
4 NEVER use petrol (gasoline) to clean parts. Use paraffin (kerosene) or white (mineral) spirits.
5 NO SMOKING!

If you do have a fire, DON'T PANIC. Use the extinguisher effectively by directing it at the base of the fire.

Paint spraying

NEVER use 2-pack, isocyanate-based paints in the home environment or home workshop. Ask your supplier if you are not sure which is which. If you have use of a professional booth, wear an air-fed mask. Wear a charcoal face mask when spraying other paints and maintain ventilation to the spray area. Concentrated fumes are dangerous!

Spray fumes, thinners and paint are highly flammable. Keep away from naked flames or sparks.

Paint spraying safety is too large a subject for this book. See Lindsay Porter's *The Car Bodywork Repair Manual* (Haynes) for further information.

Fluoroelastomers – Most Important! Please Read This Section!

Many synthetic rubber-like materials used in motor cars contain a substance called fluorine. These substances are known as fluoroelastomers and are commonly used for oil seals, wiring and cabling, bearing surfaces, gaskets, diaphragms, hoses and 'O' rings. If they are subjected to temperatures greater than 315°C, they will decompose and can be

potentially hazardous. Fluoroelastomer materials will show physical signs of decomposition under such conditions in the form of charring of black sticky masses. Some decomposition may occur at temperatures above 200°C, and it is obvious that when a car has been in a fire or has been dismantled with the assistance of a cutting torch or blow torch, the fluoroelastomers can decompose in the manner indicated above.

In the presence of any water or humidity, including atmospheric moisture, the by-products caused by the fluoroelastomers being heated can be extremely dangerous. According to the Health and Safety Executive, 'Skin contact with this liquid or decomposition residues can cause painful and penetrating burns. Permanent irreversible skin and tissue damage can occur.' Damage can also be caused to eyes or by the inhalation of fumes created as fluoroelastomers are burned or heated.

If you are in the vicinity of a vehicle fire or a place where a vehicle is being cut up with cutting equipment, the Health and Safety Executive recommend the following action:

1 Assume unless you know otherwise that seals, gaskets and 'O' rings, hoses, wiring and cabling, bearing surfaces and diaphragms are fluoroelastomers.
2 Inform firefighters of the presence of fluoroelastomers and toxic and corrosive fume hazards when they arrive.
3 All personnel not wearing breathing apparatus must leave the immediate area of a fire.

After fires or exposure to high temperatures:

1 Do not touch blackened or charred seals or equipment.
2 Allow all burnt or decomposed fluoroelastomer materials to cool down before inspection, investigation, tear-down or removal.
4 Preferably, don't handle parts containing decomposed fluoroelastomers, but if you must, wear goggles and PVC (polyvinyl chloride) or neoprene protective gloves whilst doing so. Never handle such parts unless they are completely cool.
5 Contaminated parts, residues, materials and clothing, including protective clothing and gloves, should be disposed of by an approved contractor to landfill or by incineration according to national

or local regulations. Original seals, gaskets and 'O' rings, along with contaminated material, must not be burned locally.

Symptoms and clinical findings of exposure:

A Skin/eye contact:
Symptoms may be apparent immediately, soon after contact or there may be considerable delay after exposure. Do not assume that there has been no damage from a lack of immediate symptoms; delays of minutes in treatment can have severe consequences:

1 Dull throbbing ache.
2 Severe and persistent pain.
3 Black discoloration under nails (skin contact).
4 Severe, persistent and penetrating burns.
5 Skin swelling and redness.
6 Blistering.
7 Sometimes pain without visible change.

B Inhalation (breathing):
– immediate
1 Coughing.
2 Choking.
3 Chills lasting one to two hours after exposure.
4 Irritation.

C Inhalation (breathing) – delays of one to two days or more:
1 Fever.
2 Cough.
3 Chest tightness.
4 Pulmonary oedema (congestion).
5 Bronchial pneumonia.

First aid

A Skin contact:
1 Remove contaminated clothing immediately.
2 Irrigate affected skin with copious amounts of cold water or lime water (saturated calcium hydroxide solution) for 15 to 60 minutes. Obtain medical assistance urgently.

B Inhalation
Remove to fresh air and obtain medical supportive treatment immediately. Treat for pulmonary oedema.

C Eye contact
Wash/irrigate eyes immediately with water followed by normal saline for 30 to 60 minutes. Obtain immediate medical attention.

2 Tools and Working Facilities

Introduction

A selection of good tools is a fundamental requirement for anyone contemplating the maintenance and repair of a motor vehicle. For the owner who does not possess any, their purchase will prove a considerable expense, offsetting some of the savings made by doing-it-yourself. However, provided that the tools purchased are of good quality, they will last for many years and prove an extremely worthwhile investment.

To help the average owner to decide which tools are needed to carry out the various tasks detailed in this manual, we have compiled three lists of tools under the following headings: Maintenance and minor repair, Repair and overhaul, and Special. The newcomer to practical mechanics should start off with the 'Maintenance and minor repair' tool kit and confine himself to the simpler jobs around the vehicle. Then, as his confidence and experience grows, he can undertake more difficult tasks, buying extra tools as, and when, they are needed. In this way a 'Maintenance and minor repair' tool kit can be built up into a 'Repair and overhaul' tool kit over a considerable period of time without any major cash outlays. The experienced do-it-yourselfer will have a tool kit good enough for most repairs and overhaul procedures and will add tools from the 'Special' category when he feels the expense is justified by the amount of use these tools will be put to.

Maintenance and minor repair tool kit

The tools given in this list should be considered as a minimum requirement if routine maintenance, servicing and minor repair operations are to be undertaken. We recommend the purchase of combination spanners (ring one end, open-ended the other); although more expensive than open-ended ones, they do give the advantage of both types of spanner.

Combination spanners – $^7/_{16}$, $^1/_2$, $^9/_{16}$, $^5/_8$, $^{11}/_{16}$, $^3/_4$, $^{13}/_{16}$, $^{15}/_{16}$ in. AF
Combination spanners – 5, 6, 8, 10 and 12 mm
Adjustable spanner – 9 inch
Engine sump/gearbox/rear axle drain plug key (where applicable)
Spark plug spanner (with rubber insert)
Spark plug gap adjustment tool
Set of feeler gauges
Brake adjuster spanner (where applicable)
Brake bleed nipple spanner
Screwdriver – 4 in. long × $^1/_4$ in. dia. (plain)
Screwdriver – 4 in. long × $^1/_4$ in. dia. (crosshead)
Combination pliers – 6 inch
Hacksaw, junior
Tyre pump
Tyre pressure gauge
Grease gun (where applicable)
Oil can
Fine emery cloth (1 sheet)
Wire brush (small)
Funnel (medium size)

Repair and overhaul tool kit

These tools are virtually essential for anyone undertaking any major repairs to a motor vehicle, and are additional to those given in the Basic list. Included in this list is a comprehensive set of sockets.

Although these are expensive they will be found invaluable as they are so versatile – particularly if various drives are included in the set. We recommend the ½ square-drive type, as this can be used with most proprietary torque wrenches. If you cannot afford a socket set, even bought piecemeal, then inexpensive tubular box spanners are a useful alternative.

The tools in this list will occasionally need to be supplemented by tools from the Special list.

Sockets (or box spanners) to cover range in previous list
Reversible ratchet drive (for use with sockets)
Extension piece, 10 inch (for use with sockets)
Universal joint (for use with sockets)
Torque wrench (for use with sockets)
'Mole' wrench – 8 inch
Ball pein hammer
Soft-faced hammer, plastic or rubber
Screwdriver – 6 in. long × ⁵⁄₁₆ in. dia. (plain)
Screwdriver – 2 in. long × ⁵⁄₁₆ in. square (plain)
Screwdriver – 1 ½ in. long × ¼ in. dia. (crosshead)
Screwdriver – 3 in. long × ⅛ in. dia. (electrician's)
Pliers – electrician's side cutters
Pliers – needle noses
Pliers – circlip (internal and external)
Cold chisel – ½ inch
Scriber (this can be made by grinding the end of a broken hacksaw blade)
Scraper (This can be made by flattening and sharpening one end of a piece of copper pipe)
Centre punch
Pin punch
Hacksaw
Valve grinding tool
Steel rule/straightedge
Allen keys
Selection of files
Wire brush (large)
Axle stands
Jack (strong scissor or hydraulic type)

Special tools

The tools in this list are those which are not used regularly, are expensive to buy, or which need to be used in accordance with their manufacturer's instructions. Unless relatively difficult mechanical jobs are undertaken frequently, it will not be economic to buy many of these tools. Where this is the case, you could consider clubbing together with friends (or a motorists' club) to make a joint purchase, or borrowing the tools against a deposit from a local garage or tool hire specialist.

The following list contains only those tools and instruments freely available to the public, and not those special tools produced by the vehicle manufacturer specially for its dealer network.

Valve spring compressor
Piston ring compressor
Ball joint separator
Universal hub/bearing puller
Impact screwdriver
Micrometer and/or vernier gauge
Carburettor flow balancing device (where applicable)
Dial gauge
Stroboscopic timing light
Dwell angle meter/tachometer
Universal electrical multi-meter
Cylinder compression gauge
Lifting tackle
Trolley jack
Light with extension lead

Buying tools

For practically all tools, a tool factor is the best source since he will have a very comprehensive range compared with the average garage or accessory shop. Having said that, accessory shops often offer excellent quality goods at discount prices, so it pays to shop around.

Remember, you don't have to buy the most expensive items on the shelf, but it is always advisable to steer clear of the very cheap tools. There are plenty of good tools around, at reasonable prices, so ask the proprietor or manager of the shop for advice before making a purchase.

Care and maintenance of tools

Having purchased a reasonable tool kit, it is necessary to keep the tools in a clean and serviceable condition. After use, always wipe off any dirt, grease and metal particles using a clean, dry cloth, before putting the tools away. Never leave them lying around after they have been used. A simple tool rack on the garage or workshop wall, for items such as screwdrivers and pliers is a good idea. Store all normal spanners and sockets in a metal box. Any measuring instruments, gauges, meters etc., must be carefully stored where they cannot be damaged or become rusty.

Take a little care when the tools are used. Hammer heads inevitably become marked and screwdrivers lose the keen edge on their blades from time-to-time. A little timely attention with emery cloth or a file will soon restore items like this to a good serviceable finish.

Working facilities

Not to be forgotten when discussing tools, is the workshop itself. If anything more than routine maintenance is to be carried out, some form of suitable working area becomes essential.

It is appreciated that many an owner mechanic is forced by circumstance to remove an engine or similar item, without the benefit of a garage or workshop. Having done this, any repairs should always be done under the cover of a roof.

Wherever possible, any dismantling should be done on a clean flat workbench or table at a

suitable working height.

Any workbench needs a vice: one with a jaw opening of 4 in. (100mm) is suitable for most jobs. As mentioned previously, some clean, dry storage space is also required for tools, as well as the lubricants, cleaning fluids, touch-up paints and so on which soon become necessary.

Another item which may be required, and which has a much more general usage, is an electric drill with a chuck capacity of at least $5/16$ in. (8mm). This, together with a good range of twist drills, is virtually essential for fitting accessories such as wing mirrors and reversing lights.

Last, but not least, always keep a supply of old newspapers and clean, lint-free rags available, and try to keep any working areas as clean as possible.

Spanner jaw gap comparison table

Jaw gap (in.)	Spanner size
0.250	$1/4$ in. AF
0.275	7 mm AF
0.312	$5/16$ in. AF
0.315	8 mm AF
0.340	$11/32$ in. AF/$1/8$ in. Whitworth
0.354	9 mm AF
0.375	$3/8$ in. AF
0.393	10 mm AF
0.433	11 mm AF
0.437	$7/16$ in. AF
0.445	$3/16$ in. Whitworth/$1/4$ in. BSF
0.472	12 mm AF
0.500	$1/2$ in. AF
0.512	13 mm AF
0.525	$1/4$ in. Whitworth/$5/16$ in. BSF
0.551	14 mm AF
0.562	$9/16$ in. AF
0.590	15 mm AF
0.600	$5/16$ in. Whitworth/$3/8$ in. BSF

Jaw gap (in.)	Spanner size
0.625	$5/8$ in. AF
0.629	16 mm AF
0.669	17 mm AF
0.687	$11/16$ in. AF
0.708	18 mm AF
0.710	$3/8$ in. Whitworth/$7/16$ in. BSF
0.748	19 mm AF
0.750	$3/4$ in. AF
0.812	$13/16$ in. AF
0.820	$7/16$ in. Whitworth/$1/2$ in. BSF
0.866	22 mm AF
0.875	$7/8$ in. AF
0.920	$1/2$ in. Whitworth/$9/16$ in. BSF
0.937	$15/16$ in. AF
0.944	24 mm AF
1.000	1 in. AF
1.010	$9/16$ in. Whitworth/$5/8$ in. BSF
1.023	26 mm AF
1.062	$11/16$ in. AF/27 mm AF
1.100	$5/8$ in. Whitworth/$11/16$ in. BSF
1.125	$11/8$ in. AF
1.181	30 mm AF
1.200	$11/16$ in. Whitworth/$3/4$ in. BSF
1.250	$11/4$ in. AF
1.259	32 mm AF
1.300	$3/4$ in. Whitworth/$7/8$ in. BSF
1.312	$15/16$ in. AF
1.390	$13/16$ in. Whitworth/$15/16$ in. BSF

Jaw gap (in.)	Spanner size
1.417	36 mm AF
1.437	$17/16$ in. AF
1.480	$7/8$ in. Whitworth/1 in. BSF
1.500	$11/2$ in. AF
1.574	40 mm AF/$15/16$ in. Whitworth
1.614	41 mm AF
1.625	$15/8$ in. AF
1.670	1 in. Whitworth/$11/8$ in. BSF
1.687	$111/16$ in. AF
1.811	46 mm AF
1.812	$113/16$ in. AF
1.860	$11/8$ in. Whitworth/$11/4$ in. BSF
1.875	$17/8$ in. AF
1.968	50 mm AF
2.000	2 in. AF
2.050	$11/4$ in. Whitworth/$13/8$ in. BSF
2.165	55 mm AF
2.362	60 mm AF

3 Specifications

Please note that the specifications in each section relate to each of the models upon their introduction. For changes see 'Production Modifications'. Specifications which are unchanged from one model to another are not shown under details for the later model.

Morris Minor Series MM

Built	Cowley, England from 1948-52/53 Total number built, 176,002
Engine	Cast-iron block and head. Pressed-steel sump. Four cylinders set in-line with sidevalves. Type-Morris USHM2 Capacity: 918.6cc Bore & Stroke: 57mm × 90mm Compression: 6.5/.6.7:1 Max power: 27.5 bhp at 4400 rpm Max torque: 39 lb/ft at 2400 rpm Carburettor: single SU H1 type, 1 ⅛ in Fuel pump: SU
Transmission	Rear wheel drive from front-mounted engine. 4-speed gearbox bolted to rear engine plate. Direct gear change. Synchromesh on 2nd, 3rd and top gears. Gear ratio: 1st and reverse 3.95:1; 2nd 2.30:1; 3rd 1.54:1; top 1:1. Final drive ratio 4.55:1 by semi-floating hypoid axle. Normal axle 7/37; special 8/43 axle available giving 5.286:1 overall.
Wheelbase & Track	Wheelbase: 7 ft 2 in Track: front 4 ft 2⅝ in; rear 4 ft 2⁵⁄₁₆ in
Suspension	Front: independent by torsion bar and links Rear: half-elliptic leaf springs

Steering	Rack and pinion. 2 ½ turns lock-to-lock Turning circle, 33 ft
Brakes	Lockheed hydraulic, 7 in diameter drums front and rear Front: two leading shoes Rear: one leading and one trailing shoe
Wheels and Tyres	14 in pressed-steel disc 4-bolt fixing. Tyres 5.00 × 14
Bodywork	Designed by Issigonis. Unitary all-steel construction, assembled at Cowley. 2-door and 4-door saloons and convertibles available. Headlamps initially in grille panel.

Dimensions and Weight

	Overall width	*Overall length*	*Overall height*
2-door saloon (15 ¼ cwt)	5 ft 1 in	12 ft 4 in	5 ft 0 in
4-door saloon (16 cwt)	5 ft 1 in	12 ft 4 in	5 ft 0 in
Convertible (14 ½ cwt)	5 ft 1 in	12 ft 4 in	5 ft 0 in

Electrical System	Positive earth, 12 volt, 43 Ah battery mounted on tray in engine bay. Lucas dynamo with Lucas compensated voltage control box and coil ignition. Headlamps initially Lucas single-dipping type. 3W semaphore trafficators.
Performance	Maximum speed 62 mph. Maximum speed in gears: 1st, 19 mph; 2nd, 32 mph; 3rd, 50 mph Acceleration: 0-30, 8.7 seconds; 0-50, 24.2 seconds Fuel consumption: 40 mpg (all figures for 2-door saloon)

Morris Minor Series II

Built	Cowley, England from 1952-56 Total number built, 269,838
Engine	Cast-iron block and head. Pressed-steel sump. Four cylinders set in-line with overhead valves. Type-Austin A-series, APHM Capacity: 803cc Bore & Stroke: 58mm × 76mm Compression: 7.2:1 Max power: 30 bhp at 4800 rpm Max torque: 40 lb/ft at 2400 rpm Carburettor: single SU H type, 1 ⅛ in Fuel pump: SU Type L Air cleaner: Dry gauze type
Transmission	Rear wheel drive from front-mounted engine. 4-speed gearbox bolted to rear engine plate. Synchromesh on 2nd, 3rd and top

gears. Clutch, Borg and Beck 6 ¼ in dry plate. Gear ratios: reverse 5.174:1; 1st 4.09:1; 2nd 2.588:1; 3rd 1.679:1; Top 1.000:1. Final Drive: hyphoid axle 7/37. 2-pinion differential. Final drive ratio 5.286:1. Overall ratio: reverse 27.38:1; 1st 21.618:1; 2nd 13.69:1; 3rd 8.88:1; top 5.286:1.

Wheelbase & Track

Wheelbase: 7 ft 2 in
Track: front 4 ft 2⅝ in; rear 4 ft 2⁵⁄₁₆ in

Suspension

Front: independent by torsion bar and links
Rear: half-elliptic leaf springs

Steering

Rack and pinion. 2 ½ turns lock-to-lock
Turning circle, 33 ft

Brakes

Lockheed hydraulic, 7 in diameter drums
Front: two leading shoes
Rear: one leading and one trailing shoe

Wheels and Tyres

14 in pressed-steel disc
4-bolt fixings. Tyres 5.00 × 14

Bodywork

Designed by Issigonis, unitary all-steel construction, assembled at Cowley. 2-door and 4-door saloons, Convertible and Traveller available.
Traveller rear section constructed with external ash frame and aluminium panelling, including roof.

Dimensions and Weight

	Overall width	*Overall length*	*Overall height*
2-door saloon (15 cwt)	5 ft 1 in	12 ft 4 in	5 ft 0 in
4-door saloon (15¾ cwt)	5 ft 1 in	12 ft 4 in	5 ft 0 in
Convertible (15 cwt)	5 ft 1 in	12 ft 4 in	5 ft 0 in
Traveller (16 ½ cwt)	5 ft 1 in	12 ft 5 in	5 ft 0 in

Electrical System

Positive earth, 12 volt, 43 Ah battery mounted on tray in engine bay. Lucas dynamo type C39PV/2 with Lucas compensated voltage control box and coil ignition. Headlamps Lucas double dip 42/36W. Semaphore trafficators 3W.

Performance

Maximum speed 62 mph. Maximum speed in gears:
1st, 18 mph; 2nd, 30 mph; 3rd, 45 mph
Acceleration: 0-30, 8.5 seconds; 0-40, 15.1 seconds; 0-50, 29.9 seconds; 0-60, 52.5 seconds; standing ¼-mile, 27.1 seconds
Fuel consumption: 36.40 mpg

Morris Minor 1000, 948cc

Built

Cowley, England from 1956-62
Travellers were assembled at Abingdon from 1960 to 62
Total number built, 554,048

Engine	Cast-iron block and head. Pressed-steel sump. Four cylinders set in-line with overhead valves operated. Type-APJM, then GM Capacity: 948cc Bore & Stroke: 62.9mm × 76.2mm Compression: 8.3:1 (high compression engine) Max power: 37 bhp at 4750 rpm Max torque: 50 lb/ft at 2500 rpm Carburettor: single SU H2 type. 1¼ in Fuel pump: SU type L Air cleaner: AC CL Oil Bath
Transmission	Rear wheel drive from front-mounted engine. 4-speed gearbox bolted to rear engine plate. Synchromesh on 2nd, 3rd and top gears. Clutch, Borg and Beck 6¼ in dry plate. Gear ratios: reverse 4.664:1; 1st 3.628:1; 2nd 2.374:1; 3rd 1.412:1; Top 1.000:1. Final drive: three-quarter floating rear axle. Hyphoid final drive 9/41; ratio 4.55:1. Overall ratios: reverse 21.221:1; 1st 16.507:1; 2nd 10.802:1; 3rd 6.425:1; top 4.555:1.
Wheels and Tyres	14 in pressed-steel disc 4-stud fixing. Tyres 5.00 × 14 tubeless
Bodywork	Designed by Issigonis, all-steel construction. 2/4-door saloons and Convertibles assembled at Cowley. Travellers assembled at Abingdon from 1960. Travellers constructed with external ash frame for rear section and alumium panelling including roof.
Electrical System	Positive earth 12 volt, 43 Ah battery mounted on tray in engine bay. Lucas dynamo type C39PV/2 with Lucas compensated voltage control box and coil ignition. Headlamps Lucas double dip 42/36 W. Semaphore trafficators 3W.
Performance	Max speed 75.1 mph. Max speed in gears: 1st, 23.4 mph; 2nd 35.2 mph; 3rd 60.5 mph. Acceleration: 0-30, 6.8 seconds; 0-40, 12.1 seconds; 0-50, 18.5 seconds; 0-60, 30.0 seconds; standing ¼-mile 24.2 seconds. Fuel consumption 37-44 mpg.

Morris Minor 1000, 1098cc

Built	Cowley, England from 1962-71 Total number built, 303,443
Engine	Cast-iron block and head. Pressed-steel sump. Four cylinders set in-line with overhead valves. Type 10MA Capacity: 1098cc Bore & Stroke: 64.5mm × 83.72mm Compression: 8.5:1 (high compression engine) Max power: 48 bhp at 5100 rpm Max torque: 60 lb/ft at 2500 rpm Carburettor: SU HS2 type, 1¼ in Fuel pump: SU Type L Air cleaner: Cooper dry type, with paper element Oil Filter: Full-flow, with paper element

Transmission	Rear wheel drive from front-mounted engine. 4-speed gearbox bolted to rear engine plate. Synchromesh on 2nd, 3rd and top gears. Clutch 7¼ in single dry plate. Gear ratios: reverse, 4.664:1; 1st, 3.628:1; 2nd, 2.172:1; 3rd, 1.412:1; Top, 1.000:1. Final drive: three-quarter floating rear axle hyphoid final drive 9/38 ratio 4.22:1. Overall ratios: reverse, 19.665:1; 1st, 15.276:1; 2nd, 9.169:1; 3rd, 5.950:1; top, 4.220:1
Brakes	Lockheed hydraulic. Front 8 in. diameter drums. Rear 7 in diameter drums. Front, two leading shoes. Rear, one leading shoe, one trailing shoe.
Wheels and Tyres	14 in pressed steel disc. 4-stud fixing. Tyres 5.20 × 14 tubeless
Bodywork	Designed by Issigonis, all steel unitary construction. 2/4-door saloons and Convertibles assembled at Cowley. Travellers assembled at Abingdon. 1962-64. Production then transferred to Morris Commercial Cars plant, Adderley Park, Birmingham. Traveller constructed with external ash frame for rear section and aluminium panelling including roof.
Electrical System	Positive earth, 12-volt 43 Ah battery mounted on tray in engine bay. Lucas dynamo type C40-1 with Lucas control box RB106/2 and coil ignition Lucas LA12. Flashing indicator unit Lucas FL5. Headlamps Lucas double dip 42/36 W
Performance	Max speed 78 mph. Max speed in gears: 1st, 27.5 mph; 2nd, 41.5 mph; 3rd, 68 mph. Acceleration: 0-30, 6.4 seconds; 0-40, 9.8 seconds; 0-50, 15.8 seconds; 0-60, 24.2 seconds; standing, ¼-mile, 22.9 seconds. Fuel consumption 40-45 mpg

Wolseley 1500

Engine	Cast-iron block and head. Pressed-steel sump. Four cylinders set in-line with overhead valves. Type: Austin B-series Capacity: 1489cc Bore & Stroke: 73.025mm x 88.9mm Compression: 7.2:1 Max power: 50 bhp at 4200 rpm Max torque: 74 ft/lb at 3000 rpm Carburettor: single 1¼ in SU Fuel pump: SU electric Air cleaner: AC Oil Bath
Transmission	Gear ratios: 1st, 3.6363:1; 2nd, 2.2143:1; 3rd 1.3736:1; top, 1:1; reverse, 4.7552:1. Final drive ratio: 3.73:1
Wheelbase & Track	Wheelbase: 7 ft 2 in Track: front 4 ft 2⅞ in; rear 4 ft 2⁵⁄₁₆ in
Suspension	Front: independent by torsion bar and links Rear: half-elliptic leaf springs
Steering	Rack and pinion. 2½ turns lock-to-lock Turning circle 33 ft

Brakes	Lockheed hydraulic: 9 in diameter front drums 8 in diameter rear Front: two leading shoes, 1 ½ in wide Rear: one leading and one trailing shoe
Wheels and Tyres	14 in pressed-steel disc. 4 stud-and-nut fixing. Tyres: 5.00 x 14 tubeless
Bodywork	Styled by Dick Burzi with front-end detail by Sid Goble based on floorplan and 'chassis' by Issigonis. 4-door saloon, unitary all-steel construction
Dimensions and Weight	Weight: 21 cwt Overall width: 5 ft 0 ½ in Overall length: 12 ft 7 ¾ in Overall height: 5 ft 1 in
Electrical System	Positive earth, 12 volt, battery Lucas dynamo with Lucas compensated voltage control box and coil ignition
Performance	Max speed 78 mph. Max speed in gears: 1st, 31 mph; 2nd, 49 mph; 3rd, 70 mph. Acceleration: 0-30, 6.8 seconds; 0-40, 9.5 seconds; 0-50, 16.0 seconds; 0-60, 24.2 seconds; standing, $1/4$-mile, 22.6 seconds. Fuel consumption: 30 mpg

Riley 1.5

Engine	Compression 8.3:1 Max power: 68 bhp at 5400 rpm Max torque: 81 ft/lb at 2400 rpm Carburettors: Twin 1 ½ in SU
Brakes	Girling hydraulic; as Wolseley 1500 but 2 ¼ in wide shoes and drums at front
Dimensions & Weight	As Wolseley 1500, except weight $18^1/2$ cwt
Wheels and Tyres	14 in pressed-steel disc. 4-stud fixing. Tyres: 5.60 x 14 tubeless

4 Production Modifications

Car (chassis) and engine numbers

The Car (Chassis) Number appears on the identification plate which is mounted on the right-hand side of the dash panel next to the main wiring harness grommet aperture. The practice of recording Engine Numbers changed throughout production. On very early A-series models the Engine number was stamped on a disc attached to the flywheel housing and it also appeared on the identification plate. On other models the Engine Number was stamped on a plate secured to the right-hand side of the cylinder block above the dynamo mounting bracket while it also appeared on the identification plate. On 1098cc models, it only appeared on the cylinder block.

From April 1952 until September 1962 Car (Chassis) Numbers were prefixed by an Identification Code consisting of three letters and two numbers. The first letter indicates the make and model (e.g. F = Morris Minor); the second letter indicates the body type (e.g. A = 4-door saloon, B = 2-door saloon); the third letter indicates the colour in which the vehicle is finished (e.g. A = Black); the first number indicates the class to which the vehicle belongs (e.g. 1 = R.H.D. Home Market, 2 = R.H.D. Export); the second number indicates the type of paint used to finish the vehicle (e.g. 1 = Synthetic, 2 = Synobel, 3 = Cellulose). Thus: FBA13 = Morris Minor, 2-door saloon, black, produced as right-hand drive for the home market and finished in cellulose paint. Note: The second number denoting paint type was not always used on later models.

From September 1962 until production ended a different Car Number Identification Code prefix was used. This consisted of three letters and one figure followed by an additional letter if the vehicle differed from standard right-hand drive.

The first letter denotes the make of the vehicle (M = Morris); the second letter denotes the model's engine type (A = A series engine); the third letter denotes the body type (S = 4-door saloon, 2S = 2-door saloon, W = dual purpose, T = 4-seater tourer); the fourth prefix (a number) denotes the Series of model – indicating a major change (Post '62 vehicles 5th series); the fifth prefix denotes vehicles which differ from standard RHD (L = Left-hand drive, D = De Luxe). Thus MA2S5 = Morris 1000, right-hand drive, standard 2-door saloon, fifth series. Note: Dates and car number change points are, in some cases, approximate as the manufacturers sometimes incorporated modifications before, of after, the 'official' change point. Where major production changes occured change points have been included for all models. Elsewhere the earliest known change point is given.

Production modifications

The first production Minor was a two-door saloon, car number SMM 501, engine type USHM2. Extras included a passenger-side wiper but no heater was available. Many were fitted later as kits when a heater was first offered.

Minor Tourers used the same basic shell but were originally strengthened with a length of 16-gauge steel spot-welded to the

inner walls of each sill, a small reinforcing plate was attached between each door shut pillar and inner sill and a small triangulated plate linked dash to door hinge pillar. 'Fixtures and fittings' were as for the Saloon. Rear side-screens were detachable.

Body production at Nuffield Metal Products, Birmingham, began in July 1948.

June 1949. Car No. 3389 RHD and 6142 LHD: small, round twin rear lights replace single rear lamp (mounted vertically in USA). 17580 RHD; 7967 LHD: larger squared-off variety of rear lamps fitted.

September 1949. Improved draught and water sealing. Choke control altered slightly. Seats given more forwards adjustment.

Late 1949. Front suspension tie-bar mounting strengthened 904 LHD; (5600 LHD). Rear suspension – front shackle renewable bush plates fitted – 17840 RHD; 8700 LHD. Cellulose paint replaced by synthetic enamel – 12118 RHD; 5856 LHD.
All US market cars fitted with headlamps in wings.

October 1950 – on. Four-door Series MM Minor introduced, also with headlamps situated in wings. Indicators fitted high in central door pillar instead of low down as on two-door cars. Some cars (two-door and four-door) fitted with leather front seats, Vyanide being retained in the rear. Car No. 69832 RHD; 71098 LHD – front doors closed with straps instead or cord. Four-door cars fitted with one-piece bumpers instead of earlier split-type. 72985 RHD – passenger windscreen wiper fitted as standard.

January 1951. Car. No. 83390 RHD; 81595 LHD – all Minors built with headlamps mounted in the wings with sidelamps placed where the headlamps used to be. All wing-mounted headlamps were 7 in instead of former 5 in units.

March 1951. A nickel shortage led to painted grille and hub caps being fitted – 91076 RHD; 89726 LHD. Hub caps only were restored to chrome plated finish six months later.

April 1951. Optional water pump fitted to engine, allowing use of heater. Complete cost – £16 as 'extras' but fitted as standard to four-door saloon. Car No. 83206 RHD; 81502 LHD – all cars now fitted with one-piece bumpers in place of earlier split type.

June 1951 – on. Car No. 100920 RHD; 102836 LHD – Tourer sidescreens of fixed type and revised hood fitted. Door-mounted ashtray discontinued on four-door at 131460 RHD; 126597 LHD and on two-door at 124810 RHD; 122788 LHD, replaced by fascia mounted ashtray. 139359 RHD; 139514 LHD – glove box emblem changed from chrome and enamel to plastic and bootlid lock strengthened.

September 1951. Car No. 114923 RHD; 89910 LHD – rubber bushed top suspension link introduced to cure suspension 'clonk'. Later fitted as a modification to most cars. At same time in 1952 a secondary steering rack damper was introduced.

Late 1952 – on. Series MM engine replaced by A-series engine, in export four-door car at first. Two-door saloon and Tourer still fitted with Morris 8 engine until 23 February 1953, when last Series MM Minor built.

August 1952. First ohv engine fitted in four-door saloon (sidevalve engine continued in some), 160001.

January 1953. All models fitted with ohv engine, 180001.

October 1953. New model designated 'Traveller' introduced, 216901. De Luxe models introduced featuring heater, leather seats, overriders and passenger sun visor. Two-door saloon, 221842; four-door saloon, 221803; Convertible, 221914.

January 1954. 'A' type rear axle and standard swivel pin assembly introduced, 228267. Wedge type fan belt at Engine No. 72610.

Early 1954. Sprung-type semi-bucket seats replaced by more modern, flatter far less comfortable front seats. Also around this time and until late 1954, 10,000 cars were fitted with separate rear reflectors as a stop-gap way of satisfying new rear reflector regs.

June 1954. Engine steady cable, 264013.

October 1954. Horizontal grill bars introduced. Revised instrument and control panel. Separate speedometer, fuel and oil pressure gauges replaced by single separate instrument with open gloveboxes each side: 286441, two-door saloon; 291140, four-door saloon, 290173; Convertible, 291336; Traveller, 289687. Rubber-buffered tie-rod mounted between engine and bulkhead to act as engine steady and cut out clutch judder. New larger rear light fitting incorporating reflector in lens cover fitted, 293051.

August 1956. Coloured hoods fitted to Convertible, 433571. During its production run, the Series II received few other changes but they included: discontinuation of front wing beading, hardboard replacing millboard door trim, grease nipples added to handbrake cables, shorter gear lever, repositioned pedals plus different gearbox cover and carpets to give more foot room. Car No. 433571 – on, Tourer given a coloured hood – mottled green for green cars; mottled red for all others. Seats became fixed-back for two-door cars.

October 1956. Series II discontinued. Final chassis number 448714.

October 1956. Standard and De Luxe two- and four-door saloons, Convertible and Traveller introduced, designated 'Minor 1000'. 948cc engine fitted. Single-

piece and enlarged curved windscreen and larger rear window. Dished steering wheel. Horn and trafficator control on steering column. Glovebox lids fitted. Deeper rear wings. Shorter gearlever, and deeper gearbox cover. 'Minor 1000' motif on sides of bonnet, 448801.
New type of shorter handbrake fitted with end push-button instead of side-mounted lever. Gear-lever carried in aluminium remote-control extension. Self-parking wipers, though still not of parallel movement type.

December 1956. New strengthened steering swivel pin assembly fitted, 462458.

Early 1957. Plastic gear lever knob with rubber insert, boot lid handle and lock strengthened, Car No. 463443 – on. New steering rack oil seal fitted.

March 1957. Fuel tank enlarged from 5 to 6 gallons, 487048, Saloon; Traveller, 485127.
Mud deflector plates made available for rear brake drums.

September 1957. Canvas hood on convertible replaced by plastic coated material, 524944.

November 1957. Gearlever reset and lengthened. Traveller 552906; other models, 557451.

October 1958. Courtesy light switches fitted in front doors, 654750.

December 1958. Rear spring design changed from 7 × ¼ inch leaves to 5 × ¼ inch leaves, 680464 Saloon and Tourer only.

February 1959. Early type dry paper element air cleaner, Saloon 698137; Traveller, 693918.

March 1959. Wider opening doors, self-cancelling direction indicator switch fitted to steering column. Horn button moved to centre of steering wheel. Traveller, 704254; four-door saloon, 705224; two-door saloon 705622.

September 1959. Combined inlet and exhaust manifold. Foot space between gearbox cover and clutch pedal increased. PVC interior roof lining fitted instead of cloth. Front passenger seat on two-door saloon and Traveller modified to give better access to rear seats, 750470.

During 1960. HS type SU carburettor introduced, Engine No. 9 M/U/H 353449.

January 1961. Morris Minor 1,000,000 produced as special edition of 349 cars. Special features included Lilac colour, white upholstery with black piping, 'Minor 1,000,000' badging on sides of bonnet and on boot lid and special wheel rim embellishers. 1,000,000 – 1,000,349 (these car numbers designated out of sequence).

October 1961. Flashing direction indicators incorporated into front and rear lamps. Semaphore type direction indicators discontinued. Glove compartment lid removed. Windscreen washers fitted on De Luxe models. Seatbelts anchorage points built into all models. New range of colours and upholstery offered, two-door saloon, 925555; four-door saloon, 925448; Convertible, 947088; Traveller, 925679.

April 1963. Fresh air heater introduced. Air intake on radiator cowl. Redesigned windscreen washer system, 1039564.

October 1963. Windscreen wiper blades lengthened and now work in tandem. Zone-toughened windscreen introduced. New design combined side/flasher lamps at front and rear. Extra round amber flashing indicating light fitted to rear of Traveller. New type air cleaner fitted to prevent carburettor icing in cold weather. N/S door lock fitted to two-door models. Two-door saloon, 1043218; four-door saloon, 1043752; Convertible, 1043271; Traveller, 1043226.

October 1964. New design fascia panel. Better trim and more comfortable seating. Automatic boot lid support. Glovebox on passenger side fitted with lid. Combined ignition and starter switch. Other switches modified to 'flick' type. Swivel ashtrays under parcel shelf. Crushable sun visors. Plastic rimmed interior mirror. Two-spoke safety dished steering wheel. Fresh air heater performance improved. Blocked oil filter warning light fitted. Crackle finish heater fitted – still offered as optional. Two-door saloon, 1082280; four-door saloon, 1082284; Convertible 1082717; Traveller, 1082537.

October 1966. Sealed-beam headlamps fitted. Fuse in sidelamp circuit introduced, 1159663.

October 1967. New type paper air cleaner element introduced, 1196653.

June 1969. Convertible discontinued. Final Car Number 1254328.

Late 1969. Oil filter switch ceased to be fitted. Amber warning lens fitted but not used.

1970. During the last months of production some models were fitted with an alternator instead of a dynamo.

November 1970. Saloon production discontinued. Final Car Numbers, two-door saloon, 1288377; four-door saloon, 1288299.

1971. During the last months of production some of the vehicles assembled at the Morris Commercial Cars plant at Adderley Park, Birmingham were fitted with steering column ignition locks.

April 1971. Traveller production discontinued. Final Car Number 1294082.

Footnote: Reclining seats were fitted to some vehicles though they were never fitted as standard equipment.

5 Colour Schemes

Before purchasing paint for your car, have your supplier check with a paint sample (or 'colour chip') against the original colour to ensure that you are purchasing the colour that you require.

There is a great deal of misconception about the type of paint used on Morris Minors. Only the very earliest Series MM cars were ever painted in cellulose (prior to Car Numbers 2117 RHD and 5855 LHD two-door saloons only; and 3871 RHD and 6255 LHD Tourers only) and from this time on, early in 1949, vehicles were finished in synthetic paint or 'Synobel', neither of which are suitable as a refinishing material.

'MM' Minors were fitted with matching wing piping to the front wings as well as to the rear.

Until April 1952, identification of the paint type was included in the chassis number. After the type code 'MNR', would be stamped 'SYN', or 'S', or nothing, before the letters 'SMM' and the number. 'SYN' indicated that synthetic paint was used, 'S' indicated 'Synobel', while nothing indicated that the car was painted in cellulose and should, logically, appear prior to the numbers shown in the first paragraph above.

From April 1952 to mid-1958, i.e. chassis numbers *following* those with an 'SMM' prefix, the first letter (F) shows that the car is a Minor (or O if a Light Commercial), the second letter shows the body type, the third letter shows paint colour,

the first figure shows destination or type while the second figure shows the type of paint used. Some of the information which follows is not relevant only to the Minor as it was also used on MG, Wolseley and Riley cars.

Second Letter — Body Type

A	4-door saloon
B	2-door saloon
C	Convertible
E	Van
G	Chassis/cab
H	GPO mail van
J	GPO telephone engineer's van
L	Traveller

Third Letter — Colour

A	Black
B	Light Grey
C	Dark Red
D	Dark Blue
E	Mid Green
F	Beige
G	Brown
H	CKD finish
J	Dark Grey
K	Light Red
L	Light Blue
P	Ivory
R	White
S	Mid Grey
T	Light Green
U	Dark Green

There are two distinctive eras of paint coding. The latest applies to only a handful of Travellers and Light Commercials, from 1970 on. They were given BL 'VIN' numbers, part of which is the factory paint code with the prefix 'BLVC'. VIN numbers and paint codes are attached to the vehicle on chassis number plates. All earlier paint types — the vast majority — were given a separate paint code not attached to the vehicle (except as described above). Not all of these paint colours/types are available. Pre-1970 paint colours can be difficult to match, although The Morris Minor Centre will amost certainly be able to help. Alternatively you may wish to get hold of the technical representative from International Paints or ICI who may well be able to help (contact them through your local supplier).

A list of colours used on the Minor follows but note the following. Details of colour schemes actually used are impossible to research accurately, so the following should be considered only as a close guide; and 'years' given apply to 'model years', i.e. they date usually from October of the previous year!

Note that before 1952, headlining was in cloth but from

about the 1952 model year Rexine-covered hardboard headlining was used in beige or grey. in 1953 vinyl suspended headlining was used, usually in brown or grey. From September 1959, headlining was made of PVC in pale grey or pale beige.

The 'Date' column in the following chart should be read in the following way. Where the year only is shown, this indicates a Model Year change date, which usually begins in the Autumn of the previous year and continues for around twelve months. Where an actual change date is known it is shown.

First Figure – Destination Type
1   RHD UK
2   RHD Export
3   LHD
4   North America
5   CKD (kits) – RHD
6   CKD (kits) – LHD

Second Figure – Paint Type
1   Synthetic
2   'Synobel'
3   Cellulose
4   Metallic
5   Primer
6   Cellulose body with Synthetic wings

Thus Car No. FBA 31 48, 142 means:
F = Minor
B = 2-door saloon
A = Black
3 = LHD
1 = Synthetic paint finish
48,142 = Car number

Date	Colour	Upholstery	Features
1949 and 1950	Black Romain Green Platinum Grey Maroon	Light beige with brown seat piping	Dashboard panels were gold coloured. Steering wheel mottled brown. White ring around road wheels. Door window frames and grille chrome-plated. Full width waist-line stripe.
1951 and 1952	Black Gascoyne Grey Mist Green Thames Blue	2-dr as 1950 4-dr, brown 2-dr as 1950 4-dr, green	Contrasting seat piping, wheel stripes discontinued. Waist line now a pin-stripe. March 1951-on grille painted. Hub caps painted until September 1951. Some 'accessory' chrome grilles sold.
July 1952 to 1954	Black Clarendon Grey Birch Grey Empire Green (LCVs only) Platinum Grey Dark Green Azure Blue Beige	Maroon Green Brown	
1955	Black Clarendon Grey Smoke Blue (Sandy Beige) Empire Green	Maroon Green	Sandy Beige replaced Smoke Blue, March 1955. LCVs cont. as before. Dashboard now painted in body colour (large, central speedo. dashboard). Steering wheel mottled brown, grey or blue.
1956	Black Clarendon Grey Sandy Beige Empire Green	Maroon Green	
April 1956	Black Clarendon Grey Birch Grey Sandy Beige	Red or Grey Red	Some black cars had pale grey grille bars.

Date	Colour	Upholstery	Features
	Dark Green Sage Green	Green	
	(LCVs only) Clarendon Grey Sandy Beige Bronze Empire Green	Brown	
October 1956 to 1957	As above but —	Some cars had contrasting seat piping.	Black, Dark Green and Turquoise cars now with wheels and grille in light grey. Black handbrake and steering wheel. Morris badge in horn bass.
	Turquoise Cream (Sandy Beige now discontinued)	Grey Red	
	(LCVs only) (Bronze discontinued)		
	(Traveller only) Black Clarendon Grey } Birch Grey } Dark Green	Red or Green Red Grey	
1958	As 1956/57 except: (LCVs only) Clarendon Grey Birch Grey Dark Green	Brown	
1959	At first: As for 1958 except —		
	Discontinued: Cream Introduced: Pale Ivory	Red	
Jan/Feb 1959	Discontinued: Birch Grey (not LCV) Clarendon Grey (not LCV) Dark Green (not LCV) Turquoise Pale Ivory		Grilles and wheels in off-white or cream (not LCVs). March 1959, steering wheel boss with 'M' motif. September 1959, PVC headlining in Pale Grey or Pale Beige.
	Introduced: Frilford Grey Pearl Grey	Red	

Date	Colour	Upholstery	Features
	Clipper Blue Smoke Grey	Blue-Grey	
1960	(Alternative colour names in brackets) Black Frilford Grey (Dark Grey) Pearl Grey (Off-White)	Red	Blue-Grey and Green upholstery available in nylon, De Luxe models only.
	Smoke Grey (Blue-Grey) Clipper Blue (Blue)	Blue-Grey	
	Sage Green (Light Green)	Green	
	(Traveller only) As above, except: Pearl Grey Smoke Grey	Blue-Grey	
	(LCVs only) Birch Grey Frilford Grey Connaught Green	Brown	
July 1960 and 1961	Black Yukon Grey Olde English White	Red	All rad. grilles and wheels in Old English White. Minor 1,000,000 with black carpets and draught excluders, black seat piping. Mottled grey headlining, pale cream wheels and grille, chromium wheel trims.
	Smoke Grey Clipper Blue	Blue-Grey	
	Porcelain Green	Dark Beige	
	(Travellers only) Black Yukon Green	Red	
	Smoke Grey Old English White	Blue-Grey	
	(LCVs only) Yukon Green Pearl Grey Connaught Green	Brown	
	(Minor 1,000,000 only) Lilac	Vanilla	
1962	Black Dove Grey Old English White	Tartan Red	De-luxe cars now with duo-tone seats and trim panels, second colour in Silver Beige.

Date	Colour	Upholstery	Features
	Rose Taupe	Tartan Red	
	Smoke Grey ⎫	Blue-Grey	
	Highway Yellow ⎭		
	Almond Green	Porcelain Green	
	(Travellers only) As above, except:		
	Dove Grey	Blue-Grey	
	Highway Yellow		
	(LCVs only)		
	Dove Grey		
	Almond Green	Brown	
	Rose Taupe		
1963	As above, except, Discontinued: Highway Yellow		
1964	Introduced: (not Travellers) Trafalgar Blue	Blue-Grey	
1965 to 1967	As 1964	Discontinued: Tartan Red Introduced: Cherokee Red	Duo-tone upholstery no longer offered. Heat-formed 'sculpted' panels used. Two-spoke black steering wheel, black parcel shelf.
1968 to 1970	Black ⎫ Maroon 'B' ⎬ Peat Brown ⎭	Cherokee Red	October 1970-on, wheels painted silver.
	Smoke Grey ⎫ Trafalgar Blue ⎬ (new lighter version) ⎭	Blue-Grey	
	Almond Green	Porcelain Green	
	Snowberry White	Black	
	(Police only) Bermuda Blue Police White	Black	
	(Min. of Supply only) Bronze Green	Porcelain Green	
	(LCVs only inc. Austin 'Minors') Previous cols. contd. plus probably: Cumulus Grey Everglade Green Persian Blue Damask Red Snowberry White	Not known	

Date	Colour	Upholstery	Features
mid-1970 to 1971 *(where appropriate)*	(Saloons only) As 1968-1970 (Travellers only) Aqua		
	Bermuda Blue	Navy Blue	
	Limeflower		
	Teal Blue	Limeflower	
	Bedouin	Autumn Leaf	
	Glacier White	Navy Blue or Geranium Red	
	(LCVs only) Aqua Antelop		
	Teal Blue	Black	
	Flame Red		
	Glacier White		

Some BMC and BL paint code references are available. They are as follows:

Black	BK1	
Birch Grey	GR3	
Frilford Grey	GR5	
Clarendon Grey	GR6	
Yukon Grey	GR7	
Pearl Grey	GR10	
Dove Grey	GR26	
Rose Taupe	GR27	
Cumulus Grey	GR29	Also BLVC 194
Peat	GR30	
Maroon 'B'	RD23	
Lilac	RD17	
Old English White	WT3	
Snowberry White	WT4	
Pale Ivory	YL1	
Cream	YL5	
Highway Yellow	YL9	
Turquoise	BU6	
Clipper Blue	BU14	
Smoke Grey	BU15	
Trafalgar Blue	BU37	Two shades used)
Bermuda Blue	BU40	(Police cars only)
Persian Blue	BU39	
Sage Green	GN5	(Two shades used)
Dark Green	GN12	
Porcelain Green	GN17	
Connaught Green	GN18	
Almond Green	GN37	
Everglade Green	GN42	
Bedouin	BLVC 4	
Antelope	BLVC 7	
Teal Blue	BLVC 18	
Limeflower	BLVC 20	
Glacier White	BLVC 59	
Aqua	BLVC 60	
Flame Red	BLVC 61	(Two shades used)

Before ordering paint, take advice on paint types and compatibility.

⑥ Clubs and Specialists

The following addresses and telephone numbers were believed to be correct at the time of going to press. However, as these are subject to change, particularly telephone area codes, no guarantee can be given for their continued accuracy.

Chief amongst the owners' clubs is the UK-based Morris Minor Owners' Club. It was established as the brainchild of Tom Newton, in 1977, since when have been issued in excess of 10,000 membership cards, with a current membership of well over 5,000.

A large part of the initial Club emphasis was on acquiring spares, which in the early days were collected by the cartload from the most outlandish places, and stored in a warehouse in Derby. However, with the advent of the Bath Minor Centre, and the regeneration of Minor spares and specialists on a somewhat spectacular scale over the last few years, a modified approach has occurred. The Club now has a spares consultant attached to the committee who offers advice and gives discount to members and specializes, for example, in parts for the early series MM cars which are not so readily obtainable through company channels.

This redirection of Club energies was also achieved by the formation of the Club into a limited company, during the early 1980s, to give the committee a wide-ranging brief to develop services for the members. So, for example, contact with the members is maintained by a well-produced bi-monthly magazine, *Minor Matters*, which contains a wealth of information, articles from general contributors and technical experts, tall stories, car and spares mart, and the like. Contact is also maintained by meetings at over three-dozen branches of the Club throughout the country. There is a Branch Liaison Officer ('liaison' underlined by the husband and wife team who collectively bear that title!) to co-ordinate the work of the branches, and to run meetings at which the branches can air their views with the main committee.

Minor Matters also advertizes a large selection of 'Minor' articles for sale from the regalia manager – novelties, accessories and other cosmetic dainties, all crowned with the inimitable bull crest – if you want, you can attend a social function kitted out in Morris Minoralia from head to foot!

Club addresses and officials (or at least, some of them!) change faster than we can reprint this book. See your favourite magazine for details of the many hundreds of clubs around the world.

Charles Ware's Morris Minor Centre Ltd
20 Clothier Road, Brislington, Bristol, BS4 5PS.
Tel: 0117 300 3754.
www.morrisminor.org.uk

Charles Ware's Morris Minor Centre Ltd helped enormously with the preparation of this book and are without doubt 'top of the tree' when it comes to the supply of parts, restoration, servicing and sales – in fact anything to do with Morris Minors. Over the last 25 years the world-famous centre has:

- Restored and serviced over 35,000 Minors
- Sold nearly 6,000 cars
- Valued approaching 60,000 vehicles
- Processed about 200,000 parts orders and given, at a guess, free advice to 150,000 buyers, sellers and restorers.

Their direct management team and workforce share nearly 200 years of dedicated service to the Minor. These multi skills allows them to deliver quick, guaranteed, durable solutions at the equivalent real costs of a small decent workshop.

Automec Equipment & Parts Ltd, 36 Ballmoor, Buckingham, MK18 1RQ. Tel: 01280 822818 www.automec.co.uk
Non-corroding copper brake, clutch and fuel pipes. Silicone D.O.T.S. brake fluid. Rubber lined 'P' dips, pipe flaring and pipe bending tools, stainless steel hoseclips.

Blaupunkt, Robert Bosch Ltd, PO Box 98, Broadwater Park, North Orbital Road, Denham, Uxbridge, Middlesex, UB9 5HJ. Tel: 01895 834466 www.blaupunkt.com
High quality range of in-car entertainment systems.

Charles Ware, third from right, seated, and his team

BOC Gases, The Priestley Centre, 10 Priestley Road, The Surrey Research Park, Guildford, Surrey, GU2 5XY. Tel: 01483 579857
www.boc.com
Welding gases and DIY 'Portapak' gas welding equipment

Bosch, Robert Bosch Ltd, PO Box 98, Broadwater Park, North Orbital Road, Denham, Uxbridge, Middlesex, UB9 5HJ. Tel: 01895 834466
www.bosch.co.uk
Very wide range of high quality D.I.Y. and professional power tools (and large range of Bosch automotive parts and accessories).

Burlen Fuel Systems, Spitfire House, Castle Road, Salisbury, Wiltshire, SP1 3SB. Tel: 01722 412500
www.burlen.co.uk
Full restoration service on all SU, Zenith, CD and Weber carburettors and fuel pumps. Backed up with full availability of new units, repair kits and parts.

Castrol (UK) Ltd, Burmah Castrol House, Pipers Way, Swindon, Wiltshire, SN3 1RE. Tel: 01793 512712
www.castrol.com
Consumer Technical Department can supply full information on all lubrication requirements.

Chubb Fire Ltd, Racai-Chubb House, Sunbury-on-Thames, Middlesex, TW16 7AR. Tel: 01932 785588
www.chubbfire.co.uk
Fire extinguishers for workshop and car.

Clarke International, Hemnall Street, Epping, Essex, CM16 4LG. Tel: 01992 565 300
www.clarkeinternational.com
Huge range of workshop equipment - everything from MIG welders to air compressors, bench grinders to power washers, and much more besides.

Comma Oils & Chemicals Ltd, Lower Range Road, Gravesend, Kent, DA12 2QX. Tel: 01474 564311 www.commaoil.com
Motor oil, Copper Ease grease, X-stream corrosion resistant coolant.

Dunlop Tyres Ltd. Tyre Fort, 88-98 Wingfoot Way, Birmingham, B24 9HY. Tel: 0121 306 6000
www.dunloptyres.co.uk
Manufacturers of Dunlop Classic Range tyres. See also, Vintage Tyre Supplies Ltd.

Frost Auto Restoration Techniques Ltd, Crawford Street, Rochdale, OL16 5NU. Tel: 01706 758 258 www.frost.co.uk
A huge range of specialist tools, materials and equipment purpose made for the classic car restorer. Mail order catalogue available.

Holden Vintage & Classic Ltd, Linton Trading Estate, Bromyard, Herefordshire, HR7 4QT. Tel: 01885 488 488
www.holden.co.uk
Suppliers of obsolete Lucas electrical equipment of all types. Excellent for overhaul of elderly distributors, especially where new replacements are no longer available. Mail order catalogue available, containing electrical, period accessories, etc.

Kenlowe, Burchetts Green, Maidenhead, Berkshire, SL6 6QU. Tel: 01628 823303
www.kenlowe.com
Electric cooling fans, oil coolers, pre-heaters.

Minden Industrial Ltd (SATA), Saxham Business Park, Saxham, Bury St. Edmonds, Suffolk, IP28 6RX. Tel: 01284 760791
www.minden-ind.co.uk
Rust prevention injection and spray equipment.

Moss Engineering, Lower Road Trading Estate, Ledbury, Herefordshire, HR8 2DJ. Tel: 01531 632 614
Engine reconditioning to a high standard.

Murex Welding Products Ltd, Hanover House, Queensgate, Britannia Road, Waltham Cross, Hertfordshire, EN8 7RP. Tel: 01992 710000
www.murexwelding.co.uk
Suppliers of welding products available through BOC Centres nationwide.

Namrick Ltd, Nut & Bolt Store, 124 Portland Road, Hove, Sussex, BN3 5QL. Tel: 01273 779 864
www.namrick.co.uk
Nuts, bolts, washers; a full range of fixings in plated and stainless steel.

Pirelli Tyres Ltd, Derby Road, Burton-on-Trent, Staffordshire, DE13 0BH. Tel: 01283 525252
www.pirelli.co.uk

Ring Automotive, Geldered Road, Leeds, LS12 6NA. Tel: 0113 213 2000
www.ringautomotive.co.uk
Manufacturers of a wide range of original and replacement electrical equipment.

Sykes-Pickavant Ltd, Unit 4, Cannel Road, Burntwood Business Park, Burntwood, Staffordshire, WS7 3FU. Tel: 01543 679 900
www.sykes-pickavant.com
Manufacturers of specialist automotive service and hand tools.

Vintage Restorations, The Old Bakery, Windmill Street, Tunbridge Wells, Kent, TN2 4UU. Tel: 01892 525899
www.vintagerestorations.com
Restoration and supply of vintage and classic vehicle instruments and dashboard fitting: temperature gauges rebuilt; speedometers recalibrated.

Vintage Supplies Ltd. 10G Folgate Road, North Walsham, Norfolk, NR28 0AJ. Tel: 01692 406510
www.vintagecarparts.co.uk
"Slosh Tank" fuel tank sealant and a wide range of specialist materials for the 'vintage' owner.

Vintage Tyre Supplies Ltd, National Motor Museum, Beaulieu, Brockenhurst, Hampshire, SO42 7ZN. Tel: 01590 612261
www.vintagetyres.com
Worldwide distributors of Veteran, Vintage and Classic car and motorcycle tyres. Over 16,000 in stock including Dunlop, Pirelli, Michelin, Avon and Puma.

Wurth UK Ltd, 1 Centurion Way, Erith, Kent, DA18 4AE. Tel: 08705 987841
www.wurth.co.uk
Zinc-rich primer and a vast range of the very finest workshop materials. Highly recommended by the author.

7 British & American Technical Terms

As this book has been written in England, it uses the appropriate English component names, phrases, and spelling. Some of these differ from those used in America. Normally, these cause no difficulty, but to make sure, a glossary is printed below. In ordering spare parts remember the parts list may use some of these words:

English	American	English	American
Accelerator	Gas pedal	Leading shoe (of brake)	Primary shoe
Aerial	Antenna	Locks	Latches
Anti-roll bar	Stabiliser or sway bar	Methylated spirit	Denatured alcohol
Big-end bearing	Rod bearing	Motorway	Freeway, turnpike etc
Bonnet (engine cover)	Hood	Number plate	License plate
Boot (luggage compartment)	Trunk	Paraffin	Kerosene
Bulkhead	Firewall	Petrol	Gasoline (gas)
Bush	Bushing	Petrol tank	Gas tank
Cam follower or tappet	Valve lifter or tappet	'Pinking'	'Pinging'
Carburettor	Carburetor	Prise (force apart)	Pry
Catch	Latch	Propeller shaft	Driveshaft
Choke/venturi	Barrel	Quarterlight	Quarter window
Circlip	Snap-ring	Retread	Recap
Clearance	Lash	Reverse	Back-up
Crownwheel	Ring gear (of differential)	Rocker cover	Valve cover
Damper	Shock absorber, shock	Saloon	Sedan
Disc (brake)	Rotor/disk	Seized	Frozen
Distance piece	Spacer	Sidelight	Parking light
Drop arm	Pitman arm	Silencer	Muffler
Drop head coupe	Convertible	Sill panel (beneath doors)	Rocker panel
Dynamo	Generator (DC)	Small end, little end	Piston pin or wrist pin
Earth (electrical)	Ground	Spanner	Wrench
Engineer's blue	Prussian blue	Split cotter (for valve spring cap)	Lock (for valve spring retainer)
Estate car	Station wagon	Split pin	Cotter pin
Exhaust manifold	Header	Steering arm	Spindle arm
Fault finding/diagnosis	Troubleshooting	Sump	Oil pan
Float chamber	Float bowl	Swarf	Metal chips or debris
Free-play	Lash	Tab washer	Tang or lock
Freewheel	Coast	Tappet	Valve lifter
Gearbox	Transmission	Thrust bearing	Throw-out bearing
Gearchange	Shift	Top gear	High
Grub screw	Setscrew, Allen screw	Trackrod (of steering)	Tie-rod (or connecting rod)
Gudgeon pin	Piston pin or wrist pin	Trailing shoe (of brake)	Secondary shoe
Halfshaft	Axleshaft	Transmission	Whole drive line
Handbrake	Parking brake	Tyre	Tire
Hood	Soft top	Van	Panel wagon/van
Hot spot	Heat riser	Vice	Vise
Indicator	Turn signal	Wheel nut	Lug nut
Interior light	Dome lamp	Windscreen	Windshield
Layshaft (of gearbox)	Countershaft	Wing/mudguard	Fender

Miscellaneous points

An oil seal is fitted to components lubricated by grease!

A 'damper' is a shock absorber, it damps out bouncing and absorbs shocks of bump impact. Both names are correct, and both are used haphazardly.

Note that British drum brakes are different from the Bendix type that is common in America, so different descriptive names result. The shoe end furthest from the hydraulic wheel cylinder is on a pivot; interconnection between the shoes as on Bendix brakes is most uncommon. Therefore the phrase 'Primary' or 'Secondary' shoe does not apply. A shoe is said to be 'Leading' or 'Trailing'. A 'Leading' shoe is one on which a point on the drum, as it rotates forward, reaches the shoe at the end worked by the hydraulic cylinder before the anchor end. The opposite is a 'Trailing' shoe and this one has no self-servo from the wrapping effect of the rotating drum.